The
Book
of
Eating

The
Book of
Eating

ADVENTURES IN PROFESSIONAL GLUTTONY

ADAM PLATT

ecco
An Imprint of HarperCollins*Publishers*

Portions of the chapters titled "Eating with My Family," "Travels, Part 2," "Meditations on Dieting, Final Thoughts," and "Faking It: The Imperfect Art of the Perfect Review, Part 1" were originally published in *New York* magazine as "Platt v. Fat" (September 8, 2016), "To Die For" (April 25, 2008), "Eat and Run" (Fall 2004), and "Nibbling Doubts" (August 28, 2000). Reprinted with permission.

HarperCollins books may be purchased for educational, business, or sales promotional use. For information, please email the Special Markets Department at SPsales@harpercollins.com.

FIRST EDITION

Designed by Paula Russell Szafranski
Frontispiece © Antikwar/Shutterstock

Library of Congress Cataloging-in-Publication Data has been applied for.

ISBN 978-0-06-229354-1

19 20 21 22 23 LSC 10 9 8 7 6 5 4 3 2 1

For the women in my life—KP, JYP, PXP, and SMP

Contents

Introduction

As anyone who writes about their dinner for a living knows, there are few things more subjective, or prone to myth and exaggeration, than the distant memory of an excellent meal. The same is true of a memorably horrible meal, of course, the legend of which invariably grows in horror and awfulness with each retelling. This memoir is the pieced-together record of thousands of such idealized, half-remembered events—of family dinners and picnic luncheons and summer goat roasts, which may or may not have actually been as novel or as nourishing as they seem to me now. It's a memoir of dumpling feasts and Peking duck dinners in the far-off places where I found myself living as a child, and of the kinds of strange things you come across, and even seek out, as a professional eater, like grilled chicken uterus, or raw horse sashimi, or the icy dabs of poisonous blowfish sperm, which I ingested in a state of not-so-quiet horror for a magazine story many years ago.

I've attempted to re-create these episodes as I remember them, and if I can't remember them, I've relied on the memories of others.

Special thanks to my father for his descriptions of long-ago meals and restaurants, and whose eclectic love of a good meal set the tone for my career as an eater. Thanks to his brother, Geoffrey, and to their cousins, Charles Platt and Frank Platt, "the family gastronome," for attempting to reconstruct the dining habits of their eccentric Yankee ancestors, the Choates and the Platts. Thanks to my brothers, Oliver and Nicholas Jr., for racking their brains about our long-ago food adventures in Taiwan, Hong Kong, and Tokyo, and to my mother, who spent many patient hours trying to recover the culinary nightmares from her sheltered WASP upbringing, many of which she'd managed to suppress for decades.

I've written more than I probably should about my diets, the various dining foibles of my daughters and wife, and the strange eating habits of the professional glutton, and portions and snippets of several of these articles and reviews, many of which appeared in *New York* magazine and on the magazine's website *Grub Street* are reproduced and expanded on here. Special thanks to my first editor at *New York*, Meredith Rollins, who had the daring, slightly cockeyed idea to turn me into a restaurant critic, and to Mark Horowitz and Caroline Miller for making that strange dream a reality. Thanks to Klara Glowczewska for sending me on many pleasurable junkets during her tenure at *Condé Nast Traveler*, and to Pam Wasserstein, the great Adam Moss, and David Haskell for their beneficent, hands-off support during my time as the chief eater in residence at *New York* magazine. Thanks to my longest-serving, longest-suffering editor, Jon Gluck, for shepherding a thousand end-of-the-year "monsters" into print, and to my many other colleagues at the magazine and website—Noreen Malone, Raha Naddaf, Anne Clark, Jody Quon, Alan Sytsma, and those dynamos of the food section Rob Patronite and Robin Raisfeld—for their support and guidance over the years.

Thanks to my agent, Suzanne Gluck, for exhibiting the kind

of patience that high-powered literary professionals aren't generally known for during the decade or so I spent not writing this book. Thanks also to Farley Chase for his advice on portions of the manuscript, and to Hugo Lindgren for his invaluable editing advice after gamely taking the time to grapple with the entire thing. Thanks to my occasional interns, Clare Platt, Sam Hawkins Sawyer, and Olivia Caldwell, who gamely made restaurant reservations using ridiculous fake names, diligently gathered any research I asked them for, and brought some sense of digital sanity to my disheveled, paper-strewn desk. Thanks to my diligent, long-suffering production editor at HarperCollins and to the wise, ever-cheerful Gabriella Doob at Ecco for calmly guiding this manuscript and its author to print through various stages of confusion and terror. And thanks, most of all, to Daniel Halpern, who had the idea for this memoir more years ago than either of us probably cares to remember, waited with a kind of biblical patience over the months and decades for the pages to slowly pile up on his desk, and once this confused jumble of thoughts and impressions had achieved a kind of critical mass, gave the thing a name and pronounced it done. For better or worse, none of us would be reading this book without him.

The
Book
of
Eating

1

Lunch with Gael

Remember to look for the lady wearing a very large hat," I think I hear my wife say, with a helpful, slightly wan smile, as I inspect my new jacket in front of the mirror in a nervous, slightly bug-eyed lather. One of us has read somewhere that in the mysterious Kabuki world of the professional restaurant critic, Gael Greene is famous for her extravagant hats. Hats are supposed to be Gael's calling card, her signature prop and pseudo-disguise. Over the decades, as the critic for *New York* magazine, she's been photographed sitting in the banquettes of grand restaurants, sipping flutes of champagne, peeking slyly out from under colorful wide brims of every design. She's sported so many different varieties of headgear over the years—summer straw hats, floppy felt hats, wedding hats, ship captain hats emblazoned with spinning globes and golden anchors—that I'll later hear that the restaurant people (who tend to spot the only person in the room wearing a hat every time) sometimes call her "Sergeant Pepper" in whispered tones behind her back.

My new jacket is size 48 extra-long, or possibly even larger and longer than that. I've just purchased it off the rack at a store called Rochester Big and Tall in midtown, which, in the summer of 2000, is where many of the city's prominent giants—basketball stars, ox-shouldered linemen who play for the Jets and the Giants, even Rush Limbaugh himself—purchase their fancy, Gulliver-sized threads. The jacket is boxy and coal black and looks like it's been constructed out of yards of shiny black undertaker's cloth. I'd told the bemused salesman at the fatso store that I wanted a durable, sensible garment, something I could wear to polite res-taurants and grow into if I gained an inch or two around the chest and belly. I wanted something in a dark color with the slight-est hint of polyester sheen, a jacket that could be cleaned easily, when I stained it, discreetly, with streaks of Hollandaise sauce and steak fat.

I put on this giant, flapping undertaker's garment, and Mrs. Platt and I both regard my looming reflection in the full-length mirror for a time, in studious silence. I'm the nervous worrier of the family; my wife is the cheerful, optimistic one, always liv-ing life on the sunny side of the street. We are different in many ways, my wife and I, and it won't be long before she'll grow weary of the restaurant grind, and then of restaurants altogether, and even for healthy lengths of time, of eating altogether. But at the beginning of this grand culinary adventure, our differences are complementary: she's petite, organized, and sensibly trim; I'm large, disorganized, and prone to fits of mumbling and for-getfulness. She was raised by cheery, relentlessly well-adjusted parents on a steady American diet of Pop-Tarts, tuna salad sand-wiches, and Campbell's tomato soup. I come from a family of phlegmatic, generally reserved, East Coast establishment Yan-kees who never did much home cooking in the traditional sense of the phrase. She spent most of her childhood in the same tidy redbrick colonial house, on the same street, in a leafy tree-lined suburb of Detroit. As the child of a diplomat, I spent most of my youth wandering like a displaced, upscale gypsy, from one world capital to the next. My mother-in-law once told me that the Phillipses used to eat the same sacred rotation of blue-plate specials every day of the week out in Detroit: spaghetti with to-mato sauce on Mondays; Chicken Divan smothered in cheddar cheese sauce and broccoli on Tuesdays; pork chops and apple-sauce on Wednesdays; and some variation of tuna casserole or beet and rice "porcupine" meatballs to round out the week. The Platt family's diet, however, consisted of a kind of rotating cook's tour through the countries in Asia where we lived, and we hap-pily frittered away perhaps too much time in restaurants all over the world.

"This jacket is as big as a circus tent," I say, as we stare at my new restaurant critic costume in the mirror.

"I think it will work better for you than a hat," she says.

Gael has summoned me to lunch at the new restaurant of a French chef named Alain Ducasse, which in the summer of 2000, in the cosseted, self-regarding, pre-apocalyptic world of New York City's haute cuisine establishment, is a little like being invited to Buckingham Palace for tea with the queen herself. Or if not the queen exactly, then a courtesan of long standing, one who has survived—the way Gael has over the decades through a combina-tion of talent, ambition, toughness, and more than a little sexual intrigue. Aside from her sharp palate and collection of baroque hats, Gael is probably most famous among the writers I know for her one-night stand with Elvis. ("I don't remember the es-sential details," she will write in her memoirs. "It was certainly good enough.") Gael has written pornographic novels, conducted passionate affairs with porn stars and famous chefs, and had Elvis-like flings with assorted movie stars of her day (Burt Reynolds,

Clint Eastwood). For years the major themes of her "Insatiable Critic" column have been the intertwining joys of those two social revolutions of the last half of the American twentieth century— the sexual one, of which Gael is a card-carrying member, and the gourmet revolution, which, in her colorful impressionistic style, she helped to disseminate, the way the other original *New York* magazine writers, like Tom Wolfe, Jimmy Breslin, and Gail Sheehy, did in their particular orbits.

At that time, Alain Ducasse is the most famous chef in France—and therefore the entire world—and his new restaurant, which is just being unveiled in the back rooms of the Sherry Netherland Hotel on Central Park South, is the most eagerly anticipated opening of the season, or so I've been told. My lunch with Gael is supposed to be a polite meet-and-greet session, and also a kind of ceremonial passing of the torch from one critic to the next. With some fanfare, Gael has announced that she will be retiring from the weekly grind of restaurant reviewing at the end of the summer. After an exhaustive and mostly fruitless search during which many of the candidates seem to have turned the job down, I've been chosen by the magazine's editors to take her place. The decision is a mystery to Gael ("So what exactly were you writing about before this?" she'll ask me) and to other people as well, including my mother, who, when she hears the unexpected news that her eldest son has decided, after bouncing around many other jobs in the realm of journalism and writing, with different levels of star-crossed success, to become a professional restaurant critic, will put down her cup of tea and say, to no one in particular, "That sounds wonderful, but I didn't know Adam wrote very much about food."

As usual, my mother would have a point. At the dawn of my strange, accidental career as a professional eater, I'd demonstrated a love for food and a wide-ranging appetite for culinary adventure, it's true. But I'd never subscribed to *Gourmet* magazine, or *Cook's Illustrated*, or any of the usual gastronomic bibles that my food-obsessed friends liked to pore over with manic, Talmudic intensity. I didn't save menus from the restaurants I visited, or record every morsel of every dinner I'd ever eaten in my dining journal, the way serious gourmets were supposed to do. I did have a mostly unread copy of M.F.K. Fisher's famous translation of Brillat-Savarin's *The Physiology of Taste* sitting on my cluttered desk, although I'd never gotten very far past the letter C. I vaguely knew who Auguste Escoffier was, but to my deep shame, I'd never heard of the real father of grand Continental haute cuisine, Antonin Carême, and if you'd asked me to describe the difference between mis en place and sous vide, chances are I would have stared at you in puzzled silence for a time and quickly changed the conversation.

Unlike many of the food obsessives I know, I've also never held a job in a professional kitchen, unless you count two grim weeks in college when I worked as a busboy at a restaurant in Boston, before the manager quietly let me go for what he described as "general incompetence." I have no beloved, tattered scrapbook in which I've lovingly scribbled down my favorite family recipes, and I can count the number of cookbooks my wife and I own on the fingers of one hand. The only dishes I'm able to reproduce with any reliable success in the kitchen of our little downtown New York apartment are Craig Claiborne's durable recipe for roast chicken and an enthusiastic approximation of that nomadic northern Chinese specialty, Mongolian Hot Pot, which my mother learned in China and Hong Kong in the 1960s, and which we would attempt to approximate as we set up camp in other distant parts of the world, the way the Mongols did as they roved from place to place.

"The reservation will be under the name Mrs. Rebecca Limos," Gael had said when she called over the ancient landline telephone wire, speaking in a deep, hushed voice that managed to sound both commanding and conspiratorial at the same time. I should arrive at precisely the appointed time, which I dimly recall was one o'clock. The restaurant's entrance would be in the back of the hotel, not the front. She pronounced her fake name "Leee-mooohs," drawing out the vowels in an exaggerated way. Like many famous Michelin-starred establishments, this debut restaurant in New York had a kind of waiting area before you got to the dining room, a small, elegant space appointed with gilt-edged furniture; diners could sip champagne there or nibble on petits fours and examine the ridiculously priced wine list before moving on to the main dining room once their guests arrived. "If I'm late, wait for me there," said Mrs. Limos, before ringing off.

IN THE SUMMER OF 2000, CULINARY TRENDS STILL ROLL INTO Manhattan periodically from the hinterlands (from California, from Tuscany, from Spain), but in style and structure, the idea of a proper restaurant dinner hasn't changed very much in the city since Henri Soulé opened his celebrated Le Restaurant Français at the French Pavilion of the 1939 New York World's Fair in Queens. You can still get an excellent plate of that Belle Époque delicacy, pike quenelles, at Jackie Onassis's favorite restaurant, La Caravelle, at 23 West Fifty-Fifth Street for $15. The famous Alsatian chef André Soltner still lives with his wife, Simone, above his famous townhouse restaurant, Lutèce, on East Fiftieth Street, although, ominously, he's in the process of quietly selling his four-decade-old business to an investment group from Las Vegas. With a few exceptions, like the Japanese fusion master Nobu Matsuhisa in Tribeca, the most admired chefs in the city, like Daniel Boulud on the Upper East Side, David Bouley down in Tribeca, and Jean-Georges Vongerichten, are steeped in the classic French techniques that the gourmets and experts of the small, cosseted food community still refer to in hushed, reverential tones as "haute cuisine."

The food revolutions that are about to turn this ancient aristocracy on its head—the rise of a much more populist, egalitarian cook's culture; blogs; reality TV cook-offs; a new, empowered *No Reservations* generation of diners who care more about a well-brewed cup of coffee or a superbly griddled cheeseburger than cheese soufflé prepared at their mother's favorite snooty restaurant—are still hovering out of sight, just over the curve of the horizon. In the summer of 2000, the internet is still a curious and obscure tool used in food circles around town, the way it is everywhere else, only by a small (but growing) horde of misfits and underground enthusiasts to ferret out and debate the merits of their small-time obsessions: where to find their favorite soup dumpling, or pizza slice, or bowl of Japanese noodles. In this ordered, bucolic little world, Brooklyn is still a wild and distant gastronomic wasteland that most serious-minded gastronomes from Manhattan visit now and then for a ceremonial bite of steak at Peter Luger, in Williamsburg, or dinner at one or two of the borough's iconic pizza destinations. A mercurial young cook named David Chang is studying to be a professional chef at what was then called the French Culinary Institute, downtown, although it's possible he's already hatching plans to open up a modest little noodle bar down where he lives in the East Village, serving an elevated version of the kind of pan-Asian comfort food that he grew up with, which young line cooks eat at staff meals or late at night after they get off work—bowls of Japanese ramen, spicy home-style Korean specialties, steamed buns from Chinatown stuffed with strips of pork belly—if things don't work out as planned in the ferociously Darwinian world of the traditional big city restaurant kitchen.

The future pied piper of this restive, *No Reservations* rabble of cooks and kitchen slaves, Anthony Bourdain, will publish his memoir *Kitchen Confidential* in a few months, but right now he's still putting out grease fires in the kitchen of the popular Park Avenue bistro Brasserie Les Halles. Those familiar buzzwords of the coming "slow food" revolution—"sustainable," "hand-crafted," "local," and "master forager"—are only just beginning to creep into the conversations of enlightened food people, but like most things in this curious little backwater, they are a long way from becoming part of the buzzing public imagination. TV's future *Top Chef*, Tom Colicchio, is in the process of leaving the Gramercy Tavern, the popular downtown restaurant he opened with Danny Meyer, and planning a radically subversive estab-lishment, called Craft, which will be devoted to the weighty is-sues that working chefs traditionally spend their time pondering in private—sourcing and ingredients, the rhythms of the sea-sons, how to roast the perfect country chicken or sear the per-fect Atlantic scallop. The clean, wood-toned dining room will be devoid of the usual Eurocentric, front-of-the-house frippery (oil paintings, carpets, linen tablecloths) when it opens for business the next year. Instead of recipes written in a flowery script, the spare runic menu will feature nothing but the ingredients, and patrons will be encouraged to compose their dinner themselves.

For the most part, accepted tastes in this peaceful, mannered little universe are still disseminated by members of what Nora Ephron called "the Food Establishment" in an article she'd published in *New York* in the late '60s. This small, tight-knit group of mandarins—magazine editors, critics, consultants, chefs—are as insular and exotic in their inbred, self-regarding way as the tottering aristocrats of Europe in August 1914, before the Great War broke out and the old order was swept away. The ge-nial, rotund cookbook writer from Oregon, James Beard, was a founding member of this establishment, and so was Craig Clai-borne, who arrived in New York from Mississippi after the Sec-ond World War and worked his way up from writing restaurant press releases to the lofty pinnacle of power, reigning as a feared *New York Times* critic and also the editor of its dining section. Gael Greene was a member of this fractious, competitive little group (in her precise, hilarious way, Ephron also described the many sub-establishments within the Establishment), and so was Ruth Reichl, who'd grown up in the Greenwich Village apartment next to the one where I now happened to live and was famous for wearing elaborate disguises when she went out to review restaurants for the *Times*. Reichl has recently left the paper for *Gourmet* magazine, the periodical bible of the Food Establishment for many decades, which, unbeknownst to her and everyone else, will be out of business in four years, undone by the erosion of magazine ad sales, not to mention a horde of avid food bloggers and restaurant websites, which will soon overrun the media foodscape, like herds of wild trampling wildebeest. In that summer of 2000, Claiborne has only just died, at the age of seventy-nine, after a long, slow decline into querulousness and drink. The city's most feared food snob eventually lost his taste for escargot with drawn garlic butter, choucroute garnie, and all of the delicacies he helped popularize with the great French chef Pierre Franey. Late in life, as David Kamp records in his history of mid-twentieth-century culinary manners and trends, *The United States of Arugula*, Claiborne didn't leave his apartment very much, and when he did, it was to go to Planet Hollywood on East Fifty-Seventh Street, where he admired the qualities of the club sandwich.

As it turns out, Alain Ducasse will be one of the last in a long line of accomplished, mellifluously named Belle Époque chefs—Joël Robuchon, Jacques Pépin, Gilbert Le Coze, Franey—who are greeted by members of this vanishing New York gourmet aristocracy with elaborate ceremony when they arrive in town, like a succession of visiting popes. Ducasse grew up in southwestern France and made his reputation by imbuing the seasonal Mediterranean recipes of the Côte D'Azur with a sense of intricate, often extravagant, high-minded elegance. The cookbooks I've hurriedly consulted are filled with glossy photos of shiny plum-sized scallops decked with carefully shaved black truffles, ivory-colored filets of loup de mer dappled with Ossetra caviar, and a glistening, dome-shaped version of the classic French dessert baba au rhum, scented with oranges and crowned with towering clouds of whipped cream. His restaurants in Paris and Monaco have been three-star destinations for years, and once Michelin expands its portfolio to include London, Tokyo, and New York, he will manage to gather more stars than any chef in this pompous, influential, highly subjective guidebook's history. The opening of Restaurant Alain Ducasse at the Sherry Netherland Hotel is already front-page news in the *Times*, and even back in Paris. According to some of the papers I've seen, the wait for a table is eight and a half months long, although how that figure is arrived at is difficult to say, and they claim it's growing longer every day.

But when I arrive at the appointed hour for my lunch with Rebecca Limos, the gilded little dining space in the back of the hotel seems to be mostly empty. The ceiling in the main dining room is painted white and edged along the corners in gold, like one of the private dining rooms at Versailles. The pale, mint-green carpet looks like it's been lifted from one of the guest bedrooms of my step-grandmother's house in South Hampton. The middle of the space is crowded with two black-painted, faintly sepulchral, Greco-style columns, and the decorations include a bizarre art installation of battered trumpets and trombones splattered with dried paint. I wander for a moment among the deserted tables, until the maître d' leads me politely to a little antechamber, where Mrs. Limos is perched alone on a couch, sipping a glass of what I dimly remember as champagne. I make a mock bow in my overlarge Frankenstein undertaker's jacket.

"Mrs. Limos, I presume."

"Just call me Gael," says the critic with a weary smile.

Gael isn't wearing one of her hats today. Her movements seem slow, and slightly exaggerated, and with her pale makeup, she reminds me of a stately Broadway actress out for a discreet restaurant meal between shows. When we move to our table in the mostly empty dining room, a waiter pulls out her chair with comically elaborate ceremony. He brings over a little footstool on which she places an overstuffed handbag. As I sip my water in silence, the critic takes out a crinkled little notebook and a ballpoint pen and begins, furtively, to scratch out notes under the table.

"Do you know Alain's cooking?" she asks, still scribbling away.

At this early stage in my fledgling food writing career, I don't know shit about Alain Ducasse's cooking, of course. My idea of a grand New York dining experience is lunch at our local diner in the Village, Joe Jr.'s, where a bowl of the vividly green, crouton-laden split pea soup costs $2.50 and Louie the head waiter bellows out "Good morning, El Jefe!" to the regulars when they shamble through the door. Louie knew that I preferred to sit at the end of the counter at Joe's for my solitary afternoon BLTs, and when my infant daughters grow up, he will remember the soups they like, and that the younger one always takes hers with extra crackers. Louie, who would die, tragically, of a massive heart attack, was the indispensable front-of-the-house man at Joe's. He kept order when drunks would stagger in off the street, and he had a knack for calming down the unconventional West Villagers who frequented the place, like "the Tattoo Lady," whose face was covered in a pattern of intricate tattoos, and another regular who had a habit, when she was overwhelmed by the cares of the world, as New Yorkers often are, of screaming out her order—"Eight coffees, light and sweet!"—at the top of her lungs.

"Is there a lunchtime price fixe option?" I hear myself say to Gael as I scan the almost cartoonishly large menu, attempting to conjure up witty and knowledgeable avenues of conversation. Unlike at Joe Jr.'s, a single veal chop costs $76 at Monsieur Ducasse's establishment, and it doesn't take a professional critic to figure out that the prices are bordering on the insane. To get a taste of the chef's famous truffled chicken breast, you have to fork over $66, all for a dish that, later on, when I revisit the restaurant on my own expense account, I'll describe as tasting like some strange, denatured form of steamed pork.

"I believe the word is pronounced 'preeee fixxxxxe,'" says Gael, elongating the X with a soft hiss of her teeth.

"I hear the chef's baba au rhum is quite wonderful," I say, exaggerating the word "rhum" in a ridiculous-sounding faux French accent.

"Why don't we try something savory first," she says gently.

The savory dishes begin to arrive at our table minutes later, served by a succession of stiff-backed gentlemen, who are dressed like palace butlers in starchy, smoke-colored suits. They appear at the table like ghosts as each course is served, then drift away in the restaurant gloom. I have dim memories of a pasta dish, possibly, and a wan-tasting salad, and of two pale miniature roulades of sole that appear to have been blanched in tepid bathwater for an hour or two too long. I take tiny little bites of my lunch and make innocuous comments like "This seems lovely" and "*Mmmmmmmm*, I really enjoy the texture here," while Gael tastes her food with an increasingly sour look on her face and puts down her fork, occasionally, to scribble a few notations in her crinkled little book.

In her dyspeptic cover story review, the critic will pronounce my roulades of sole "pathetic" and compare the grandly named Ducasse creation Prawns à la Royale to "simpering baby food." She'll call attention to the breast of squab, which is served deboned and cut into delicate, liver-colored rounds roughly the size of cough lozenges, and explain that in France, prior to roasting, the baby birds are gently strangled in order to preserve the deep crimson color of the meat. As the strangled birds are served, one of the whispering waiters will appear from the gloom to offer a selection of special squab-cutting knives laid out, like cigars, in a ridiculous satin-lined box. "Were Ducasse to try that gimmick in Paris," she'll write of this stunt, and others, "I think they'd roll him through town to the guillotine."

As we contemplate our lunch in increasingly stilted silence, Chef Ducasse suddenly pops out from the kitchen, as if on cue. The chef is smaller than I imagined, and like lots of hardworking restaurant cooks, he has the pale, ghostly complexion of a submarine captain who spends months at a time submerged in a small space, away from the sun. Seeing us at our window table, he effects a look of shocked surprise, and then opens his arms wide, like a man who's greeting long-lost friends.

"Mon amie Gael!" Ducasse cries out to the suddenly startled-looking Mrs. Limos.

"Is it really you?" says Gael, effecting her own look of mock surprise.

They buss each other on both cheeks, like two friendly European matrons.

As Ducasse hovers over the table in his spotless chef's whites, Gael raises one of her bejeweled hands and waves it languidly in my direction. "This is my friend Mr. Duffy," I think I hear Gael say as I rise in my flapping dark jacket to shake the great man's hand.

"Call me André," I hear myself say.

"Welcome, Monsieur Duffy," he says.

What name did Gael actually use to introduce me during that first critic's luncheon long ago? Who really knows? Who really cares? From that day forward, in my fevered imagination, the legend of André Duffy was born. During my long career, I will book tables under a whole array of odd crackpot stage names. I'll make reservations under "Branch Rickey" and "Tyrus Cobb" and whatever else comes into my head. I'll run through the names of deceased relatives, former girlfriends, and the names of formerly eminent, long-dead politicians like Huey Long and Sir Edmund Burke. But "André Duffy" always struck me as having the proper balance between authority and farce. I'd reserve tables under Monsieur Duffy's name for a month or two, until the restaurants around town made a note of it, and I even ordered him his own credit card on which to tabulate the vast sums accruing to his expense account.

I liked to imagine the Great Duffy strolling the avenues on his endless gastronomic rounds with a silk handkerchief tucked into his jacket pocket and a pair of sky-blue suspenders holding up his size 44 expandable trousers. He's a boulevardier of the old school, fluent in the Romance languages and capable of getting around the markets of Chinatown with a smattering of Cantonese. He's familiar with the house specialties at L'Arpège in Paris and Brennan's in New Orleans, and he has a fondness deep in his artery-clogged heart for the ancient trencherman specialties—whole hog North Carolina barbecue, icy buckets of Belon oysters from Brittany, heaping piles of Alsatian choucroute garnie. The Great Duffy repairs to his favorite spa in the hills around Lausanne each year to diet on mineral water and stalks of celery, while rereading the parts of the food canon he loves—Brillat-Savarin on the many signs of gluttony, A. J. Liebling on his beloved Rhône wines, Julia Child on the proper way to cook an omelet. He keeps his statin pills secreted away in a small gold box shaped like a seashell and carries a silver-tipped cane, which once belonged to his grandfather, to help with a recurring touch of the gout.

In my mind, Duffy started out as an amusing alter ego of

course, a way of laughing off, and in many ways protecting myself from, the strange and slightly comical role that the restaurant critic has always cut in the public imagination. But in
time the fantasy of André Duffy and his gastronomic exploits
and the reality of my daily routine in the trenches as a professional critic would blur together in all sorts of slightly unsettling ways. I never stuffed silk cravats in my breast pocket or
carried a silver-tipped cane, but it wasn't long before the real
Adam Platt began to suffer from a touch of gout and began
to keep his statin pills in a plastic box by his bed rather than
a little gold case shaped like a seashell. It wasn't long before
he developed a healthy sugar addiction, along with a taste for
unhealthy, cholesterol-saturated offal products and a tendency
toward perhaps a few too many goblets of Liebling's beloved
Rhône wines. I never wore sky-blue suspenders on the job, but
my next purchase at Rochester Big and Tall, after the jacket,
was an expandable webbed leather belt favored by rotund country club golfers, which grew and shrank with the size of one's
trousers, and soon I was returning to the big man's store up on
Sixth Avenue again and again to browse the aisles for easy-to-
clean polyester dress shirts, more plus-size jackets, and other
tools of the trade.

After a few more pleasantries, Ducasse disappears back into
his kitchen with a perplexed look on his face. With her cover
blown, Mrs. Limos's mood seems to grow a little darker. I don't
ask what kinds of "disguises" have worked best during the course
of her career, or whether other critics around town are on a first-
name basis with the cooks they cover. I don't ask why she's decided to retire after all these years, or what her favorite food
is, or what she likes to cook on off days at home. Later on, after
I've endured my own share of strained dinners at a seemingly
endless stream of mediocre restaurants, making conversation
and answering the same questions from friendly people I barely

know—friends of friends, well-heeled New Yorkers who have bought dinner with the critic at their school auctions—I'll have a better understanding of this strange, mannered world from Gael's point of view. I'll understand that there isn't glamour in every restaurant dinner, and that after a couple of decades in the trenches you'll get to know certain chefs, and they'll get to know you. I'll understand that she's probably gone to some trouble to secure this table, and that she could have invited one of her friends instead of this bumbling giant dressed in his badly fitting suit. I'll understand that in the end, while her guests are making conversation and dribbling sauce onto the tablecloth, she has a job to do.

After a wave of harsh reviews from the New York critics, Ducasse will do away with the squab knives and a few of the other gimmicks, including the practice of presenting his startled guests with a selection of pens on a satin pillow with which to sign their obscenely large bills. He will lower his prices a little and change his executive chef several times. But it won't matter. In the broader sweep of the city's dining history, his timing couldn't have been worse. Tastes are changing all over town to a simpler, more egalitarian brand of dining, and New Yorkers will roll him to the proverbial guillotine anyway, along with many of the other revered French chefs around the city. The next year, La Caravelle stops serving its fluffy pike quenelles forever. The Las Vegas group that buys Lutèce closes the restaurant down and abandons the space in André Soltner's famous townhouse, although the chef and his wife keep living in the apartment above it. Restaurant Alain Ducasse closes quietly, three years after it opened, and is replaced in the back of the musty Sherry Netherland Hotel with a coffee shop. The chef will open three more restaurants in New York, but only one of them, a midtown brasserie called Benoit, will survive. Most of the reviews of that simpler, scaled-down project, named for the famous brasserie that Ducasse restored in Paris, will be lukewarm (including mine), although on her blog Gael, grudgingly, has some kind things to say about the quality of the sautéed skate.

A MONTH AFTER MY LUNCH WITH GAEL, I'LL USE ANDRÉ DUFFY'S freshly minted credit card at another French dining establishment on East Fifty-Second Street called Le Périgord. The restaurant has been open since the Francophile glory days of the 1960s, and it will survive the coming fine-dining apocalypse thanks mostly to the loyal patronage of European diplomats who work at the nearby United Nations and a scattering of devoted grandees and cave dwellers from the staid, spacious apartment buildings around Sutton Place. I know that the proprietor, Georges Briguet, has recently hired a young new chef from Belgium because I've read about it in the "openings" section of the magazine, and I still have a dim idea that serious restaurant critics are supposed to review French restaurants. I book a table for two, at lunchtime, just as Gael recommended I do, because it's usually easier to get a table at a popular restaurant during lunch. For moral support, I invite my mother, an Upper East Side resident of the old school who grew up among gently aging dowager restaurants like this and has a keen appreciation for tables set with white linen and fresh roses, waiters dressed in dusty tuxedos, and classic, slightly archaic delicacies like Dover sole and soufflés tinged with a little extra Grand Marnier.

I put on my critic's jacket, which after only a few weeks on the job is already stained with streaks of gravy, spilled wine, and pork fat. I arrive at the restaurant before my mother does and announce my name to the maître d', who happens to be Monsieur Briguet himself, dressed that afternoon the way he always is: in a black bow tie and stiff-cuffed white shirt. The restaurateur looks me up and down, the faintest trace of a smile on his face, and then says, with elaborate courtesy in his possibly exaggerated accent, "Follow me, Monsieur Duffy." The snug, bustling dining room smells of baked bread and freshly cut flowers, and the tables are filled with serious-faced gentlemen in charcoal-colored suits and gaggles of well-dressed women from the neighborhood sipping glasses of Brouilly wine from the Beaujolais country with their lunch, just as I'd seen Parisian ladies doing at lunchtime when I visited Paris.

Monsieur Briguet leads me to a small, slightly cramped table near the kitchen door, which it soon becomes clear is his little restaurant's equivalent of deepest Siberia. As waiters come rushing in and out of the swinging door, he asks if I'd like a little wine with my lunch. I tell him I'll wait for my guest before ordering the wine, but could I please see the menu? Monsieur Briguet returns to the table and hands me the ancient, beautifully scripted menu, along with the wine list, which is embossed in weathered leather and seems as thick and heavy as an old-fashioned phone book. I pretend to examine the menu for a time in studious silence, while Monsieur Briguet hovers over my cramped little table by the kitchen with what I later imagine is a look of imperious, Gallic distraction on his face. "What's good today?" I finally say, shooting my cuffs the way I think André Duffy might do and smoothing a few bread crumbs from my shirt. Monsieur Briguet smiles a faint smile. "You tell me, Monsieur Duffy," he says, with an exaggerated little bow. "You're the critic."

2

Eating with My Father

Like cruise ship captains and candy-makers, restaurant critics are often being told they have the best job in the world, even if the darker side of the daily grind—the health issues, the struggles with finding a thousand different words for "delicious," the repeating *Groundhog Day* sense of creeping monotony as one familiar baked salmon entrée succeeds the next—makes many things about the job less glamorous than they seem. This mantra becomes one of the quiet perks of the job, however, and it's often followed by questions about how we got into the business, and how one should train for, or even possibly obtain, such a dream occupation. A background in cooking is helpful, I always say, although since I'm not much of a cook, I quickly add that your job as a critic is to sample all kinds of elaborate recipes, not to create them, so it's more helpful to take pleasure in eating and also to develop a sturdy constitution for the rigors of what one of my colleagues used to wearily call "tying on the old feed bag."

What food snobs used to delight in calling "a sophisticated palate" is probably helpful too, although in my experience, a delicious dish is not difficult to spot, and a truly exceptional palate is a rare thing that takes a combination of talent, practice, and hard work to develop, the way a golfer hones a perfectly grooved golf swing. A modest talent for writing and expression is something any critic needed back in the predigital print and publishing world where I came from, along with a distinctive, settled point of view. There are different tricks for mastering these skills, I suppose, but if you want to develop that crucial constitution for sturdy eating at an early age, along with a curiosity and appreciation for the endless, uplifting pleasures of a good meal, it helps to grow up with a worthy role model. And it doesn't hurt to be dropped into the middle of an ancient and mysterious culinary culture at a young and impressionable age, with two ravenous younger brothers and a hefty little boy's appetite.

For someone who occupied the staid, unruffled world of international diplomacy for most of his working life, my father always had an impressive, wide-ranging, slightly eccentric appetite for a good meal. From an early age, he told his plump, impressionable sons stories of the favored, delicious foods of his own chubby youth—steamed lobster fished from the chilly waters of Maine, dense, bacon-filled tomato sandwiches in the summertime, crunchy peanut butter (as opposed to the viscous smooth kind), and always his beloved mayonnaise, which he purchased in large vats and spread with religious devotion on everything from summer tomatoes to canned sardines to bizarre mystery lunchmeats of every imaginable kind. Hellmann's was his mayonnaise of choice, but he also worshipped an obscure Swiss brand called Thomy, which back in the 1960s and '70s you could buy in handy metal tubes. Where other dignified WASP gentlemen packed flasks of whiskey or their collection of traveling pipes when they went off on business trips or diplomatic excursions, my father would pack a few tubes of Thomy mayonnaise in his travel bags for emergency use (though he usually had a flask of whiskey too). My father enjoyed other exotic garnishes, especially Worcestershire sauce, and a spicy sauce from Jamaica called Pickapeppa, and although I never saw him cook an entire proper meal, on our birthdays when we were growing up he would splash these favorite condiments on toast, sausages, and soft-boiled eggs, together with a hint of vermouth, and present us at breakfast time with what he liked to call, with elaborate ceremony, our special birthday "Daddy Egg."

My father collected favorite restaurants in all of the scattered destinations where we lived when we were young, whether it was Taiwan, where we first moved when we went to Asia in the early 1960s; or Hong Kong, where we moved after that; or the random restaurants of 1970s Washington, DC, like the Yenching Palace on Connecticut Avenue, with its illuminated art deco interior and sticky, vividly orange bowls of sweet-and-sour pork, or Blackie's House of Beef downtown on M Street, where J. Edgar Hoover and his cronies used to unwind after a hard day at the office over gin cocktails and bloody slabs of prime rib. My father sometimes brought back menus from his travels, including one emblazoned at the top with the red seal of the People's Republic of China, from a banquet held in Richard Nixon's honor during his famous trip to China in the winter of 1972 at the Great Hall of the People, where the assembled dignitaries dined gamely on a grim-sounding dinner of "Bean Curd Junket," "Chicken Dices in Chili," and "Stewed Meat Balls." Sometimes he brought back strange spirits from his adventures: bottles of cheap yellow Mehkong whiskey from Thailand, jars of "snake wine" from Taiwan, and fiery Moutai from Beijing, which came in a white ceramic bottle with a red ribbon tied around the top and tasted, he told us, like "liquid razor blades."

Like many seasoned world travelers, my father was a firm

believer in the diplomatic and cultural benefits of a fine meal—it was the easiest and most immediate way to connect with any strange new city or country where you happened to find yourself, he liked to say, and also the easiest way to summon up a sense of well-being and calm when everything around you seemed to be trending in the opposite direction. Later on, when he served as the US ambassador to the kind of challenging posts that big-money political donors tended to avoid (Pakistan under Benazir Bhutto, the Philippines under Cory Aquino, the tiny, beautiful southern African republic of Zambia), he explained that one way he projected a sense of diplomatic happiness and unflappable calm during his challenging working day was by doing what a public speaking expert had advised him to do early in his career during times of trouble and stress. "Think about what makes you happy," the wise expert had said. So, before giving a speech or entering into a difficult diplomatic negotiation, he'd dream about the joys of a proper lobster dinner, with drawn butter and a side of crunchy potatoes, which he ate when he was a young boy during the summers his family spent up at their small vacation house in Maine—a state of happy, beatific, Buddha-like calm that he called "Lobster Face."

My father got many of his quirky culinary habits and tics the way people get most things—from his own parents, both of whom came from a long line of Yankee toastmasters, amateur cooks, and cheerful, cocktail-loving inebriates. If my mother's family, the Maynards, were the more traditional, dour Puritans when it came to food and cooking, then the Platts and my grandmother's family, the Choates, were jolly Anglicans, devotees of the famous eighteenth-century scholar and cleric Sydney Smith, who famously described his idea of heaven as "eating foie gras to the sound of trumpets." Unlike some families, the Platts and the Choates enjoyed one another's company, and they liked to convene in the evenings at the appointed time to sip their ritual cocktails and then repair to the dining room to shout at each other cheerfully over a nourishing dinner. Over the years both families collected favorite recipes, patronized favorite family restaurants, and sang their favorite family songs in loud, merry, and sometimes drunken voices. They enjoyed crackly standing rib roasts served with all the trimmings at Christmastime and ceremonial haunches of lamb, brushed with rosemary and mustard sauce, for Easter. They devoured their ritual Thanksgiving turkey every fall, dined on platters of shad roe fished from the Hudson in the springtime when the fish were running up the river from their home base of New York City, and engaged in all sorts of strange and comforting dining rituals when they left Manhattan every June to visit their rambling, increasingly dilapidated country estates up in the green hills of New England.

Sitting around in the evenings sipping drinks during their sacred cocktail hour, my father and his large collection of siblings and cousins would sometimes recite the names of the venerable family fressers, the way wistful old baseball fans remember the starting lineups of their favorite childhood team. There was my father's grandmother, Eleanor Hardy, who came from a family of Boston sea captains whose clipper ships sailed the spice routes between Asia and the Americas. She sang Hindu lullabies to her children at night and gathered them in her rumpled bed in the morning for breakfasts of buttered toast drizzled with honey. There was Great-Uncle Charlie, who returned from life as a cowboy rancher out west with a facility for baking rhubarb pies, and cousin Frank, the family gastronome, a collector of classic New York restaurants and speakeasies who had the staccato delivery of one of his favorite mid-twentieth-century comedians, Sid Caesar, and who carried in his head a whole rattlebag of obscure cocktail recipes, tall food tales, and snatches of poetic verse. Cousin Frank would sometimes arrange communal lamb and goat roasts on Labor Day at the family house up in New Hampshire, and he had a fondness for tripe, calves' brains, and other gently sim-mered offal delicacies long before nose-to-tail cooking achieved the height of gourmet sophistication thanks to chefs like Tony Bourdain and the famous master of the genre in London, Fer-gus Henderson. There was my father's grandfather, a prosperous Manhattan architect named Charles A. Platt who, back in the early 1900s, well before the scourge of vegetable snobbery swept the country almost a century later, had fresh earth shipped up from Connecticut for the planting of the vegetable garden at his summer house in New Hampshire. The elder Platt developed a rigorous system of composting for his garden that his ancestors follow even today, and his devotion to fresh salad was so intense that his friend Sanford White Jr. wrote a sonnet about it, which he had framed and hung in his country kitchen.

There were my father's formidable aunts on different sides of the family, Lena and Mabel, learned and eccentric women of the Eleanor Roosevelt school who had their own strongly held habits and opinions on how to enjoy a fine meal. Aunt Lena was a cook, of sorts, who gave her favorite dishes colorful names like "Train Wreck" (an apparently delicious chicken basted with 7-Up) and "Cry Like a Child" (her famous beef stew). She taught my father how to appreciate the finer points of a well-roasted haunch of roast beef ("save the fatty crackle bits for last"), and after dinner she liked to light up a long cigar and enjoy healthy drafts of sherry procured from the famous S. S. Pierce provi-sions store on Copley Square in Boston. Aunt Mabel Choate had traveled widely in Asia and was an expert on the intrica-cies of Chinese gardens, which she re-created, complete with an ancestral family temple, at her house up in the Berkshires. She was a stout woman who strongly believed, my father liked to say, that good health depended on the vital organs being sur-rounded by a thick layer of fat, and she fattened up her nephews and nieces who came up from the city to work on the farm in the summertime with a diet of fresh eggs in the morning and rashers of country sausages, followed by all sorts of buttery, creamy, gravy-laden, locally grown specialties for lunch and dinner. My father remembers that Aunt Mabel wore a large collection of gold and copper bracelets on her wrists that tinkled loudly when she walked, which meant that you could hear her coming down the garden path from a good distance away. She told stories to her impressionable young nephew about the banquets and dinners she'd attended in Imperial China, where it was the custom not to clap or murmur in appreciation of a delicate dish after a fine meal, but to burp as loudly as you possibly could.

Aunt Mabel's family, the Choates, were known for their prominent noses and shocks of wild red hair; several of them became prominent politicians, educators, and barristers around New England and New York. Like the Platts, the Choates had their own firm ideas about what constituted a good meal, and when my father's parents were married, the two clans used to engage in long culinary debates that ran down through the generations. There were arguments on the proper way to eat your summer corn (a vigorous uncle named Penrose, who married into the Choates, spent a lifetime espousing what he called the "typewriter" method) and on what to name the best fatty bits of a crown roast ("crispy" said the Choates; "crackle" said the Platts). There were discussions on the best kind of raw bar shellfish to eat frosty and fresh (Long Island cherrystones of course) and the best way to extract the proper sweetness while cooking a lobster (gentle steaming of course). There were debates on the most noble form of chowder (New England versus Manhattan), what kind of seafood to put in your chowder (cod fish versus clams), and how to garnish your bowl of steamy chowder once it was ready to eat and on the table (with sizzled, finely chopped bits of salt pork of course).

Often these discussions were moderated by my grandfather

Geoffrey, who was arguably the Babe Ruth of this ancient, ancestral lineup of eaters, drinkers, and bon vivants. We called our grandfather "Grappa," which also happened to be the name of his favorite Italian liqueur, so the name was fine with him. Like many people of his privileged class and generation, he found comfort in rituals, and he took pleasure in creating them all his life. He had a ritual fondness for hats: fedoras in cold weather and straw panamas banded with strips of checked cotton in the summertime, when he walked up and down the avenues wearing his panama from Brooks Brothers on Madison Avenue. As a card-carrying member of the booze-loving Prohibition Generation, he had ritual toasts for different occasions and ritual drinking songs, which he liked to sing at the top of his lungs while keeping time by conducting with a single finger in the air, like an old-time bandleader. Before going out for the evening, he liked to slug down a shot of stiff drink, which he called a Rammer, and for as long as I knew him, he and my grandmother Helen, who was a voluble member of the Choate clan, observed the cocktail hour seven days a week, beginning more or less exactly at 6:30 p.m., often with an extra-dry Beefeater or Marie Brizard gin martini at their side, and a bowl of cheddar-flavored Pepperidge Farm goldfish crackers, which my grandfather purchased in bulk from the grocery store.

LIKE HIS FATHER AND MY FATHER AND COUSIN FRANK, GRAPPA was a diligent eater of the traditional New York school, who patronized restaurants and dining clubs and beefsteak parlors throughout the city. He liked veal saltimbocca hammered to a papery thinness, stewed innards served in all sorts of traditional ways, and pike quenelles prepared the way French cooks did them in the grand midtown restaurants, which he considered the ultimate expression of a certain kind of civilized gourmand comfort food. Whenever we went to visit our grandparents in New York, Grappa would buy us hot dogs on the street, smothered with mustard and sauerkraut, and hot roasted chestnuts twirled in sheets of newspapers, and when we stayed with them in Maine, or up in New Hampshire, or out in their house in Mount Kisco, he'd convene ritual dining clubs to celebrate his favorite foods. There were lobster clubs and fish cake clubs and the famous "Fish Ball Club." This august institution met only at breakfast time and revolved around our mutual regard for Mrs. Paul's frozen fish balls, which, during the culinary hellscape of the early 1970s frozen TV dinner era, Grappa believed to be a kind of miracle dish. In the mornings—sometimes early in the morning, before he took the train into the city to work—Grappa would carefully heat the fish balls to a ritual 425 degrees until they were suitably toasty and rock-hard, and then, still dressed in his bedroom slippers and baggy flannel robe, call the Fish Ball Club to order. There was a Fish Ball Club proclamation, which I've forgotten, and after we'd finished reciting the proclamation in solemn tones, he would lead my brother and me in a loud rendition of the Fish Ball Club song, "Fish Balls to You." Dressed in our leather slippers and baggy cotton pajamas, we'd sing "Fish Balls to you, Fish Balls! Fish Balls! Fish Balls! Fish Balls! Fish Balls to You!"

Sometimes the Fish Ball Club would convene out in Westchester, where Grappa lived with our grandmother in a rambling house of his own design (like his father, he was an architect), filled with big bay windows and large brick fireplaces that smelled of wood smoke even in the summertime. Sometimes the Fish Ball Club would convene up in Maine, on an island called North Haven out in the middle of Penobscot Bay, usually in between our visits to the local market, for bags of root beer barrels and other penny candies, and carefully orchestrated lobster dinners that Grappa called "Lobster Wallows." These family banquets tended to unfold according to the same sacramental routine: with the dressing of the salad (always blue cheese), followed by the sacred crisping of the potatoes (with olive oil, salt, and a scattering of rosemary) and the breaking of the lobsters over the sink, a ceremony Grappa often performed wearing the same big rubber lobsterman's gloves that my father would wear when he presided over lobster dinners, and that my brothers and cousins and I still use today. On very rare occasions the Fish Ball Club might even convene at the old Platt summerhouse up in New Hampshire, where Grappa was born, on the second floor, in a sun-filled room facing south down the valley. Built by his father, the architect, in the upper reaches of the Connecticut River Valley, it was located on a ridge of farmers' fields above the river between the towns of Plainfield and Cornish, New Hampshire, overlooking Ascutney Mountain and the distant church steeples of a town called Windsor, Vermont.

I've never thought of these old country houses as family estates, but over the years I suppose that's what they've become. According to my own unofficial count, close to fifty people have access to the house in New Hampshire, and if you show up on a summer weekend, any combination of them might be there, having traveled from places as distant as California, Washington State, and Peru. Other architects as well as artists, like the illustrator Maxfield Parrish and the sculptor Augustus Saint-Gaudens, worked and owned houses in the area, and the group, many of whom were friends of Grappa's father, Charles, were known informally as the Cornish Artists Colony. Like his friend Saint-Gaudens, whose house and studio were up the hill, Charles was a neoclassicist who read Ovid in the original Latin and had traveled widely in Italy. Over the years, as his practice down in New York grew, improvements were made to the house, often in a neoclassical way: a large room called the Parlor was built for entertaining, and he added garden terraces modeled after the country villas around Italy, which he'd visited as a young man, and even a columned porch area called the Piazza, framed with cracked bubblegum-colored frescoes embroidered with painted grapevines.

Long ago, it used to take the first Platts seven hours to travel up to their country house by train from Grand Central Terminal—which is about how long it can take their modern ancestors to navigate the same trip through the weekend rush-hour traffic outside of New York or Hartford or Boston, with their cavalcades of children, guests, and family dogs. Usually you arrive late at night, and depending on the season, the air will be filled with the smell of pine trees and wood smoke or, in the late spring or early summer, of blooming lilacs. Once you finally arrive, where you sleep is a matter of serendipity. You could find yourself in "the back," above the kitchen, where I slept with my brothers and cousins when I was young and my father and grandfather slept when they were boys. You might end up in the North Room, so-called because it faces north and gets little light, or, on special birthday or anniversary occasions, in my great-grandfather's room, with its weathered oil paintings and views out over the garden to the pine trees and the blue-green mountain in the distance. Or, on crowded holiday weekends, you could find yourself curled up in a sunny room on a musty couch in a cigar-colored space called the Boys' Room, peering at cracked first printings of Rudyard Kipling or Max Beerbohm with your knees tucked up under your nose.

Sooner or later when you visit the Platt house up in Cornish, however, you'll end up in the kitchen, with its smooth-topped butcher block breakfast table, and its rattling drawers filled with all sorts of anthropological wonders, like ancient egg-beaters, rusted carving knives, and dark cast-iron pans as thick and weathered as soldiers' helmets. The cupboards are stacked with cocktail glasses and patterned china plates, some of them from long-ago weddings, and above the breakfast table are narrow shelves of cookbooks, winnowed down over the decades to the bare essentials. There's a scuffed *Joy of Cooking* dating from 1973, its yellow, stain-covered pages falling from the spine and covered in illegible notations. There are well-worn copies of Elizabeth David's *Summer Cooking* and Ada Boni's *Talisman Italian Cookbook*, a precursor to Marcella Hazan's famous Italian books. (The ingredients for the stock in Boni's Thrifty Fish Soup, a Depression-era dish, are 2 pounds haddock, 1 medium onion, 1 stalk celery, 1 bay leaf, 2½ quarts water, and 1 teaspoon salt.) There's also an early edition of *Fannie Farmer*, with an introduction by James Beard, as well as its own precursor, the classic Yankee volume *The Boston Cooking School Cook Book*, which Fannie Merritt Farmer first published in 1896, with its intricate canning charts and carefully measured recipes for chowders and buttery "two crust" country pies.

When I was growing up, the Master of the Salad at the Platt house was my father's cousin Charlie, who made his own highly particular version of this ancestral dish in a big oil-stained wooden bowl, which had been presented to him by the groomsmen on his wedding day. In the kitchen before large family dinners, there being no TV in the old house even today—or back then video games or iPhones—we would often gather around to watch Charlie conduct the ritual rubbing of the fresh bulbs of garlic into the bottom of the bowl with a large spoon, the scattered crumblings of rock salt and blue cheese for the base, and then the final benediction of the olive oil, which Charlie, an avowed atheist, poured solemnly and from a great height, like a priest performing an ancient sacramental rite.

Charlie was the Salad Master of Cornish, but if it was a classic New Orleans Sazerac you wanted, or a quirky disquisition on the best vintages of mid-twentieth-century French wines, or a lesson in the correct way to dig a barbecue pit, or the perfect recipe for Timballo di Lasagna alla Modenese (which he once typed out for me and mailed along with the blizzard of other notes and cards he habitually sent around to his friends and family on the subjects that interested him, and which I still have, stuck like an ancient biblical parchment on the bulletin board above my desk), the person to consult was cousin Frank, the family gastronome. Frank's father, my grandfather's brother Roger, was a schoolteacher and a man of regular and steady dining habits that sustained his "substantial" physique (the term he preferred over "fat," Frank used to say). Frank's father and mother had a regular extra-large booth to accommodate their substantial size at Hamburger Hamlet in New York, where they lived, and his father enjoyed the occasional late-night snack, the way my grandfather and my own father often did: standing naked except for his underpants, late at night, in front of the open refrigerator. "Is there anything better than eating cold mashed potatoes by the icebox on a hot summer's night with your son?" Frank remembers him asking late one evening, when the young boy had discovered his father stuffing his craw by the light of the antique refrigerator filled with gently melting blocks of ice. "No, Pop, I don't think there's anything better in the whole world than this," Frank replied.

Cousin Frank told stories about possibly mythical cocktail drinks, like the Tammany Hall Martini, made with whiskey instead of gin by the Irish ward bosses downtown, and about aged waiters and the restaurants they inhabited in his vanished corner of New York—like the original Longchamps on Madison Avenue, or Lüchow's down by Union Square, where his father took him to taste forgotten German delicacies like smoked eel, or platters of herring smothered in mustard sauce, or, on special occasions, generous helpings of Beluga caviar, which the waiters served on a bed of crushed ice for $8.75. He remembered dinners of sautéed foie gras at Lutèce and dining on cassoulet in the famous painted dining room at Le Côte Basque on Fifty-Eighth Street, where the waiters would brush the top of your bowl with streaks of mustard from an earthenware pot. He remembered visiting the original Ritz in midtown, where his parents took him when he was five years old to sample the magical invention of the head chef, Louis Diat, called vichyssoise, and how the waiters stacked up a pile of phone books for him to sit on when the cool, creamy, delicious soup arrived at the table. He'd visited the original French Pavilion at the World's Fair in 1939, when he was a little boy, and later in life he became friends with the author of the Madeline books, Ludwig Bemelmans, who gave him drawings of giant red lobsters and chefs wearing their tall, leaning white toques, which he'd hang proudly on the walls of the study in his dark, rambling apartment on Park Avenue and Eighty-Sixth Street. Cousin Frank was in the publishing business, and he befriended M.F.K. Fisher and André Soltner, among many other poets and writers, and he liked to tell the story about the time he dined with A. J. Liebling himself at the Lobster, a now-vanished restaurant on Forty-Third Street. The great man devoured two whole lobsters for lunch in a moody silence, Frank happily reported, sucking the last shreds of meat and juice from each shell, as practiced lobster eaters do, and after lunch he ducked in to a local diner to buy an extra cheeseburger for the road, along with an extra milk shake or two.

The Platts weren't bad cooks, and my grandmother especially prided herself on the recipes that she'd learned from the chefs at Cordon Bleu. They had a habit of collecting favorite restaurants wherever they went, however, and sometimes it seemed to me, as an impressionable young eater, that the real die-hard New Yorkers among them, like Grappa and cousin Frank, had a favorite restaurant for each meal of the day. When not consuming fish balls in the morning, Grappa dropped into the kind of diners that were plentiful around the city in those days, like my local,

Joe Jr.'s, on Twelfth Street, or Neil's on the corner of Lexington and Sixty-Ninth Street, where my father still likes to sit at the bar to read the morning paper and sip his non-barista cup of $2 coffee. The Oyster Bar, with its curved, bunkered ceilings beneath Forty-Second Street in Grand Central Terminal, was the favored Platt venue for a quick big-city luncheon. Grappa liked to sit at the original bar in front of the shuckers and cooks, not in the tourist-filled dining room and never, God forbid, at the low-slung Formica-topped counters that the owners installed during one of their misguided expansion periods, although Frank was partial to that counter, especially when his favorite server, Mae, was on duty. In the summertime, they'd order a dozen Blue Points over ice and, if they were fresh and plump, a platter of the Long Island cherrystones. If it was a brisk, wintery afternoon, the famous oyster pan roast was the favored Platt dish, and we would sit at the bar together and watch the chefs in their tall white hats mix the oysters together with sweet butter and flagons of cream, the way they still do today, and then pour the silken concoction over slices of bread and finish each bowl with a sprinkling of paprika.

The favorite Platt restaurant for a ceremonial family dinner was Giovanni's, an old Italian establishment run by Pramaggiore Giovanni, an avuncular, balding gentleman from the Piedmont region of Italy. Like André Soltner's Lutèce, over on East Fiftieth Street, Giovanni's occupied the bottom floors of a narrow townhouse, on Fifty-Fifth Street between Madison and Park, and like Soltner, the proprietor lived with his family in an apartment above the restaurant. Also like Soltner, Giovanni went to the markets every morning with a shopping bag, and the food his restaurant served was an elegant big-city version of the classic regional cooking he'd grown up with as a child. Like most of dining New York in the days before superstar chefs, destination restaurants, and the democratic madness of the internet, Giovanni's was a place of settled order and habit, where the same neighborhood regulars appeared at their favored tables night after night. Early on, during the Depression, Grappa and his brother Bill had done architectural work for Giovanni, and because money was tight, they'd agreed to be paid in kind with a string of dinners. Over the years, as the economy recovered and the restaurant prospered, Giovanni's became an informal clubhouse for the Platts, who held birthday and wedding parties there and a long series of booze-filled weekend luncheons. When my father turned twenty-one, he was given twenty-one meals at Giovanni's, and many of his cousins received the same coming-of-age gift. Over time Giovanni became an honored friend of the family who attended weddings, christenings, and funerals; when one of Frank's children was born, the old restaurant man appeared at the hospital carrying a frosty jug of vichyssoise for Frank's wife, Judy, which he considered the most nutritious potion possible for mother's milk.

A dinner at Giovanni's tended to follow the same ritual pattern. After making the market rounds in the mornings, Giovanni would be stationed by the door in the evenings, dressed in a blue blazer and exuding the professional restaurateur's practiced brand of good cheer. John the bartender was a veteran of the war and had the habit of calling regulars by their military rank. He called my uncle Bill "the Commander" and my grandfather "the Major," and John usually mixed Grappa's regular rum sour or a martini made with 110 proof Marie Brizard gin as soon as he walked in the door. Cousin Frank remembers that the wallpaper at Giovanni's was yellow "like the color of old gnocchi" and that the antipasti cart always followed shortly after the drinks. My grandfather was partial to the clams en gelée or possibly a small bowl of eggplant caponata off the menu, followed by a plate of gnocchi à la Romana or, if he was feeling expansive, maybe a helping of the veal saltimbocca, which the kitchen prepared in the classic Roman way with flattened veal cutlets, slivers of salty prosciutto, and a finish of buttery masala sauce. Dessert was either a properly boozy tiramisu or a strange brandy, berry, and cake concoction that Giovanni, who called it Strawberries à la Platt, enjoyed taking a match to at tableside. (According to Frank, there were other flaming strawberry dishes named after other faithful regulars of the restaurant.) After the meal, Giovanni would come to the table with a bottle of grappa alla ruta, which was scented with a special mountain herb from back in the Veneto, and the two gentlemen would sip their digestifs in little glasses and tell stories before retiring for the evening.

Giovanni closed down his restaurant in the late 1970s, after a long successful run, and moved with his family out to the suburbs. With the proceeds from selling the Madison Avenue townhouse, according to Frank, he'd bought the home of the owner of the Stork Club, Sherman Billingsley, which was not far from where Grappa lived out in Westchester, and he brought the best of the Veneto and Piedmont wines from the restaurant to his new house in the country and kept them in the cellar. He and Grappa and Frank would gather at his house with their families to drink dusty bottles of Amarone and inky red Barbarescos and dine on specialties from the home country, like braised wild boar, which was so soft, Frank remembered, that Giovanni would cut it the traditional way—using stiff pieces of string. I never tasted this famous wild boar dish, and I only visited Giovanni's restaurant once, when we went to New York from Hong Kong, on home leave. Compared to the food we'd been feasting on in Asia, the refrigerated jellied clams and tubes of cannelloni stuffed with undersalted ricotta seemed a little on the bland side of the flavor spectrum. But for my father, going back to the old dining room with its rolling antipasti carts and yellowing wallpaper had an elemental effect. Throughout our wandering childhood, he would always be searching for that mythical place where we could order off the menu, chat with the owner, and summon for his own family the sense of permanence and community and celebration he'd known at Giovanni's back home.

Growing up, we'd hear stories about Giovanni's, sometimes as we sat out eating Mongolian barbecue under the stars in Tai-chung, or during one of our dinners at a strange colonial estab-lishment called Jimmy's Kitchen in Hong Kong. Sometimes we'd hear about Giovanni's at Peking duck restaurants in Beijing, or at Blackie's House of Beef, the traditional steakhouse in Wash-ington, DC, where assorted politicians and power brokers of the old city dined on prime rib and sipped their gin cocktails. We'd hear about it at our favorite sushi restaurant in Tokyo, where the Platt boys first tasted a mysterious, silky, orange substance called uni, which the proprietor explained was excavated from the in-sides of prickly raw sea urchins and shipped down to Tokyo in little wooden boxes from Japan's northern island of Hokkaido.

We never found our mythical Giovanni's, of course. Or we'd find it for a little while and then pack up and move on to another country, and when we'd return to modern Beijing for the Peking duck or to Hong Kong for a meal at the Repulse Bay Hotel, or visit the original Jimmy's Kitchen in Hong Kong (where my brother and father and I ordered some withered pork bangers and a dank, tasteless bowl of mulligatawny soup not long ago), the menu would be a little different, the food wouldn't be as we remembered it, and that fleeting sense of intimacy that you get as a regular would be gone. During my career as a frenetic professional eater, I've been doomed to repeat this same endless cycle, although sometimes I still dream about that mythical joint filled with familiar faces from the neighborhood, a place where I can order a leisurely dinner without looking at the menu, at my usual table, on my usual night, a place where the kitchen staff don't recoil in alarm when the critic walks through the door. Over the years I've taken my daughters to the Oyster Bar in Grand Central to sample the legendary oyster pan roast ("These oysters are a little overcooked, Dad") and to the old French restaurants uptown in the hopes that they'll develop a taste for cousin Frank's favorite tripe ("This isn't really my thing, Dad"). My father is always happy to try new places, and sometimes he will come along on these expeditions, especially to restaurants that specialize in northern Chinese cuisine, or his beloved Peking duck, or helpings of steak tartare mixed tableside in the classic French manner, with egg yolk, chopped capers, and plenty of Worcestershire. But, unlike me, he's still a regular at heart, and so he visits Neil's diner for his short-order breakfast, and I like to think that every once in a long while he drops in at the Oyster Bar at lunchtime to get a sense of the rhythms of the old bustling city. He still convenes dining clubs for his grandchildren up in Maine in the summertime, and although the club song is the same as the one my brothers and I chanted loudly on those winter mornings with our own grandfather out in the New York suburbs many years ago, tastes have changed over the years, and both he and his raucous brood of grandchildren seem to prefer boxes of "brown 'n serve" maple-flavored pork sausages to the timeless frozen pleasures of Mrs. Paul's.

3

Eating with My Mother

"You boys must have some very bizarre and mixed-up food memories," my mother said to me once as we looked through the old family photo albums together. My mother was an observer by nature, a collector of sensations and images and fleeting moments that struck her as true or beautiful in her Proustian way as she traveled through life, and I'm probably the most Proustian of her large, Rabelaisian sons. We are the worriers of the family, and we often like to watch the world at a critical distance, or at least from a safe remove, standing toward the side of the room. My mother kept a series of journals during her exotic overseas travels with my father, and, for a time, when I was trying to duplicate this kind of life, so did I. Our pinched handwriting style, experts will tell you, is a sign of introversion, although her tiny, neatly ordered characters were always much more legible than mine. She was shy as a child growing up, and so was I. My father and brothers have busy, restless temperaments, but for whatever reason, my mother and I can spend long stretches of time sitting in one place, watching the clouds change shape in the sky. Toward the end of her life, she had arthritis in all of her joints and problems with her circulation, first in her legs and hands, and finally in her heart. She took what she liked to call her "puffs" of powerful chemical-laced medicine several times a day from an inhaler contraption that sat by her bedside. After a lifetime of travel, she and my father rarely went on their excursions anymore to Shanghai, or to Tehran to tour the great mosques, or to Cambodia to cruise the Mekong River and view the temples at Angkor Wat. On summer weekends, and even in the winters when the weather was clear, they would drive together across the Hudson to their small house by a green marsh next to the river, where she liked to sit out on the porch overlooking the water, there where the river narrows and bends southward past the city and out to the sea, and watch the flocks of birds come and go across the sky on their long migrations up and down the coast.

My mother began putting together photo albums of our family travels shortly before we moved to Asia in the early 1960s, when my father was sent to Taiwan as a young diplomat to study Mandarin. She compiled them in her deliberate fashion as we moved over the years from Canada to Hong Kong and back to Washington, DC, to Beijing and Tokyo, to southern Africa and Manila, and to Islamabad, Pakistan, where we all flew in one Christmas and drove up to the Khyber Pass to snap photos of the border guards dressed in their plumed hats left over from the British Raj and take portraits of the Platts, looking across the border toward the craggy mountains of Afghanistan. In the end, there were eleven volumes in all, lined up side by side on a long shelf in the apartment: a Talmudic record of her family's exotic wanderings. Over the years the linen covers have grown smooth and faded with age, like worn pieces of coral. The album pages are filled with notations and dates, written out in her small, neat hand, with crinkled pieces of wax paper set between the pages to keep the prints from sticking together. My original birth certificate is pasted in one of the books from the George Washington University Hospital in Washington, DC, with its tattered edges and shadowy gray imprints of two tiny feet. She titled a photograph from the summer of 1960 of the future plump-faced restaurant critic, sitting with his mouth open and both hands on a dining room table, "Adam Anticipating His Lunch." There are photos of graduations and weddings and misty views of mountain hikes and long-ago picnics in places like the Ming tombs, outside of Beijing, and the Great Wall of China, sites that were mostly deserted ruins in the days when they lived in China. There are fuzzy snapshots of vanished twentieth-century ocean liners and coal-burning steam trains, and many of the kind of artful, atmospheric still-life pictures my mother loved to take—of flower vases, of views from Victorian hotel windows, of the little bowls and trinkets she'd pick up at different markets, many of them patterned in her favorite colors, blue and white.

We'd moved to Asia in the winter of 1962 from Windsor, Ontario, across the border from Detroit, where my father got his first government job, at the age of twenty-three, processing visas on the Canadian border. He had joined the Foreign Service with dreams of glamorous postings to the grand embassies of Europe, but after his time on the visa line, he'd changed his mind. China was in the midst of its dark Maoist age, and during the Joe McCarthy/Roy Cohn witch hunts of the 1950s, an entire generation of Foreign Service China hands had been purged from the State Department. Unlike in Europe, which was crowded with ambitious young diplomats fluent in German, Russian, and French, there were opportunities in Asia, especially for those who were willing to go through the tortures of learning a language like Chinese, which took two years of training at a special government institute in Taichung, a small city on the eastern coast of the island. The first year of Mandarin study was devoted to learning the intricate spoken tones of the language; during the second year students learned how to read and write Chinese characters. My father liked to say that you didn't really know a language until you started to dream in it, and by the time they left Taiwan two years later, my parents would both be dreaming in the mellifluous, singsong sounds of Mandarin Chinese.

My mother couldn't remember how they found the classic Japanese-style house on the outskirts of Taichung. She guessed that it had been built by a Japanese merchant or official when the Japanese occupied the island in the decades leading up to World War II. In many ways, it combined the classic touches of Japanese architecture with the functional style of a well-to-do Chinese family home. A double-door gate out front was painted a bright firehouse red, which is the color of good luck and good fortune in China; it opened onto a classic Mandarin courtyard, surrounded by a series of rickety wooden walls, with living quarters for our cook, Mr. Yu, and his family in the courtyard. The house had two living rooms downstairs, one covered in traditional Japanese tatami matting and the other a Western-style room, which my mother decorated with curving rattan peacock chairs that looked like they'd been lifted from the set of a James Bond swinger spy movie from the 1960s. From the bedrooms upstairs, there were long views toward what my mother described in her letters back home to New York as "the marvelous heap of rumpled blue mountains beyond the town."

This new world was filled with all sorts of strange wonders. Turning the pages of the family photo albums, you can see the colors of the pictures slowly change from bleak black-and-white shots of snowbound Canadian streetscapes to bright color photographs of gardens and street markets and cloud-shrouded mountains. In our new neighborhood there were pig farms and an eel farm filled with dark green pools of water covered with lily pads, and in the mornings farmers would herd dust-covered water buffalos down the road beyond the house, out into the fields. Every morning my brother Oliver and I were pedaled off to kindergarten at the local Presbyterian church, bouncing out between the rice paddies in the back of a metal pedicab powered by an energetic elderly man on a bicycle. On the weekends, we wobbled on the backs of our parents' bicycles to the local markets, where we bought bags of steaming pork and scallion dumplings and long stalks of sugarcane, which vendors shaved with long knives or squeezed through a rusty wheeled press to produce little plastic cups filled with sweet sugarcane juice. The markets sold live snakes, which were cooked in medicinal soups, and soupy bowls of breakfast porridge laced with salty eggs or dried fish or little bundles of pork floss, and all sorts of magical tropical fruits we'd never seen before, like long green papayas filled with mysterious-looking pods of black seeds, hairy coconuts, yellow watermelons, and waxy orange-green star fruits, which had the tartness of lemons and the sweet, chewy consistency of summer plums.

In those decades after Mao's revolution, Taiwan was filled with all kinds of dislocated refugees from the suddenly vanished capitalist economy on the Chinese mainland: limousine drivers, jewelry makers, bankers, butlers, and hundreds of accomplished cooks and restaurateurs who'd been on the wrong side of the war and whose livelihoods had dried up in Chairman Mao's China. The most famous of these culinary masters was Peng Chang-kuei, who ran the banquets operation for Generalissimo Chiang Kai-shek in the capital of Taipei and who would later introduce a grateful New York dining public to the glories of General Tso's chicken. Even in our little town, you could find accomplished cooks trained in the mysteries of everything from Cantonese dim sum to Imperial dishes from the Emperor's Court like Peking duck. Our family cook was the gentlemanly and talented

Mr. Yu, from Shandong in northern China. In addition to many of the home-style specialties, like lo mein tossed with chicken or shrimp, different kinds of dumplings, and pork dishes stewed, fried, and simmered in endlessly delicious ways, he knew how to prepare comparatively tedious Western classics, like chocolate chip cookies, bacon and eggs for breakfast, and on special occasions carefully layered cakes, which he covered, like a first-class pastry chef, with waves of sugary frosting.

In the old photo albums, there's a photograph my mother took of Mr. Yu carrying one of his frosted vanilla cakes across the garden on my fifth birthday, and another photo of him standing in front of the painted red gate outside the house one morning with me and my brother, the two of us dressed in white pinafore smocks with little red Chinese characters on them that spelled out the name of our nursery school. Mr. Yu gave us Chinese names—"Big Tiger" (Da Hu) and "Second Tiger" (Ar Hu)—and after school we'd visit him and his wife, Mei, in the kitchen to practice our Mandarin and watch him turn a pile of leftovers (yesterday's rice, eggs, sweet fatty slivers of "la chang" sausage) into a sizzling meal of fried rice, with what seemed like just a flick of his wrist. We watched him conjure up pancakes from flour and water, dapple them with green onion tops from the market, and fry them in the wok for savory after-school snacks. With my mother, he taught us how to make pork dumplings by combining pork with vinegar, scallions, and soy, depositing spoonfuls of the mixture on carefully rolled-out dumpling wrappers, wetting the round edges, and then folding them in a half-moon shape and crinkling the edges together like the ridge of a seashell. We watched Mr. Yu shape large "Lion's Head" meatballs out of ground pork, plenty of Shaoxing wine, and a mash of onions and ginger. We watched him roll little cigar-sized spring rolls, stuffed with bean sprouts and shreds of chicken, that tasted as different from your standard

American-style carryout egg roll as a delicate cheese blini does from the heavy, leaden microwave burritos we'd buy later at the grocery store chains back home.

In Canada and the United States, we'd subsisted on the grimly forgettable casserole and lunchmeat delicacies of postwar America, but in Taiwan my brother and I grew fat on Mr. Yu's magical cooking and ate, in retrospect, like two portly little food critics. Instead of gobbling breakfast cereals in the morning, we took to commenting on the quality of our morning noodles, and we took trips to the market, where we consumed golden, crunchy cruller-like strips of fried dough called *youtiao* for breakfast, sometimes dipped in cups of soy milk, or wrapped in strips of flat, white rice noodles, or eaten by themselves in twirling cones of newspaper. Instead of bacon and breakfast sausages, I became obsessed with eggs: chicken eggs brought in fresh from the farms around the house; large, salty duck eggs with their vivid orange yolks; and the darkly mysterious Thousand-Year Eggs. Buried for weeks in a mixture of salt, hulled rice, quicklime, and soy, these eggs, with their slightly seductive suggestion of danger (yes, quicklime is not good for you) and translucent, darkly jellied texture, were a fine introduction for a hungry and impressionable four-year-old boy to the mysterious, rewarding, lifelong pleasures of adventurous eating and to that strange, addictive taste I would hear described many decades later as "umami."

Having endured her share of grim, overboiled, unadventurous dinners as a child, my mother had never experienced cooking like this before. Like her husband, she'd grown up in the sheltered world of Manhattan's Upper East Side, and both of her families had deep roots in what Newland Archer, in Edith Wharton's *Age of Innocence*, describes as that "hieroglyphic world" of knickerbocker New York. She never talked much about these family roots, and it was only after she died and I was putting together her obituary that I found out that one of

her ancient relatives had commanded the cavalry escort that accompanied Ulysses Grant to accept Robert E. Lee's surrender
at Appomattox in the spring of 1865. Her mother's family, the
steelmaking Burdens of Troy, New York, made a fortune providing horseshoes to the Union Army during the Civil War,
and her grandfather ran a publishing house and was a friend of
Wharton herself. Both of her parents were figures straight out of
an F. Scott Fitzgerald novel, and they met in the most Gatsby-
ish way possible: on the North Shore of Long Island, where their
families owned neighboring summer estates whose rooms were
filled with French antiques and whose lawns, I used to imagine,
were long and green and flowed together down to the water.
Her father was a talented and genial Wall Street banker who
owned a succession of sailing yachts and power boats, several of
which he named after his only daughter. Her mother, an only
child, lost her father in a hunting accident when she was young,
and she never felt quite at home, my mother said, as a member
of the formal WASP family into which her own mother would
eventually marry. My grandmother was a glamorous debutante
as a young woman, with pale skin and large, blue eyes, but the
sense of wistful, elegant shyness she cultivated in her youth
seemed to harden into an air of stern disapproval as she entered
motherhood and middle age. She was beloved by our New York
cousins, but my brothers and I didn't see as much of our Maynard grandmother when we were living abroad, and we used to
call her "Pilgrim Granny," after the grim, unsmiling Puritans
we'd read about in history books. Pilgrim Granny suffered from
various maladies, and like my mother's father, she would die at a
relatively young age, in her early sixties. There were no sacred dining rituals on that side of the family that I ever heard about, or
raucous cocktail toasts. My most vivid food memory of Pilgrim
Granny is of visiting her for a formal Sunday lunch, after she and
my grandfather had parted ways, sitting down to a table set with

rows of silverware on either side of the plate and little stacks of over-refrigerated butterballs, which were stamped out from an antiquated wooden butterball mold by a friendly cook who wore a frilly white apron tied around her starched black dress.

Sheila Maynard grew up in a redbrick townhouse on Manhattan's Upper East Side, not far from the home of my great-grandfather Choate, who was also partial to homemade butterballs and stodgy formal sit-down dinners, and on special occasions her family would also visit Giovanni's down on Fifty-Fifth Street, just as the Platts used to do. For more casual meals, they'd visit Hamburger Heaven on East Seventy-Ninth Street, where they'd eat messy cheeseburgers with all the trimmings, she told me, or they'd dine on cream cheese sandwiches at the New York chain Chock full o'Nuts, in which her father, who prided himself on being a healthy eater before the era of healthy eating was fashionable, was an investor. Walter Maynard was the managing partner of a Wall Street investment bank, and a governor of the New York Stock Exchange, and during the war he'd been a member of the Royal Air Force Bomber Command in London, the group that orchestrated the flights of B-52s that pulverized Hitler's Germany. Unlike some of his blue-blood friends, he preferred bread "with bits of seed in it," my mother remembered, and he liked to sweeten his coffee like a frontier cowboy: with spoonfuls of honey and blackstrap molasses. He was an avid gardener and a director of the New York Horticultural Society, which may have been why his favorite place for a celebratory meal toward the end of his life was the flower-filled dining room at Le Grenouille, on Fifty-Second Street. He believed that the most civilized dish in the world was grilled Dover sole with drawn butter and just a touch of lemon, although he would confound the waiters there, and in other fancy joints around the city, by asking for a bowl of bran cereal for dessert instead of the usual sugary pastries and soufflés.

My mother was always diplomatic on the subject of Pilgrim

Granny's cooking skills, which apparently did not evoke the usual warm childhood memories of flapjacks for Sunday breakfast, platters of roast chicken with all the trimmings, and fresh baked wheels of apple pie. As a little girl, she developed an aversion to garden vegetables from the family farm, which tended to be oversteamed and sometimes contained boiled caterpillars in their sodden depths. Her childhood bedroom was patterned with dark wallpaper painted with more garden vegetables—eggplants; string beans; long, twisting ears of corn—and she told me that she used to dream at night that the vegetable stalks and vines were creeping down from the walls and twisting around her bed, until she woke up in a cold sweat. Once when I asked her to try to summon up happy images from this food-challenged youth, she told me a similar strange Alice in Wonderland tale about a lunch at one of the Astor family estates called Ferncliff, up the Hudson River in Rhinebeck, New York. Her parents were apparently distant friends of Vincent Astor, who had inherited Ferncliff when his father went down with the *Titanic*, and one Sunday they went to family lunch at the house, which sat at the end of a long and twisting driveway, on top of a hill overlooking the river. There must have been some kind of renovation under way at the estate, which was famous for its indoor swimming pool and supersized ballroom, because as they drove uphill, past the gates, through the long alley of trees, they could see volumes of musty leather books stacked up in tall towers on the lawn. The lunch was a very formal affair, held in the large dining room, with crystal goblets at every place setting and butlers, in full black-tie regalia, standing behind every chair. My mother doesn't remember what they ate for lunch at the Astors', but there were tiny bottles of ketchup at every place setting, and afterward Mrs. Astor asked the children to take any book they wanted from the lawn. My mother took the heaviest book she could find, a large volume of *Webster's Dictionary* bound in calfskin, and she used it to preserve the collection of wildflowers that she picked that summer, by pressing them between the heavy pages, lined with sheets of wax paper.

My mother was just twenty years old when she made the rash decision to leave college, get married, and set sail on a life of adventure and risk around the globe. She would return to college in time, earn two degrees, and build an impressive, far-ranging career working with refugees and adopted children, and developing a variety of programs for the United Nations and other international organizations in the field of crisis management and post-traumatic stress. And out in Asia, away from the judgmental gaze of Pilgrim Granny and the narrow cosseted world of finishing schools and debutante balls that she'd grown up in, the magical, madeleine moments began to pile up one by one. "We always knew these were the good old days," she liked to say as we turned the pages of the photo albums together, one by one. The Taiwan book is one of the earliest and most tattered of the volumes. It was made in Italy of more delicate, less durable paper than the other books; instead of linen, the cardboard cover is patterned with rows of gray-and-white deer, and the pages have the worn, slightly falling apart feeling of delicate parchment paper. It has the snapshot of my brother and me in our nursery school pinafores, standing with Mr. Yu and squinting in the sun before going off to school. There are pictures of the dumpling-making sessions with Mr. Yu, pictures of the food markets, and pictures of the weekend picnics the family took by bicycle, riding out between the rice paddies to visit little villages up in the hills. There are photographs of the Platt boys eating fat, round bao-dze dumplings on a trip up into the mountains, which run through the middle of Taiwan island, and a photo of the famous Grand Hotel in Taipei, a giant multistory structure that is rimmed with red columns, in the traditional Imperial style, and looks a little like an Imperial cruise ship stuck, like *Fitzcarraldo*'s famous opera house, on the side of a jungle-covered hill. The hotel was one of the ceremonial centers of diplomatic Taipei (the banquet kitchens were featured in Ang Lee's excellent food-themed movie *Eat Drink Man Woman*), and my parents stayed there when they went to Taipei to attend a garden party given by Generalissimo and Madame Chiang Kai-shek. The Generalissimo, who had ruled China during the tumultuous years leading up to the Second World War and then retreated to Taiwan after Mao's revolution in 1949, was a doddering old gentleman by then, my mother remembered. He was dressed in his military uniform, and his wife, who was one of the famous Soong sisters from Shanghai, wore a long silk dress patterned with elaborate, carefully sewn flowers. While the Generalissimo stared off into the middle distance, Madame Chiang asked animated questions about life in the USA and they all ate cucumber tea sandwiches rolled flat, with their crusts cut off, in the classic English style.

As we flipped through the parchment pages toward the end of her life, my mother liked to remember other things about those early days in Taiwan. She remembered attending banquets at the Palace Hotel in dining halls the size of the Astors' lawn, and that after her steady diet of Chock full o'Nuts back home and hamburgers on Madison Avenue, the cooking there and in other restaurants around Taiwan seemed like a kind of miracle. In addition to Mr. Yu's cooking, there were restaurants serving fiery specialties from China's spice-loving interior provinces, such as Hunan and Sichuan, and restaurants serving refined coastal delicacies from Shanghai like soups made with spider crabs or freshwater eels. There were the famous soup dumpling restaurants, which like General Tso's Chicken, were first popularized in Taiwan, where you sipped the gently cooked pork broth from the spoon before popping the rest of the dumpling into your mouth, and restaurants that served a Shanghai dish called Beggar's Chicken, which you had to order days in advance. The cooks stuffed the chicken with chestnuts, mush-rooms, and handfuls of sticky rice, wrapped it in lotus leaves, and baked it slowly inside a ball of clay. When it was ready to be served, they brought the ball of baked mud to the table and let you crack it open with a small hammer, to get at the soft, melt-ing bird inside. There were Cantonese dim sum restaurants in Taipei and Taichung and restaurants devoted to one dish only, like our favorite Mongolian barbecue—a communal beef and lamb barbecue buffet tossed with vegetables and different sauces by the cooks on giant, curving, charcoal-heated braziers and then served, with messy ceremony, between fresh-baked sesame seed buns. Mongolian barbecue isn't actually from Mongolia, it turns out. Like Chef Peng's famous chicken, the dish evolved in postwar Taiwan as a fusion mash-up between Japanese style teppanyaki, which was popular during the Japanese occupation, and the lamb barbecue that the Mongolians brought with them to northern China during their invasions from the west.

Our favorite Mongolian barbecue restaurant was out in the countryside, between the hills that you could see from the up-stairs windows of our house and the bustling center of the pro-vincial city. The cooking was done in a low-slung building set out in the rice paddies, and driving toward the restaurant from a distance, you could see threads of smoke curling from the flat roof, up over the tops of the trees. Mongolian barbecues are al-most as popular in Taiwan these days as pancake houses are in the United States, although modern fire and health standards require that the lamb and beef now be frozen and the stoves heated with gas. When we lived in Taichung, however, the meat was fresh, or semifresh, and the grilling was done over charcoal fires that the cooks would tend with large bamboo fans. Din-ers collected their lamb or beef in a bowl, then mixed it with vegetables like cabbage, fresh scallions, and coriander, a strange, miraculous herb that ever since those days has always tasted like the essence of exotic Taiwan to me. We'd mix the meat and vegetables with soy and sesame oil and splashes of sugar water and rice wine, then hand our bowl to the grill men, who'd spread out the contents on the domed braziers with long spatulas and sizzle them in billowing clouds of steam. The smoke from the fires would keep the mosquitoes away, so in the summertime we'd eat outside, where you could hear the cicadas and frogs out in the rice paddies and watch the fireflies lighting up the tops of the trees. My brother and I would eat the meat hamburger-style, in sesame buns, and wash our dinner down with soda pop. Then we'd put bottle rockets in the empty soda bottles, shoot them out over the rice paddies, and watch the fireworks pop in the evening sky.

The closest home-cooked approximation to Mongolian barbecue we ever managed to find in Taiwan—without sending the kitchen up in flames—was another communal northern Chinese delicacy called Mongolian hot pot. The dish is cooked fondue-style, like all of the other regional hot pots that flourish around China, although in those days the stoves were small, charcoal-burning chimney ovens made out of brass. The chimney had a mouth in the bottom for the flaming charcoal, and a small moat, filled with water, was forged around its center, which led to a smoky tapering top shaped like a chimney. When the charcoal fire at the bottom of the brass stove got going, the water heated to boiling and diners, using chopsticks, gathered around and also cooked pieces of beef in the simmering broth, into which we'd put tofu, wood ear mushrooms, fans of cabbage, and tangles of glass noodles. When the beef was done, we dipped it in a sesame-based sauce that we mixed ourselves—just as in the classic Taiwanese Mongolian barbecue experience—from sugar, soy, sesame oil, splashes of rice wine, and plenty of chopped scallions and coriander, which were all arrayed around the table in blue-and-white rice bowls.

After leaving Taiwan, my parents would collect Mongolian hot pots in the markets of Hong Kong and Beijing, where they lived in a tall, dusty apartment block not far from Tiananmen Square. When we moved back to Washington, DC, my mother perfected several of the family-style dishes from Mr. Yu's repertoire—stir-fried rice with eggs and onions, frozen peas, and slices of processed American hot dog; an excellent version of cold sesame noodles in which she often substituted peanut butter for sesame paste; and pork and scallion dumplings, using sacrilegious frozen skins purchased in Chinatown instead of rolling them out from scratch the way Mr. Yu did. And when a crowd of guests came over, whether gathering for a special family occasion or to warm up a cold winter night, my mother liked to get out the family hot pot. The Platts had an impressive collection of these contraptions in the end. Lined up along the top of the kitchen cupboards in the different houses we occupied during our extended family travels were a half-dozen chimneyed brass ovens, in different sizes and states of disrepair, that my mother would set up the way other cooks displayed their favorite antique pots and pans. I took one of the little brass smokestacks with me after I graduated from college, as a memento. I even kept it for a while, getting it out for my little parties to try to re-create a sense of family and community as I moved from apartment to apartment, and even country to country, during my long bachelor years, the way children who grow up rambling from one place to another tend to do.

WE LEFT TAIWAN IN THE WINTER OF 1963, AND THERE'S A PICTURE in one of the faded parchment pages of the actual propeller airplane we took when we left. It had the curved, gleaming, silver exterior of a spaceship, and it made the famous approach into Hong Kong's original Kai Tak Airport flying so low over the tenement rooftops of Kowloon that you could see people cooking lunch through their kitchen windows. My mother doesn't remember what happened to our Japanese house in Taichung, or our favorite Mongolian barbecue, both of which I'm sure vanished long ago under a patchwork of skyways and housing developments. She never went back to Taichung, although she remembers that by the end of our time there both she and my father were dreaming in Mandarin. Her father never made the long trip to visit us in Taiwan, although he would come out to Hong Kong with his second wife and put up at the Mandarin Hotel downtown, where the city's most famous tailor, A-Man Hing Cheong, cut several charcoal-colored business suits, made from expensive British wool, to his exact specifications. Pilgrim Granny never visited either, although for Christmas one year she sent soldier costumes to me and Oliver direct from FAO Schwarz on Fifth Avenue, complete with plumed helmets, swords, and silver pieces of armor. My mother took photographs of us waving our swords at each other in the dusty garden of the Japanese house and sent Kodachrome copies back home to New York.

That last winter in Taichung, President Kennedy was shot. My mother remembers that it was Mr. Yu who came out from the kitchen with the news. "Something terrible has happened to your president," he said to my parents, in perfectly intonated Mandarin, so that the children wouldn't hear the news in English and get upset. Mr. Yu left for America not long after we flew off for Hong Kong and settled with his family in the suburbs of Washington, DC. One evening when we were living back in Washington, subsisting once again on a diet of casseroles, irradiated Swanson's TV dinners, and bags of roast beef sandwiches and greasy double cheeseburgers from the local Roy Rogers up on Wisconsin Avenue, my father and I went to visit him in the Italian restaurant where he worked preparing fettucine Alfredo and platters of chicken parmesan for the discerning gourmands of Bethesda, Maryland. Mr. Yu still had the manners and bearing of a courtly Mandarin gentleman, but his dark hair was growing gray around the temples and he cut an incongruous figure, dressed in his starched chef's whites and surrounded by portly red sauce waiters and rows of cheap, straw-covered Chianti bottles. He said that he'd worked in several Chinese restaurants around Washington, but that the heavy style of cooking—the thick burrito-bomb egg rolls; the soupy, vulcanized omelets of egg foo yong; the gallons of cornstarch and MSG—was as foreign to him as this heavy, Americanized version of Italian food. He still cooked dumplings and fried rice and little blini-sized spring rolls for his family at home, but his children had American names now, he said with a faint smile, and even their tastes were beginning to change.

Toward the end of her life, my mother's tastes began to change too, although she never lost her fondness for those delicacies from long ago, back in the good old days out in Asia. A few of the brass hot pots are still set up on top of the kitchen cupboards in my parents' little house by the Hudson, although when my mother prepared the dish when her grandchildren used to visit during the winter holidays, she used a small portable gas cooker that she found in one of the Korean supermarkets down the road in New Jersey. She'd gather packs of frozen sliced beef from the same supermarket, along with a head of Napa cabbage, a bag of wood ear mushrooms, sprigs of coriander, fresh scallions, and a few spools of glass noodles, which she said the shopkeepers in the Korean market called "cellophane" noodles nowadays. We'd boil the water and make the special sauce to our different tastes from the bowls of sesame oil, soy, chili, and sugar, spread out on the kitchen table. When the water was bubbling, we'd simmer the meat with our chopsticks, just like Mr. Yu taught us to do, then add the vegetables, which take some time to cook, followed by the noodles, which slowly soak up the flavor of the broth. At the end of the meal, after the meat and vegetables and tofu had been cooked and eaten, my mother would slowly stir the stew of noodles and beef juices and vegetables together with a little of the leftover sesame sauce until it thickened into a soup and then serve it as a settling digestive, the way soups are often served at the end of a Chinese meal. It was her favorite part of the dish, she used to say, and on a chilly winter night in suburban New York, with the bright moon rising outside over the river, it still tasted the way it did all those years ago—exotic and magical and strangely soothing, the way the best home cooking tends to do.

4

Eating with My Brothers

Some tourists like to collect seashells on their journeys, or shards of pottery, or nostalgic postcards from the distant places they've visited, like the Pyramids of Giza or Timbuktu. But ever since those early days in Taiwan, I've always equated the glamour of travel and living in far-off lands with the eternal joys of a good meal. A good meal is always a pleasure when you travel, but for the Platt family, nosing around markets in strange cities and grazing in local restaurants and on a variety of bizarre street food was a way of finding our bearings during those peripatetic years and comforting ourselves as we moved endlessly from one place to another. My brothers and I grew adept at living off the land during the 1960s and early '70s as we roamed the world, mostly in our tight-knit family unit but also sometimes alone or in pairs, on trains, ocean liners, and creaky single-aisle Pan Am jets, which in those days stopped in Honolulu and Alaska to refuel as they made their way across the wide

Pacific Ocean. Food was a constant comfort during our roving life on the road, and even a necessity, when we settled down for a year or two and then moved on again. It drew us out of what my father called the "expatriate cocoon" and gave us the illusion that all travelers crave: that we were connected, in some tenuous way, to the strange, foreign world around us.

In Hong Kong, where we moved in the early winter of 1964 after our sojourn in Taiwan, the third of the voracious Three Tigers, Nicholas Jr., who would be called "Sanhu," was born in the Catholic hospital across from the apartment where we lived. Thereafter, what had been a gentlemanly eating partnership between two brothers began to evolve into a slightly more frenzied, free-for-all food fight. As with most siblings, we developed our particular well-choreographed roles early on and tended to reprise them again and again. I was the dutiful, entitled eldest son, the consummate teaser and critic who strategized behind the scenes, made lordly pronouncements and needling observations that were generally ignored, and attempted, not always successfully, to coerce my bumpkin younger brothers to do my bidding. Oliver was the jolly, charismatic front man from an early age. The future actor charmed strangers with his antic personality and impersonations (he was famous in the family for his uncanny imitation of an angry water buffalo), negotiating prices when we visited the markets, and sweet-talking cab drivers, flight attendants, and assorted other strangers when we were sent off alone to the airport by our parents or weary grandparents to fly between Hong Kong and the USA. Sanhu was the coddled, plump-cheeked youngest son, a future journalist and financier who was hand-fed all sorts of delicacies from birth by an adoring gaggle of cooks and babysitters and who used to be carried from place to place so often on picnics in the countryside and trips around the city, that we called him the "Baby Dalai Lama," after the original child prophet, who just years before, in the winter of 1959, had been carried over the mountains out of Tibet to India by a worshipful and devoted band of monks.

In Hong Kong, we lived on one of the middle floors of a spacious colonial-era apartment building at the bottom of Old Peak Road, a twisting two-way street that winds up to the top of the Peak on Hong Kong island, where the British colonial officials and original Taipan business tycoons moved to escape the oppressive heat and smell of the city down below. The exterior of the building was painted the tropical yellow of an overripe mango, and the rooms were spacious and filled with light. A long veranda at the front of the apartment had bright, windy views down to Hong Kong's famous harbor, which in those days was filled with ferries, fishing junks, and huge gray American battle ships that cruised in from the war in Vietnam and dropped anchor among the smaller boats. We'd ride our tricycles up and down this wide porch, and at night, when the weather was cloudy, we could hear the sounds of foghorns drifting up from the harbor as we lay in our beds. My parents bought a share in a China blue–colored sailing junk called *The Star Elephant*, which had two eyes painted on its bow for good luck, and rumpled orange sails that unfolded when you raised them, like the ribs of a bamboo fan. On the weekends, we would take *The Star Elephant* on picnic cruises around the islands, and every few years we would rent *The Sea Dragon*, a much larger junk, from one of the prominent antiques dealers in town. With the family of a journalist we knew, we'd cruise for days out among the little fishing harbors and deserted beaches in the green rural country beyond the city called the New Territories, which lead up to the border between the royal colony and the vast, forbidden region still referred to in those days as "Red China."

In those last years of the British Empire, there were a few more cricket pitches scattered among the old Chinese neighborhoods of Hong Kong and Kowloon than there are today. The southern side of the island, around Stanley and Repulse Bay, was where the Japanese army invaded in December 1941, and you could still find faded stitches of bullet holes on the walls of some of the older buildings. A green vintage Spitfire warplane from the Battle of Britain was on permanent display at Memorial Square, by the harbor where you caught the Star Ferry over to the Kowloon side, and the British colony still had a governor who lived in a cream-colored mansion just down the hill from our apartment and who appeared in public every year on the queen's birthday wearing a curved black admiral's hat fringed with ostrich feathers. Many of the banks in the city were still guarded by Sikhs from the northern Punjab region of India—giant, stern-faced gentlemen left over from the British Raj who carried sawed-off shotguns and wore their great beards tied up behind their necks under tall, colorful turbans. The finest grocery stores in the colony were still stocked with sturdy, imperishable delicacies from the queen's empire: lard-crusted pork pies wrapped in brightly colored wax paper; cans of sausages and pickled chestnuts; pots of mango chutney and anchovy relish; sticky, tar-thick Marmite in squat, yellow-lidded jars; and rows of raspberry jams and marmalades from venerable London purveyors like Fortnum & Mason, their labels emblazoned with Her Majesty's royal seal.

Every morning, while the Baby Dalai Lama took his ease at home, Oliver and I went down the road to the Victoria Barracks Infant School in the center of town, which in its curious customs and sense of formal tradition was almost as strange and foreign as the Mandarin-speaking nursery school we'd attended in Taichung. We dressed in pressed white cotton uniforms in the summertime and scratchy woolen jackets and socks in the win-

ter, and soon the Mandarin I'd learned in Taiwan was replaced
with a pidgin Cantonese that mingled now and then with comic,
plummy English accents as I gobbled pork pies at lunchtime and
attempted to learn how to use a cricket bat during recess time at
school. My mother enrolled me in the British Boy Scouts, which
required another ridiculously proper, scratchy uniform, and she
began making notes in her diaries about all of the mysterious al-
lergies that the delicate, increasingly cranky young Adam seemed
to be developing—to wool, or strange foods, or unseen specks of
dust in the air. The Platts became members of the Royal Hong
Kong Yacht Club, and sometimes on the weekends the family
would take picnics down to the beach on the far side of the island and watch my father row back and forth among the junks
and sampans in long, cigar-shaped boats with other gentlemen
of the empire in traditional, English-style rowing regattas. On
Sunday mornings, we would dress in jackets and ties and go off
to St. John's Anglican Church, which had been built the century
before, on a little rise above the harbor, and still survives today
among the forests of glass towers in central Hong Kong. Potted
palm trees were set up around the altar at St. John's, the pews
were made out of polished wood and swatches of woven rattan,
and enormous ceiling fans turned slowly in the rafters as the
congregation sang Victorian hymns and read passages from the
St. James Bible. After the service, the members of the congregation would gather on the lawn in their straw hats and patterned
cotton dresses and engage in friendly conversation while nibbling on digestive biscuits and sipping cups of watery tea.

But this was the mid-'60s, and beneath this layer of civil
manners and polite good cheer the old order was beginning to
fray noticeably around the edges. During typhoon season, fierce
storms blew in off the South China Sea, and we'd cover the rattling windows around the apartment with big strips of tape to
keep them from shattering. One year it rained so hard for an

entire week that one of the apartment blocks built into the steep mountain down the road came loose from its foundations and tumbled down the hill, killing hundreds of people. The Vietnam War was intensifying month by month, and China was in the midst of Chairman Mao's Cultural Revolution. There were bombs going off around the city, and one afternoon, after school, my mother took us down through the park below the apartment to crouch under the trees and watch crowds of young Red Guard demonstrators in front of the Governor's Mansion, chanting slogans of the revolution and frantically waving copies of the Chairman's Little Red Book. Our father, whose job as one of the colony's large community of "China watchers" was to decipher these events by reading newspapers from the mainland and interviewing refugees coming across the border, would come home in the evening with stories about the factional fighting getting so violent in the mainland cities that bodies were floating down the Pearl River from Canton, out into the waters around Macau and the northernmost parts of the harbor. Journalists who had young families and were covering the war in Vietnam for the big American papers and magazines were based in Hong Kong in those days, and they would come back from the war front telling stories about wearing flak jackets during bombardments and surviving wild helicopter rides. These stories sounded dashing and adventurous to an impressionable young boy like me, but looking at the family photographs of these young war reporters many years later, you can see the faraway, shell-shocked look in their eyes.

Sometimes at Christmas my parents would invite servicemen from the ships down in the harbor to the apartment for a proper holiday dinner, and I remember that once a friend of my mother's brought an actual marine lieutenant to visit the apartment. The marine's hair was shaved close in the classic jarhead cut, and he wore a row of regimental ribbons on his chest. When I stupidly asked the marine if he had ever killed anyone during the war, my mother let out a little gasp and the officer looked down politely at his well-shined shoes. Not long after that, she told me that the nice marine who came to tea had died while on patrol somewhere along the Vietnam border with Laos.

I was always doing awkward things like that during the years we lived in Hong Kong. I caught pneumonia and came down with various other maladies, real and imagined. I got seasick on the junk excursions and carsick as we drove the narrow winding roads in our little VW sedan; one time during mango season I ate so many delicious tropical mangoes that I broke out in a rash of hives. I'd suffer wheezing asthma attacks, which my mother treated by running steamy hot water in the bathtub and having me sit in it for hours, gasping for breath under a wet towel. I got stomachaches and headaches at the regimented British schools and brought home a steady stream of C and C+ report cards, which my mother collected in a folder that I still keep in one of the stacks of papers on my desk. "Adam's absence on leave has been detrimental to his progress in school," reads a report from the Victoria Barracks Infant School from the summer of 1965. "On his return he was rather unsettled, but he is beginning again to put some effort into his work." Young Adam's delicate mood was not improved by the stout, fearsome headmistresses who ruled these very British institutions. These formidable ladies had comic Dickensian-sounding names like Miss Warmsley and Miss Handyside, and spoke in the hooting accents of the colonial empire. They dressed for work in stiff tweed skirts and jackets, and sported the tall, tightly wound beehive hairdos you see in photos from the 1960s of the wives of Russian cosmonauts. They seemed to enjoy barking at their students in commanding, regimental voices, especially the ferocious, pink-faced Miss Handyside, who presided over the second school I attended after leaving the military barracks. If you misbehaved, which for me seemed to be quite often, she would summon you to her office and, after a stern lecture, whack you on the palms of your hands, or the backs of your legs, with a long wooden ruler or the back of a hairbrush.

My best friend at this new school was a jolly, round-faced Hong Kong boy named Horace, who wore thick horn-rimmed glasses and had a taste, the way my brothers and I did, for the antically named Willy Wonka–style British candy treats of the day. After being terrorized by Miss Handyside, Horace and I would sometimes muffle our anxieties with soft Jelly Babies, crunchy Malteser chocolate-covered malt balls, and rattling boxes of the English equivalent of M&Ms called Smarties, which came in long, colorful cardboard tubes. In Hong Kong, you could find candies with names like Taveners Liqourice Cuttings, or Parma Violets, or Fizzers, which came two to a pack and turned your tongue different shades of yellow, pink, and blue. You could find chewy candies flavored with currants that got stuck in your teeth, and Sherbet Fountains, which you squeezed like toothpaste from yellow and orange plastic tubes. My brothers and I devoured every kind of chocolate bar wrapped in the sainted purple paper of the Cadbury Company, which had received its royal warrant from Queen Victoria herself back in 1854—Cadbury Flakes, Cadbury Double Deckers, Cadbury Curly Wurlys, and Cadbury Dairy Milk bars by the hundreds, which came in golden tinfoil wrappers and were pocked here and there with nuts and raisins and deposits of caramel. We ate Boland's Custard Cream cookies, with filigreed Victorian designs on top, and chocolate- and nut-topped ice cream cones called Nutty Nibbles, which were wrapped in tight sheets of paper and tinfoil. We also consumed a steady stream of local Chinese delicacies, like the salty, dried sweet and sour plums that came in little plastic bags; wisps of "dragon's beard" candy made from spun sugar; and blocks of sweet puffy rice, which we bought after school from the vendors who sold them in the park under the shade of giant, brightly colored parasols.

If you wandered the crowded streets of the Central District behind the big office buildings around the harbor, you could find jumbles of food stalls selling all kinds of other local delicacies, like pig's blood simmered into blocks like some strange, savory Jell-O; bowls of steamy breakfast congee; and warm paper bags filled with squid balls or barbecued octopus tentacles stuck on little bamboo sticks. Interspersed between the street markets were the big air-conditioned tourist hotels like the Hilton, the Mandarin, and the Peninsula on the Kowloon side, which were famous for their high British teas, beginning punctually every afternoon in the lobbies, and for the éclairs, fresh-baked crois- sants, and sugary palmiers shaped like elephant ears, all served in their pastry shops and stacked in glittering glass displays like in the patisseries of Paris. There were ersatz New York delis in Hong Kong that served watery versions of matzo ball soup and a passable pastrami sandwich; crowded old British sailor pubs with names like Wellington's Inn and the Mariner's Rest, where the patrons played darts while dining on scotch eggs and pints of brown ale; and dimly lit Italian grottoes, where the rafters were hung with empty Chianti bottles bound in thatches of twine and the calamari the cooks served up was brought in fresh every morning from fishing junks out in the South China Sea.

In Taiwan we had experienced the glories of proper Chinese cooking for the first time, but in Hong Kong the Platt boys were introduced to the magical, endlessly theatrical pageantry of res- taurants. For a taste of northern Chinese specialties—like shreds of crispy orange beef, bamboo trays of steamed xiao long bao soup dumplings stuffed with ground pork and fresh chives just like the kind we'd enjoyed in Taiwan, or strips of cool Xian-style noodles covered with sesame sauce—we visited the American Restaurant, a weathered, aqua-colored establishment a few blocks from the harbor in the Wan Chai bar district. There were floating seafood restaurants in Hong Kong decorated like circus tents with strings of lights, where you could watch waiters scoop your dinner live from bubbling green tanks, and crowded dim sum parlors, where we were encouraged to pick all sorts of strange, tongue-twisting delicacies—rolls of rice noodles in sweet soy sauce, translucent har gow shrimp dumplings, little log-shaped spring rolls of every kind—from carts that floated by the table in an endless happy procession, like little boats on a canal. Unlike in Taiwan, there were Western-style restaurants in Hong Kong: French restaurants, Japanese restaurants, Italian restaurants, and strange, colonial hybrids like Jimmy's Kitchen, a sailor's canteen dating back to the 1920s, which served sturdy Western delicacies like Waldorf salad and crocks of onion soup covered with gooey caps of melted Gruyère cheese. The original Jimmy was an American sailor who'd washed up in Shanghai after the First World War and opened a short-order joint for seamen on Broadway, a street in the Bund section of the city, across from the old Savoy Hotel. Another American, Aaron Landau, brought the franchise to Hong Kong, where it still operates today in a shadow version of its former self, serving eight varieties of curries and vindaloos, a rib roast, which back then was probably flown in frozen from Australia and carved off the bone on Sundays; and a stout all-day English breakfast composed of two eggs, pork bangers, black pudding, roast tomatoes and beans, and a rasher of greasy fried bread.

Sometimes, on a birthday or a special anniversary, we'd pile into the little family VW and drive over the twisty roads to the Repulse Bay Hotel on the south side of the island, where a mix of tourists, wealthy Hong Kong businessmen, and local dignitaries left over from the empire gathered on weekend afternoons to peer out at the sandy beach through the trees across the road, over their pressed sandwiches and cups of tea. Like our apartment, the building was painted in shades of tropical yellow and had faded green-and-white canvas awnings leading up to its entrance, like the awnings you might see at a British lawn tennis club. The hotel dated from the 1920s; Somerset Maugham had stayed there, as well as Sean Connery during his James Bond period, and in classic Hong Kong fashion, the building would be torn down decades later by developers and then built again as an ersatz, Disneyland version of its former self. But in those days the rooms still had a faintly glamorous, slightly faded feel. There was a dark bar filled with wicker furniture and a long, screened-in veranda, which was set with linen-covered tables during lunch and dinner. The menu was filled with exotic Continental specialties more notable for the rituals surrounding them than for their actual taste: duck flambé, escargot set in their slippery reused shells and baked in garlic butter, and puffy soufflés spiked with raspberries or Grand Marnier, which my mother would sometimes attempt to duplicate at home. My favorite dish was the house version of steak tartare, which was mixed tableside by serious-faced waiters who spoke in exaggerated, possibly fake French accents and always looked to me, in their stiff suits, like magicians conjuring a magic trick.

Hong Kong has always been one of the world's great culinary melting pots, and living there, the Platt boys developed all sorts of curious and eclectic eating habits. The breakfast eggs were flown in from Australia, our father told us, and to mask their bland flavor we mixed them with Worcestershire sauce, the way he liked to do, and ate them with fat British bangers and wedges of toast slathered, on occasion, with mango chutney, fermented tofu, or spoonfuls of yeasty, sharp-tasting Marmite. Our cook in Hong Kong was Mr. Wong, a courtly gentleman who, unlike

Mr. Yu in Taiwan, hadn't worked extensively in restaurant kitchens. He came from the rural province of Anhui in the mountains
of central China, and he and his wife, Tao, would tell us stories
about life in the wild countryside filled with panda bears and
bamboo forests and wild tigers that now and then came down to
the villages to maul people working in the fields. His specialties
were the home-cooked comfort specialties of the Chinese canon:
leftover rice tossed with eggs and bits of sweet sausage and scallions, pork and chive dumplings, and red-braised pork, which he
made with chunks of fatty pork belly, stewed to a soft tender-
ness with caramelized sugar and sweet Shaoxing wine in a thick
earthenware crock. Mr. Wong and his family had an apartment
near Wan Chai, Hong Kong's red-light district. On holidays—
like the Moon Festival in the springtime or the Lantern Festival
in February, which marked the end of the Chinese New Year—
we'd visit them and go shopping in the markets for roast duck
and the addictive strips of sticky, candied barbecued Cantonese
pork called char siu, and until they were banned in the city during the Cultural Revolution bombings, we'd shoot bottle rockets
and set off long, popping strings of red firecrackers.

Our parents dutifully took us to visit the cultural sites
around the city, but they were aware at that point that, given a
choice, their hungry sons would rather spend their time touring
the local bakery or seafood restaurant than an aged temple or
colonial-era museum. As we roved around the world, whether on
weekend trips from Hong Kong to the old Portuguese colony of
Macau or back to the United States to visit the family, excursions
to the market and communal dinners in gently crumbling far-off
hotels became a subtle exercise in morale-building and crowd
control. One year, instead of flying back to the United States for
our home leave by the usual network of cramped Pan Am flights
via Tokyo and Honolulu, my parents organized a weeks-long
excursion overland from Asia back to New York on a series

of slow-moving trains and ocean liners so that we could get a feel for the vast spaces of the world and experience the stately rhythms of pre–jet age travel. We boarded one airplane, from Hong Kong to Tokyo, but then took a small steamship from Yokohama across the Sea of Japan to the Russian port town of Nakhodka. From there, we made our way slowly west by train, across the broad expanse of Russia on the Trans-Siberian Railway, to London and eventually across the Atlantic, on an ocean liner called the SS *United States*, before arriving at the piers of Lower Manhattan. The highlight of this long journey was the Trans-Siberian Railway, which took a week to chug slowly through seven time zones to Moscow. Several of the trains we took along the way were pulled by steam locomotives with the Communist hammer and sickle emblazoned on their noses, and some of the antique railway cars we slept in were trimmed, as in the days of the czars, with polished wood and fitted with fluffy comforters, which would be covered in the mornings with a thin film of soot from the coal-burning engine outside. The dining cars were beautifully appointed too, in the Orient Express style, and every day the same grumpy attendants would hand out elaborate menus filled with enticing-sounding dishes like chicken Kiev and then inform the hungry Platt brothers, with a sad shake of the head, that the only items available from the kitchen were viscous Soviet-era egg dishes and bowls of warmed-over borscht. So when the train stopped at the little Siberian villages along the way, my parents would lead foraging expeditions up and down the station platforms, gathering loaves of country bread, cold salami sausages, and fresh yogurt decked with bits of honeycomb, which we happily consumed as the train rumbled slowly across the endlessly unspooling landscape filled with wheat fields and long, frozen forests of birch trees, interspersed here and there, as my mother wrote in her diary, "with streams running clear, the color of root beer."

My mother's diaries from that long-ago trip are filled with all sorts of food allusions like this, as well as bemused remarks on the struggle to keep her ravenous brood properly fed. She carried candy bars and jars of peanut butter in her purse as emergency rations. When provisions ran perilously low for the Platts on the Siberian steppes, my father and his Russian-speaking friend from the embassy would trade airline bottles of Jack Daniel's for our sausages and loaves of bread. At the Hotel Siberia in the icebound city of Irkutsk, there was no breakfast to be had, so we found a vendor selling warm pierogi on the street and scoops of grainy ice cream; according to my mother's diary, we all gobbled down these treats while stamping our feet to keep warm in the bitter cold. Back on the train, chugging toward Moscow, she recorded an epiphany regarding a late afternoon rainbow and a jar of pickled mushrooms. "Our prize purchase of the day was at the last stop before dark," she scribbled as the train headed west through scenery that reminded her of the Russian novels she'd read in college and the movie *Doctor Zhivago*, with its puffing steam locomotives and endless snowy landscapes.

We had been sitting in the compartment looking at the most brilliant double rainbow—a magnificent arc showing the whole color range from yellow to purple, arching over the grey sky and lush green wooded hillside. As the train stopped, the rainbow disappeared and we all leapt out. We found a lady selling home preserved mushrooms and bought some for 50 kopecks. They came in a fat, greenish glass crock, and were the most delicious aromatic combination of dill, garlic, onion, all cool as the evening outside, and completely exotic. We had them with some caviar on the heel of a loaf of bread leftover from lunchtime and felt very satisfied indeed.

I've never been back to Russia since that trip, but I can still remember the dark, rustic earthiness of those pickled mushrooms at that chilly train station out on the rolling steppes of Siberia—a taste that, for me, is still the essence of that country. Strangely enough, steak tartare is the dish I always equate with Hong Kong, along with bottles of frosty San Miguel beer from the Philippines, which we drank in the noodle stalls when I traveled there from my high school in Tokyo to play in a local basketball tournament. After our frequent home leave visits in New York, the city always tasted to me like pastrami sandwiches from the real Lindy's deli, on Broadway, or the rich, creamy texture of the oyster pan roast at the Oyster Bar under the sidewalks at Grand Central, and it smelled like the smoky, slightly stale roasted chestnuts sold by vendors, to this day, around Times Square. When I think of Beijing, where my parents moved in the early 1970s after leaving Hong Kong and spending a long stretch of time in Washington, DC, I think of platters of boiled dumplings from a venerable dumpling house in Ritan Park not far from the Great Hall of the People; the sticks of sugared red crab apples called tanghulu, which we'd buy on the street as a snack in wintertime; and the taste of crunchy duck skin and the smell of fresh scallions that you get when you take the first bite of that famous local delicacy, Peking duck.

We left Hong Kong after living there for five years, but returned to Asia in the summer of 1973, when my father was assigned to the first US diplomatic mission to open in China since the Second World War. Foreigners entered the country by train from Hong Kong, and I remember that, as the steam locomotive began its slow passage north from the border, making those familiar chugging sounds and puffing clouds of smoke, we all peered out the windows and snapped Polaroid pictures of the passing fields and rice paddies the way the Apollo astronauts snapped photos of the moon. We spent our first night in China at the Dong Fang, a vast, empty, dimly depressing Soviet-era hotel in Guangzhou. To orient the family in this strange land, my parents did what they often did—they took us out to the local restaurants. On our first night in China, we visited the PanXi, Guangzhou's most famous dim sum parlor, which was built in a slightly rundown imperial garden and reputedly served a thousand different kinds of dumplings. Beijing was a low-slung city in those days, bisected here and there by wide imperial avenues. It was hot during the summers and windy and bitter cold in the winters, and year-round the air was filled with dust and the smell of charcoal smoke rising from a million heating stoves and braziers around the city. Even in China's capital, people weren't used to the sight of big, looming foreigners, and occasionally they would gather to stare at the giant Platt boys as we lumbered down the street. The few diplomats and journalists who lived in Beijing were confined to a dusty compound not far from the emperor's Imperial Palace. Our apartment overlooked the Avenue of the Long Peace, one of the same wide roads the government tanks would roll down a decade later on their way to Tiananmen Square. We were assigned a cook, who my parents decided was actually a low-level intelligence operative, because all he knew how to make were fried eggs and a strange dish he called "peanut pie." One afternoon they came home to find him taking a nap on the dining room table, which was as hard and about as comfortable as a traditional wooden Chinese bed, with the tablecloth pulled up snugly under his nose.

My brothers and I visited a dust-filled swimming pool near the compound that summer and patronized the Friendship Store, which was for foreigners only and stocked with strange things: communist-era tchotchkes, winter hats with big flapping ears lined with rabbit fur, wristwatches emblazoned with the image of Chairman Mao, and bolts of cheap-looking silk. After we'd exhausted the limited pleasures of the Friendship Store, we spent most of our time visiting approved tourist destinations (usually with a large picnic basket in hand) and exploring the city, looking for interesting things to eat. We frequented ancient dumpling houses and a Mongolian barbecue joint whose dome-shaped braziers, my father used to say, probably hadn't been cleaned since the Qing dynasty, in order to preserve the particular smoky flavor of the meat. The best place for spicy Sichuan food in Beijing was the Sichuan Fandian—located in a discreet compound near Tiananmen Square—frequented by Sichuan officials connected to Mao's successor, Deng Xiaoping. Even in those days, the Peking duck restaurants were so numerous that we gave them names: the Sick Duck (because it was near a hospital), the Dirty Duck (because the floors were dirty), and the Big Duck, which was the famous, seven-story-tall Quanjude Peking Duck restaurant; even in the depths of Chairman Mao's Cultural Revolution, it served hundreds of plump, perfectly crisped ducks every day, with all the trimmings.

When I returned to Beijing many years later, I went back to the Big Duck, which still serves thousands of ducks a day and still occupies a large seven-story building at its original address in the Qianmen shopping area, which is not far from the dusty apartment block where we lived. According to the restaurant's website, there are now more than fifty franchised and company-owned Quanjude Peking Duck outlets in China, and instead of grimy, stained Mao-style jackets, the chefs now wear tall, French-style toques and use fancy cutlery to carve the duck in front of you on a shining metal tray. What hasn't changed is the mixture of honey, ginger, and rice wine used to baste the ducks just as they did back in 1864, when the restaurant's original owner, Yang Quanren, hired a chef from the Imperial Palace (who brought the recipe with him). The crispy duck skin is still served with spring onions and stacks of neatly rolled, house-made bao bing pancakes. Sitting in the restaurant—surrounded now by ring roads and new office towers wreathed in smog—the meal still tasted the way it did all those years ago back in Chairman Mao's Beijing. It tasted like comfort, community, and the essence of imperial grandeur to me, all mingled together with the excitement and mystery of travel in one timeless, crunchy, delicious bite.

5

After Leaving China: Japan

After the China years, the Platts moved on to Tokyo, where I spent my last two years of high school. We lived in a tidy two-story house covered in white stucco, which looked like it had been built, like many houses around the city, after all the wooden buildings burned down during World War II. Tokyo in the 1970s was much the same as it is today—a vast patchwork of villages and neighborhoods knitted together by a network of train lines and raised highways. Life proceeds in these neighborhoods just like it does in a small village—according to an endlessly refined pattern of customs and rituals conducted at a discreet distance from the bustle of the city and often hidden from view. In our little neighborhood of Hiroo in the central part of the city, not far from the US embassy in the fashionable shopping district of Roppongi, there was a public bath by the train station. The giant, pale-skinned Platts would go there sometimes on weekend evenings to soak with the rest of our politely horrified neighbors in the steaming hot water, with wet towels draped over our heads. Back home and lying in bed on a cold winter night, you could hear the slow squeakings of creaky wooden carts pushed by old peddlers selling hot toasted sweet potatoes and calling out their wares in high, croaking voices. There was a pickle shop in the neighborhood where we bought colorful, tart oshinko pickles made from cucumber and bulbs of garlic to eat with our bowls of thick, sticky Japanese rice, procured from an ancient rice shop nearby. There was a soba shop by the train station where, for an extra few yen, you could get a single, fat, slightly soggy tempura-fried shrimp to go with your bowl of noodles after school; and at the local yakitori house, cooks wearing towels around their heads tended classic bincho charcoal grills, fluttering smoke-stained fans made of woven bamboo, just like at the barbecue back in Taichung. You could get spindles of charcoal-grilled baby squid at this restaurant and fatty grilled pork belly threaded, like twirling pinwheels, with shreds of shiso leaf, although the real specialty of the house was chicken. The variety of chicken preparations was so bountiful throughout Tokyo—crispy wings; chewy cockscombs; charred, Chiclet-sized hearts; folded ribbons of skin sizzled in sweet yakitori sauce; even the hen's uterus in a soy-based yakitori sauce, with the unborn, barely cooked yolk bobbling on the end of the stick—that at some of the restaurants, I discovered later when I revisited them on eating excursions for various magazines, customers were provided with a small, pocket-sized map of the bird, with each part labeled in neat Japanese characters.

The famous national food manias—for French pastries and retro cocktails and antic cooking shows like *Iron Chef*—many of which would spread around the world from Tokyo, were still decades away back in the early '70s. Nevertheless, many of the elements of this madcap gastronomic renaissance—the obsession with detail and style, the love of ceremony and presentation (in

Japan both then and now, elaborate hundred-dollar boxes of the perfect apple, or the perfect mango, are traditionally presented as gifts), the deep traditions of craftsmanship and technique, the predilection for fads, and the tendency to move in large packs— were already very much on display in Japan. Decades before ramen noodles became an obsessively photographed trophy food for a generation of globe-trotting gastronauts and high-profile cooks, the Platt boys were happily slurping the different varieties of miso and shoyu ramen and comparing the relative merits of noodle broths made from chicken parts and those made using the more classic collection of pork bones. We snacked on crunchy fried potato croquettes at train stations, and for dinner in the wintertime we dined on mountains of breaded pork katsu cutlets, which, in the local katsu shops, were either served on little silver wire trays with decorous piles of shredded cabbage on the side or cooked "katsu don" style and served with a sweet mash of eggs and onions over mounds of rice. We complained about the quality of the Japanese gyoza dumplings, which tended to have more cabbage filling in them than the pork and scallion variety we'd grown up on in Taiwan and Hong Kong. We bought brightly wrapped lunchtime bento boxes for the long train trips we were always taking around the country and triangular rice snacks, called onigiri, folded in strips of dried nori seaweed, with little deposits of dried fish or pickled ume plums in their center. Instead of Hellmann's, we spread smooth, umami-rich dabs of Kewpie mayonnaise on our lunchtime boiled eggs and tuna sandwiches, along with bottles of a sweet plum sauce called Bulldog. Fifty years later, Kewpie is all the rage among New York chefs, and although I remain a devout Hellmann's man, in the Platt tradition, I still like to buy the occasional bottle from the local Japanese grocery store, along with some Bulldog to squirt on my fried pork cutlets or furtive afternoon bowls of steamy, sticky Japanese rice.

As in New York, everyone gets around by subway in Tokyo, and like New York, the city is a festival of cheap snack delicacies designed to be consumed quickly and on the go. Because we commuted an hour and a half each way every day to the American School out in Chofu, a northwestern suburb, my brothers and I would graze up and down the Hibiya, Shinjiku, and Sendai lines, like buffalo following the ancient food trails. At the Chofu station after school, you could buy the aforementioned fried potato croquettes, crunchy and hot, in greasy wax paper bags, and if you were still feeling hungry, or possibly just a little sad, skewers of meatballs fried in panko crumbs, all squirted with more Bulldog sauce, would hit the spot. There were noodle joints everywhere, but my favorite was a small soba shop by the Hiroo station where you could get the buckwheat noodles cold in the summer, served on bamboo trays, with a tangy sweet ponzu sauce for dipping. My favorite yakitori shop ended up being a place in Shinjiku surrounded by noisy pachinko parlors, where I used to go after basketball games with friends or on weekends to order platter after platter of chicken thighs and crispy fat chicken skin brushed with a sugar-and-soy-based mirin sauce, which we washed down with tall frosty bottles of Kirin beer.

Like today, the more refined dining establishments in Tokyo tended to be discreet and hard to find, and even if you managed to find them, you couldn't reliably get a seat without a written introduction from a well-connected regular customer. The best cooks and chefs practiced their craft behind small bars, rarely advertised themselves to the outside world, and greeted you by name after a few visits—provided they let foreign-speaking gaijin through their doors at all. There were small tempura bars where devotees of aged tempura masters lined up for hours to experience that ineffable state of tempura nirvana called hitoshimeri (literally, "a delicate wetness"), which the cooks achieved, I would later learn, not by watching the tempura but by listening to the sizzling sounds the ingredients made as they cooked in the oil. Much later on, during my days as a professional eater, a business friend took me to a teppanyaki grill restaurant called Shiozawa. The small basement restaurant in the Ginza shopping district had no sign on the door, and inside the walls were lined with bottles of Grand Cru wines from Burgundy and Bordeaux, each with the name of one of the regulars marked on its label. Before you even asked for your own bottle of Grand Cru Bordeaux, the price of a set-course grilled Kobe beef dinner started at $400 per guest. When we sat down, there were only a few other guests—a couple of older gentlemen, dressed in Savile Row suits, sat with their silent, unsmiling escorts at the bar, which was built in a square shape around the flat-topped grill. I remember the first course was spoonfuls of Iranian caviar on toast, followed by pieces of fresh abalone sizzled in butter by the genial chef, who wore a red scarf around his neck and a tall paper toque on his head. "Who knows about this place?" I asked my friend as we sipped our goblets of Bordeaux, waiting for the Kobe beef to arrive. "Nobody knows about this place" was his reply.

Shiozawa has since closed, but there have long been thousands of similar anonymous little establishments in Tokyo that are run by cooks and chefs practicing their craft in anonymous shopping centers, in back alleys, or, as the famous sushi master Jiro Ono still does today, by an entrance to the Ginza subway station. Then as now, sushi was a great delicacy in Japan, and once a month, on a Sunday evening, the Platts would pay a visit to our own private Jiro, a friendly, loquacious gentleman named Noike-san, who ran a small sushi bar not far from Tokyo University in a neighborhood called Ichigaya. Besides introducing us to the wonders of uni, Noike-san also showed us different grades of tuna belly, which he bought on his early morning visits to Tokyo's famous Tsukiji fish market. Like all traditional sushi chefs, Noike-san had his own signature recipe for the smooth, faintly sweet slice of egg omelet called tamago, the traditional conclusion to a sushi meal. If we were still hungry, which we usually were, he'd improvise a variety of hand rolls made with chopped yellowtail and scallions, or more uni folded into cones of rice and gently toasted nori seaweed, or a small spoonful of tart, salty-sweet plum paste called ume, which he dressed with cuttings of fresh shiso leaf that left a minty taste in the back of your nose.

Not that we considered ourselves overly obsessed with food at the time. After moving from strange city to strange city every few years like a family of vagabonds, the Platt brothers had a semblance of a normal teenage life in Tokyo. We wore bell-bottom jeans fitted with wide leather belts and scraggly, shoulder-length hair. Unlike the dysfunctional, weed-addled, all-boys New England boarding school I'd attended while my parents were in China, the American School in Japan was a re-freshingly functional place, with a homecoming queen and a school prom and normal American kids from places like San Diego, Detroit, and Dallas. Like them, I zoned out for hours listening to Led Zeppelin on huge, snowball-colored Sony head-phones, drank industrial amounts of excellent Japanese beer, and experimented with a hash substance called Buddha on the golf course outside of school. I was the slow-footed backup center on the varsity basketball team, the genial, shambling player whose shorts were perpetually falling down and who came off the bench to provide comic relief for the crowd long after the game had been won or lost. I took the daughter of a Baptist missionary to the senior prom, wrote articles for the school newspaper, and read weathered, month-old copies of the *New Yorker* and *Rolling Stone* slouched in my favorite beanbag chair in a corner of the library. We still have the faded white leather yearbook from

1976, which has a picture of me in this posture, above a quotation from the Taoist philosopher Lao-Tzu that, to the horror and amusement of my wife and daughters, reads: "In not doing, all things are achieved."

In accordance with the ageless wisdom of Lao-Tzu, however, Tokyo turned out to be a kind of nirvana for a future slacker restaurant critic. There my brothers and I were introduced to different kinds of instant ramen and learned to pronounce mysterious words like "omakase" and "umami," and, more than anywhere we'd lived before, the city was filled with culinary expeditions and adventures of every kind. You could dine on strange nose-to-tail delicacies (it was in Japan that I first learned that really bad meals are as interesting as really good ones) and take the train out to Kappabashi, a distant neighborhood in the eastern part of the city where you could buy the perfectly rendered plastic replicas of every kind of food imaginable used as displays in restaurant windows all over Japan—cheeseburgers, ice cream cones, Kobe beef steaks, and uncannily rendered pieces of fried chicken. You could amble around the glittering depachika food halls of the grand Tokyo department stores, like Mitsukoshi and Takashimaya, where my mother liked to wander the aisles admiring the trophy apples and mangoes, nestled in their carefully constructed boxes, and the rows of bento boxes wrapped up like Christmas presents, while her large sons sidled off to the butcher displays and ogled the Bavarian hams and strings of fat sausages that were flown into Japan—where meat products were a scarce luxury—from the finest butchers in Germany.

One winter we traveled up to the northern island of Hokkaido to eat sushi in Sapporo and soak in the bubbling hot sulfur springs of a town called Niseko, which is an international skiing destination now, but in those days was a one-lane village surrounded by mountains piled with rumpled blankets of snow. In the spring my mother and I rode the bullet train down to Kyoto, where we toured the temples in a snowstorm. The price of a night's stay in one of the city's traditional inns was a tenth of what it is today and included a breakfast of grilled fish, eggs, and rice mixed with salmon roe and pickles, all arranged in different antique lacquer boxes. We would make the early morning trip to Tokyo's Tsukiji fish market, which even in those pre–Travel Channel days was an obligatory tourist pilgrimage, like rising to see the Pyramids at dawn. We watched the chefs and cooks wander among the bubbling tanks of sea creatures with their baskets, and attended the morning bluefin auction where the brokers, dressed in their smocks and gum boots, moved among the silvery, headless carcasses on the concrete floor, calling out prices and ringing their bells. Afterward we'd eat bowls of noodles for breakfast or sample the sushi— Spanish mackerel touched with ground daikon radish, or sweet, pearly, impossibly fresh white shrimp shiroebi, hauled in fresh from Toyama Bay in northern Japan—which was sold in little stalls and restaurants around the market for half of what the fish would cost a few hours later for lunch or dinner at the gourmet sushi restaurants around town.

The late 1970s was also a golden era for traditionalist sumo wrestling fans in Japan, and because we followed sumo, my father took us one morning to tour a wrestling stable. For the Platt boys, this visit was a special kind of nirvana, like visiting the Yankees' clubhouse during spring training or obtaining a pass to watch boxers train before a big fight in Vegas. In those days, wrestlers from Japan populated the top ranks of the sport, instead of the giant foreigners, many from Mongolia, who dominate the sport today. Our hero was the first foreign-born sumo to compete in Japan, a genial Hawaiian giant named Jesse Kuhaulua whose fighting name was Takamiyama. Sumo is a highly technical art, filled with different holds and leverage points, but Takamiyama, who was famous for his bushy sideburns and easy Santa

Claus disposition, specialized in grabbing smaller wrestlers by their brightly colored mawashi girdles and merrily bulldozing them from the ring. Jesse arrived in Tokyo as a portly young man and grew to enormous size on the special high-protein hot pot called chankonabe, which the masters who ran stables fed their wrestlers four times a day, starting early in the morning, to maximize calorie intake and fatten them up for battle. At the wrestling stable with our father, we watched these portly giants slap each other in the unheated ring and roll around in the dust, and afterward we shared a giant pot of chankonabe with them. Several bowls of the famously thick, sticky, sugar- and fat-laced beef and vegetable stew added up to roughly 10,000 calories, and it had an addictively sweet savory taste, like some ancient trencherman's form of Sunday supper ragù.

I've been back to Japan many times since leaving for college in the summer of 1976, and more than any of the places where we lived during that wandering childhood in Asia long ago, it looks and feels the same as it did back then. Many of the subway cars are still painted the same colors, and if you want to circumnavigate the city, it's still best to avoid the cab drivers, who get lost driving down the twisting alleyways, and to take the green-painted Shinjiku line, which runs in an oval ring around the central part of the city. Takamiyama retired years ago and now manages his own sumo stable, but if you want a taste of chankonabe, it's available in various styles in many different restaurants now. Our house in Hiroo had been replaced by a small apartment block the last time I visited the old neighborhood, but the public baths were still there, and so were the crowded shops of the Harajiku district. Mr. Noike closed his sushi restaurant long ago, but if you have connections and several hundred thousand yen in your pocket, Jiro and his acolytes are still producing chaste ten-piece omakase dinners at his now-world-famous restaurant by the subway entrance in Ginza.

In the fickle ever-changing world of food fashion, Tokyo seems to have replaced Paris as the epicenter of the chic and style, and the city is a destination not just for diners but for worshipful chefs. They come from their kitchens around the world to purchase Japanese knife blades and soak up knowledge on foraging techniques from the wizened mushroom and herb masters in the forests and mountains of central Japan. A few years back, my editors sent me out to cover one of these highly publicized pilgrimages, a six-week pop-up organized by the famous Danish chef René Redzepi. Pop-ups aren't something I usually write about as a working critic. They're never around for very long, and most are designed not so much with the dining public or groundbreaking recipes in mind but as publicity for up-and-coming chefs or high-profile cooks who are between projects. Redzepi had left his world-famous Copenhagen restaurant, Noma, and he was happy to take the Mandarin Oriental hotel's offer of room and board for his seventy-five cooks and other kitchen staff in exchange for six weeks of Nordic Japanophile dinners and all the frenzied attention that the world's most renowned chef and a luxury hotel in the new culinary capital of the world could generate.

I flew into Tokyo in the evening and spent the night in one of the Mandarin sky box suites, looking out at the blinking office lights of the city, drinking glasses of Suntory whiskey, Bill Murray–style, in a jet-lagged daze. The waiting list for seats in the dining room was sixty thousand names long, one of the breathless hotel officials told me, and dinner was fully booked for the entire Redzepi run. However, they set up a lunchtime spot for the visiting critic propped up on a stool at the pass, between the hot, clattering kitchen and the dining room, which was decorated in a cursory way with Nordic furs thrown here and there over the backs of the chairs. The chef, when I met him for my odd meal, was genial and soft-spoken and dressed in his starched chef's whites, surrounded in his narrow little kitchen by his lean, serious-faced cooks, many of them with whiskers and tattoos. He looked a little like the diminutive captain on the bridge of a newly launched Scandinavian vessel far from home, and they looked like his crew.

The first dish of my meal, as I wrote at the time, was a bowl of slightly bitter strawberries, followed by a stunned, still-wriggling (and curiously waxy-tasting) Hokkaido shrimp dotted with ants, which one of the cooks happily told me were foraged "by this cool ant dude in Nagano." The ants were supposed to give the dish a little acidity, but they didn't taste much like anything at all. They were followed by a decorative creation that looked like loops of orange ribbon candy but turned out to be thin bands of shaved monkfish liver, which tasted icy, salty, and faintly primal, as though hauled directly from some freezing Arctic sea. My strange jet-lagged lunch proceeded with fiery orange segments of sea urchin wrapped in steamed cabbage, slices of hakkori pumpkin paired with salty spoonfuls of Fukuoka caviar, and a serving of Scallop Fudge, a magically strange substance made from foraged beechnuts, kelp, and dehydrated scallops. The main course was a roasted wild duck, which had been caught, the cooks told me, according to ancient custom: by hunters using nets in the marshlands just south of Hokkaido.

AS I BLEARILY ATE MY DUCK WITH THE HEAT OF THE KITCHEN AT MY back, peering out at the crowd of mostly Japanese diners politely picking at their thousand-dollar meals, Redzepi stopped by now and then to chat. He said he preferred the term "restaurant internship" to "pop-up," and that although he'd visited Japan before, this was the first time he'd stayed in the country for a long period. When I asked him if he and his cooks had gotten out into the city to eat, his eyes lit up. It was a revelation, he said, to spend an extended amount of time immersed in a food culture much larger than his own. He told me about a sushi stand at Tsukiji where for $80 three people could get twenty pieces of sushi each, along with a few cans of beer. He told me about a bar he'd visited where the bartender muddled a special breed of tomato from the south of Japan to make his Bloody Marys, and another where the bartenders made their own Campari from scratch. He told me about the tempura he'd tasted at a little place by the Sumida River that had forever expanded his knowledge of how a fried shrimp could taste, and he told me about a ramen stand near a subway station, not far from the hotel, where the cooks had mastered, after years of practice, a certain spicy, chili oil–laced version of ramen noodles. "Oh, you definitely have to go there," the chef said, sounding, it occurred to me later, the way I did back in the day, when I was roaming the train stations of Tokyo with my brothers, looking for another meal. "Those damn noodles will definitely blow your mind."

6

The Birth of a Critic, Part 1

My mother would sometimes say that although her frowning, oversized son hadn't planned to grow up to be a dyspeptic restaurant critic, she wasn't all that surprised that things worked out for him the way they did. I'd caught pneumonia shortly after arriving in her arms at the George Washington Hospital, in Washington, DC, and was suddenly rushed away, in her dramatic retelling, and placed by the doctors in an incubator, which she always called "that Little Glass Box." I can't have been happy about my time in the box, it's true, and I would eventually emerge apparently recovered and in the pink of health. A few months later, however, the family legend of Grumpy Adam was officially sealed when the famous Di-Dee-Wash Man came to call. Di-Dee-Wash was a laundry service that picked up used cotton diapers in those days before disposable Pampers and delivered them fresh the next day. To build brand loyalty, the Di-Dee-Wash deliverymen apparently carried cameras and took snapshots of their cute little diaper-soiling customers, which they presented to their parents as keepsakes. My mother happened to be out of the house when the Di-Dee-Wash Man arrived with his camera, which may have explained the glum look on young Adam's face as my father propped me up on my elbows in a pile of rumpled baby blankets. The gloomy portraits were preserved in one of the earliest of the tattered family photo albums under the title "The Best Adam Could Do for the Di Dee Wash Man." Much later on, they would frame the three black-and-white photos and give them to me as a birthday present. When the magazine decided to "reveal" the identity of their restaurant critic and the scowling cover image of their son the restaurant critic appeared on the newsstands decades later, my parents merrily sent me the image with one of the uncannily similar Di-Dee-Wash photos attached below it.

When you write judgmental, sometimes unflattering things about people for a living, the presumption of grumpiness comes with the territory, of course. You get used to the outraged reactions after a while, like mosquito bites in the tropics, or the burn marks that collect up and down the arms of any busy professional line cook. Until he sensibly stopped reading reviews of his work altogether, my brother the actor would mutter imprecations under his breath, the way most actors tend to do, about the dead-end pontificators who terrorized the theatrical community in New York and whose grim, unhappy lives shaped their terminally dark, negative views of the world. It was true, I would tell him, that the long hours and low pay of the solitary writing life didn't always inspire a sense of effusive good cheer, and I admitted that journalism tended to attract its share of questioning, skeptical characters. It was also true, however, that like, say, the forced consumption of a thousand bland grilled salmon entrées day after day after day, the repeated viewing of hundreds of mediocre movies or Broadway plays could cause even the most enthusiastic connoisseur to fall into occasional bouts of jaded despair.

Ironically, of course, the best, most grizzled professional critics tend to be animated over the long haul by a cockeyed sense of enthusiasm for the things they write about. The fearsome, glowering theater, restaurant, and movie critics I've met over the years—Mimi Sheraton and the famous "Butcher of Broadway," Frank Rich, who made their reputations terrorizing unfortunate restaurateurs and actors for the *Times*, and that master of what my father the diplomat used to call the grumpy "boiled-owl" expression, Jonathan Gold, out in Los Angeles— never seemed to me to be glowering or fearsome at all. A kernel of the Scrooge-like Di-Dee-Wash spirit is helpful, of course, especially to establish a sense of authority and a strong, consistent point of view. The best critics, however, are storytellers—even anthropologists. Rich's collected reviews weave a social tapestry of the '80s theater world in New York. Gold wandered the strip malls and boulevards of Los Angeles for decades, sifting through the thousands of dumpling stands in the San Gabriel Valley, the Thai curry parlors along Sunset Boulevard, and the roadside hot dog and taco joints up and down Pico Boulevard not only to amass for his readers useful tips on where to find the best Oaxacan moles or midnight burritos, but also to convey a sense of what it meant to be alive during a certain time and place in the sprawling city of Los Angeles.

Long before I was a portly, overfed food writer, I would hand out Jonathan Gold's collection of early "Counter Intelligence" columns to aspiring writers, whether or not they were interested in finding the best burritos in LA, and to New York friends who were going out to LA and might be interested in a single volume that captured a bit of the essence of that famously unknowable city. As I wrote on *New York*'s food site, *Grub Street*, after Gold died suddenly of pancreatic cancer at the age of fifty-seven, I'd bought my first copy somewhere, maybe at LAX, while on a random freelance magazine assignment out in LA. Hunched, cackling, in my tiny seat in the back of the plane, next to a genial man from Delhi who unrolled chapati cakes from a large silver metal tiffin tin as we crossed over the great wide middle of the USA, I read Gold's atmospheric little tone poems about the restaurants he came across during his daily rounds, like "the hilarious, barbecue-less LA Toad in Koreatown," where the maître d' looked like a skull-headed version of Christopher Walken. Or his story of devouring wet tacos filled with simmered tongue and crumbles of chorizo at midnight at the stand out back of El Gran Burrito on Santa Monica Boulevard, alongside laborers and tradesmen coming off their shifts for a late dinner, where the master describes the elusive "fire energy chi" of taco bliss, which disappears "seconds after the tacos are served, and unless you're at a first class place, you'll never experience it at all."

I would meet Jonathan Gold in person a little later on, toward the beginning of my time as a food critic, when I was still attempting to navigate my way around a world that seemed to be full of almost too many possibilities—too many restaurants to visit; too many delicious (and less than delicious) things to stuff down your throat before feeling jaded and overfed; too many horrible, hackneyed adjectives and descriptors to avoid ("thrilling," "eatery," "toques," "melting" [still one of my favorites], "succulent," "morsels," "unctuous," "delectable") before, invariably, you started repeating yourself and sounding less like the lofty writer of lucid prose that you imagined yourself to be and more like a tired old hack. This was many years before documentary movies were made about the great man and his pilgrimages up and down the boulevards searching for taco nirvana in his battered pickup truck, before he became the first restaurant critic ever to win a Pulitzer Prize, and before he'd become famous not just as the wise man of the food culture of Los Angeles but as a kind of poet who captured and described the essence of the city itself.

The Platts were on vacation in Tuscany one summer with an editor friend who had signed Gold, possibly years before, to one of the several book deals he had over the years. Like lots of his editors, our friend hadn't yet seen much in the way of chapters from Gold, a grumbling and tortured writer who composed his atmospheric little arias and tone poems on the strip mall cuisine of LA for the newspaper every week, the way Bach wrote his organ music for church every Sunday morning, but famously had a more difficult time with the longer, more symphonic-length pieces, which he spent months and sometimes years avoiding and often never finished at all.

I don't think my editor friend ever got her manuscript in the end, but she managed to wheedle us an invitation to lunch at the Tuscan farmhouse to which Gold and his family retreated in the summertime to get away from deadlines and bedeviling editors "and to ponder the more important things in life," I wrote in my *Grub Street* piece. "Like fire-grilled Florentine beefsteaks, unfussy Tuscan wines, and the quality of the soft, gently gamy tripe sandwiches which he liked to consume during his trips to the San Lorenzo market in Florence."

I remember that it was a sunny afternoon, and that the house sat at the end of a winding, predictably difficult-to-find country road. When we finally arrived, we were met by the large Mr. Gold dressed in a flowing cotton shirt, with wisps of hair blowing about his shoulders, and his cheerful wife, Laurie Ochoa, who led us to a table set for lunch out on the patio, under the shade of an arbor of green leaves. "I remember," I wrote, that "my own little girls were comforted by the sight of a restaurant writer who was possibly larger than their father ('I think he might even eat more than you, Dad,' one of them said)." As we ate our lunch of green salad, country cheese, and twirls of respectably fattening, cream-soaked pasta that he'd made himself, the famous critic sat at the head of the table, dispensing bits of wisdom about the food writing life with a look of owlish contentment on his face.

Did Mr. Gold believe in diets for restaurant critics? "Hell no, he did not," I wrote.

How many times did he visit places before writing about them? He couldn't remember, but it was an awful lot. Did the bad meals he'd had over the years outnumber the good ones? Of course, they did. He'd recently finished a stint in New York writing for *Gourmet*, so which was a better eating town, LA or New York? New York for technique and general excellence, LA for atmosphere, authenticity, and variety, the great J. Gold said. He'd just been to Florence, for those tripe sandwiches, and to the town of Carrera, not to look at the towering chunks of marble, but to tour the famous caves filled with gently aging hunks of lardo. "Were they worth a special detour?" I asked, as my wife shielded her eyes, and my editor friend started looking nervously at her watch. "Oh, yes, you must go immediately," he said, with a happy, distant twinkle in his eye, looking, it later occurred to me, like a great art critic and connoisseur describing a last visit to Giotto's frescoes in Assisi, say, or the Sistine Chapel.

Gold cultivated the quiet, slightly awkward air of someone who was just as happy making observations and comments about the state of the world around him as he was sitting silently for long minutes at a time listening, in a distracted way, to the ideas pinging around inside of his head. Between periods of silence, he told me that he'd studied to be a concert-level cellist before falling into the punk rock scene and writing music reviews, an occupation that evolved slowly into writing about his other passion—roaming through the diverse, endlessly fascinating foodscapes of LA and devouring everything in his path. Like most critics, he thought the occasional panning of a restaurant was necessary to maintain a sense of credibility, but coming from the world of low-end cheap eats restaurants, he found that people were less interested in reading about bad burritos than in finding out where they could get the really good ones. I later heard that he'd called one of the *New York* editors, after he'd left *Gourmet*, and asked, in an offhand way, if the magazine was interested in hiring him to do my job. I'm still a little puzzled why they didn't offer it to him on the spot, although it may have explained why he didn't ask me many questions at all, until the very end of our pleasant lunch. At that point, he took a sip of his wine and fixed me with one of his quizzical looks. "So how did a fellow like you get into the food writing game?" J. Gold said.

I can't remember what I told him, but the truth is that being a restaurant critic, especially in a city like New York, turned out to be the perfect occupation for a writer with a sturdy constitution and a confused jumble of Proustian associations rattling around in his head. I was probably the first professional food critic ever to graduate from Georgetown University's School of Foreign Service back in my hometown of Washington, DC, which was filled in those pre–Tony Bourdain days, before touring the night markets and beer halls of the world became the height of fashion, with a curious mixture of the sons and daughters of overseas oligarchs, beer-swilling students who seemed to hail mostly from sprawling gray suburbs of Long Island and New Jersey, and a smattering of earnest future UN officials and international bureaucrats. It was my vague idea to become a globe-trotting reporter, like the correspondents who would recount their adventures as we sat in the evenings on our veranda in Hong Kong, or maybe a writer for one of the tattered magazines I used to read in the beanbag chairs of the little library during my dissolute, well-fed years at the American School in Japan.

I had dropped out of college for a year and taken a job as a copy assistant at the *Boston Globe*, back in the days when big-city newsrooms were filled with the faint smell of cigarette smoke and the *clickity-clack* of beat-up IBM typewriters. In those days, reporters typed stories in duplicate, then handed the finished sheets to a copy assistant like me, who rolled the sheets into a battered plastic container and sent it with a *whump* sound down to the typesetters, and eventually the printing presses, via a medieval system of pneumatic tubes. I worked the late-night weekend "lobster shift," which began on Thursday afternoons, when the newsroom was in a clattering deadline frenzy, and ran into the night on Saturdays and Sundays, when the noise of the typewriters and the threads of tobacco smoke faded away and all you could hear in the newsroom was the buzzing of the rows of tired fluorescent lights and the occasional distant ringing of a soon-to-be-antiquated push button telephone. The reporters and editors were mostly pale, grumbling men, I remember; dressed in their suspenders and wrinkled polyester suits, smoking the occasional unfiltered cigarette drawn from a pack wrapped in crinkled cellophane, they looked a hundred years old to me.

I sat near the paper's small obituary section, across from one newsroom character who, I remember, had only one arm and dressed for work every day in a darkly rumpled black suit, like the caricature of an obituary writer out of a Ben Hecht play. He pecked at the typewriter with his one hand, usually grumbling to himself and with a perpetual scowl on his face. If it was a busy afternoon, the death notices of beloved schoolteachers from Waltham or prosperous judges and merchants from the North Shore of Boston would start piling up on his desk. By the time I arrived in the afternoon, there would often be one or two notices left to type up, so in between fetching cups of coffee and sending rolls of copy down the pneumatic tubes, I would take calls from bereaved relatives talking in the deep twanging accents of South Boston and Dorchester. Then I'd start pecking out the notices myself, one key at a time, often grumbling to myself and with a frown on my face, until late in the evening, when the newsroom fell quiet again and everyone went home for the night.

After finishing Georgetown with a C-plus in Mandarin, I went to Asia by myself and rented a small studio with white-washed walls and iron grills covering the windows, set among rows of terraced vegetable fields outside of a fishing village on Lama island, just south of Hong Kong. An elderly blind woman lived in the studio below me, and at night, as the mosquitoes buzzed around my head, I could hear her talking to herself in Cantonese as she drifted off to sleep. I took the ferry to work every morning through the busy harbor, past trawlers and fishing boats and the kind of wooden junks that I'd sailed in as a boy, though most of them were now used, with their sailing masts cut off, as motorized party boats for company picnics and private oligarch events. I wrote confused, often heavily edited stories about China trade policy and export-import business regulations for a now-defunct research company called Business International, where a young graduate named Barack Obama would also work when he got out of college before he found bigger and better things to do. I roamed around the city with a new generation of expatriates—dissolute young bankers, aspiring foreign correspondents, and pale-faced pub crawlers from the dark, wet cities back in the UK who were trying, like me, to conjure up the old magic of the adventurous, entitled expatriate life out on the last distant fringes of the empire. We haunted crowded little discos in Wanchai and Kowloon and played American football on Saturday mornings on the grassy infield oval of the Jockey Club racetrack, which the colony's original Scottish taipans had laid out in a flat crook of land below the hills, just south of the central part of the city, called Happy Valley. I rode up and down on the Peak Tram and posed for pictures in front of our old mango-colored apartment building at the bottom of Old Peak Road. I haunted many of the same restaurants where the Platts had been regulars during the 1960s—the Luk Yu Tea House for Cantonese dim sum, the Mandarin Hotel for overpriced afternoon tea, and the American Restaurant in Wanchai, with its battered green neon sign hanging above the entrance outside. At the American, the same cranky waitstaff laid out sweet pickled cucumbers on the table and little bowls of peanuts before lunch arrived, and the kitchen still served familiar northern delicacies like crunchy-bottomed pork and chive dumplings and strips of cool, wide-cut liang pi "cold skin" noodles the color of candle wax, and poured over them a thick, vinegar-laced sauce made with soy, chili oil, and crushed white sesame seeds.

Not surprisingly, many of my memories of these early, mostly failed attempts at "serious" journalism are framed around the comforts of a good old-fashioned expense account feed. I left Hong Kong after a year and went to journalism school in New York City, and then began working as a magazine writer in Washington, DC. On assignment back in Asia for a right-leaning publication called *Insight*, I dropped into the ramen and yakitori shops around our old neighborhoods in Hiroo and Azabu and checked in, like the pretend big-time journalist I thought myself to be, to the Okura Hotel, which had been the place where all the potentiates and bigwigs had stayed during the '60s and '70s. In its basement was one of Tokyo's finest sushi restaurants, called Kyubei, where the women on the waitstaff dressed like courtiers at the Imperial Palace, in rustling silk kimonos, and just off the Okura's lobby, with its pendulous, triangle-shaped chandeliers and midcentury modern Japanese-style *Mad Men* interior, was the Orchid Bar. This was the dissolute expatriate hangout of choice in Tokyo long before Bill Murray wearily lifted a glass of whiskey to his lips at the yet to be built Park Hyatt bar in Shin-juku. With its roster of exotic cocktails and fabulously colored tiki drinks, the menu at the Orchid Bar read like an anthropo-logical tour through the high-end gin dens of mid-twentieth-century Asia. Sitting in the cool gloom of the room among the groups of salarymen and the hard-drinking foreigners in their tropical hula shirts, and watching the barmen pour glasses of whiskey from the rows of backlit bottles glimmering against the wall, it was easy to imagine yourself as an extra on the set of an early James Bond film.

Back in New York, I had lunch at the Four Seasons Grill Room for the first time, at the suggestion of Philip Johnson him-self, whom I interviewed for a magazine profile at his office in the Lipstick Building on Third Avenue. An elfin figure, nattily dressed in a Pierre Cardin suit and wearing round, Coke bottle Corbusier glasses that made his tiny head look huge, Johnson spoke in short complete sentences, I remember, and jumped from topic to topic like a butterfly. "Order the chocolate dessert. Tell them I sent you," said Johnson, who was eighty-one at the time and would continue to dine in the famous landmarked room that he'd designed most afternoons at his usual corner table on the south side of the room, number 32, until he died years later at the age of ninety-nine.

Later on, when I worked in midtown as a rewrite man at *Newsweek*, I'd sometimes go back to the Grill Room at lunch-time and prop myself up at the corner of the bar next to one of the cathedral-sized windows, with their tall, gently billowing chain-mail curtains hanging down like tapestries, and take in the strange anthropological scene. Like any bustling, renowned restaurant during its heyday, the Four Seasons Grill Room was more evocative of a certain time and place than any musty archi-tectural landmark or tourist-filled museum. Sometimes one or two of my *Newsweek* editors were sitting along the banquettes on the east side of the room, where Johnson, Henry Kissinger, and the rest of the favored regulars would array themselves at lunchtime, like walruses on a rock. Long martini lunches were still one of the jaunty rituals of that mercifully vanished power lunch era, although I don't remember seeing a cocktail cart perambulated around the offices of *Newsweek* during my short, gloomy tenure there, at least not like the one that supposedly rolled through the offices of the Time-Life Building toward the end of the week to help ease the pressures of the deadline crunch. There were plenty of heavy drinkers on staff, however, including my editor, a sweet and talented gentleman who would sometimes disappear on Friday evenings into his corner office— where he was rumored to stash a bottle of booze stuffed in a brown paper bag, which he'd pull on late into the evening while editing his section of the magazine.

When I moved up from Washington to take the job, I'd imagined living the kind of leisurely existence that was still possible in those vanished days of print magazine writing— exploring different stimulating topics of the day and drifting from one story to the next in the manner of the main character in Calvin Trillin's novel *Floater*, a book he based on the time he spent as a writer at *Time*. I was soon disabused of that notion by *Newsweek*'s editor in chief at the time, a tinpot martinet of the old school named Maynard Parker, who kept a battered army helmet and other macho mementos from his time as a swashbuckling war reporter in his office for all of his troops to see. Maynard was probably a decent person if he liked you well enough, but having risen to the top of the totem pole of corporate journalism, he was now famous for his quixotic, dictatorial leadership style, and for terrorizing those poor cowering souls who annoyed him on the various rungs down below. One of his favorite ways to amuse himself, late at night on deadline, was by picking on lowly, hapless rewrite editors like me.

In fairness, I was not cut out for that brand of corporate deadline writing, which, if you were a bottom-dwelling junior editor, involved long hours of lounging around the musty midtown offices, in the way Trillin described, waiting for reporters to write up their files on plane crashes and palace coups from various distant corners of the globe. While the reporters happily chased down their stories, the editors and rewrite staff stewed back in New York, flipping through the newspapers, guzzling their martinis at lunchtime, or, in my case, staring idly at the office wall, which was covered with strange, vaguely menacing stains left by the previous unfortunate occupants. The office next to mine was a bleak fluorescent space occupied by a genial, red-faced man whose expanding belly was beginning to strain the buttons of his blue, corporate-issue oxford shirts. I called him Crunchy, because, as a Friday deadline loomed and Maynard stalked up and down the halls barking commands like Captain Queeg aboard his doomed, unhappy ship, he would pour out a fistful of Tylenol tablets from the collection of plastic bottles he kept in his desk and, without benefit of a glass of water, crunch them whole. As my junior stories got picked at and bounced back week after week, I started crunching handfuls of aspirin too, not to mention drinking to excess (although the most martinis I ever managed at lunch was two). Nevertheless, my paragraphs grew smaller and more incomprehensible as one deadline week succeeded the next, and eventually, as I sat in front of my oversized Wang word processor in a paralyzed sweat, they disappeared altogether.

I quit that dream job shortly before the authorities wheeled me from the building, babbling in tongues, and not long after my hasty, unplanned departure, my aspirin-crunching neighbor, who was a much more learned, facile journalist than I was, would die tragically from what I later heard was a sudden, massive coronary event. I returned to Washington, DC, where I spent a solitary year ghostwriting the memoirs of Joseph Alsop, a formidable Washington columnist of the old school. At the end of his life, Alsop had heart trouble and what he called "a spot of lung cancer," which kept him from attempting to write his own book. So in the mornings, he would sit in an overstuffed chair in his Georgetown townhouse and reminisce about the genteel, vanished world of the capital city while puffing, like FDR himself, on one cigarette after another set in a long cigarette holder carved out of ivory. Joe Alsop had been a feared and controversial character in his day—an avid New Deal Democrat, a friend and relative of the Roosevelts, an intimate of Jack Kennedy and LBJ, a fierce Cold Warrior in the Winston Churchill mold, and a staunch supporter of the war in Vietnam—and even by the standards of the imperious globe-trotting columnists of the time, he'd lived an eventful life. He'd made his reputation as a reporter at the *New York Herald Tribune*, covering stories like the famous Charles Lindbergh baby kidnapping trial during the 1930s, and he'd been taken prisoner when the Japanese invaded Hong Kong at the beginning of World War II. A closeted gay man, he never talked to me about his sexuality, and he left out of his memoirs a notorious incident that took place in Moscow during the depths of the Cold War: he was caught in a classic intelligence honey trap set by the KGB after he'd picked up a bellhop at a local hotel. When confronted with photographs, he'd alerted a college clubmate from Harvard, who happened to be the US ambassador to the Soviet Union, and then returned to Washington, where he continued to write indignant anti-Soviet columns in the classic cold warrior mold. The story would later find its way into books about Alsop and his brother, Stewart, and even into a Broadway play about his life called *The Columnist*, starring John Lithgow.

Alsop had all sorts of quirky interests—in the Greek and Roman classics, which he read in the original, in the sciences, in Chinese history, in archaeology and the history of art

collecting—and he was also an avid gourmet in the true sense
of that word: he was preoccupied with the history and anthro-
pology of food and cooking, and with the restorative pleasures
of a civilized meal. He was famous for the parties he gave at
his home in Washington, including one for John Kennedy on
the eve of the inauguration in 1961, when he served the young
president and his guests that mid-Atlantic regional delicacy
terrapin soup prepared by the cooks at the Maryland Club
in Baltimore and transported to Washington by car in great
plastic tubs. Alsop was one of the few traditional WASPs I
knew who considered proper old-fashioned Yankee cooking to
be something more than the usual overbroiled chunks of roast
beef on Sundays, interspersed with appetizers of stale Triscuits
and cottage cheese, all washed down, repeatedly, with hearty
swigs of gin. He came from a family of old Connecticut Yan-
kees, and he liked to talk for hours about growing up on his
father's gentleman's farm outside of Hartford, near the town of
Avon. The Alsops had dressed for dinner every Sunday in long
formal dresses and full tuxedos. They'd dined on old-fashioned
specialties like steamed marrow bones with pickled chestnuts,
grilled liver with cream sauce and buttered potatoes, platters
of roasted lamb with mint sauce, and broiled chicken doused
in egg sauce and dressed, for extra fatty pleasure, with strips
of crisped country bacon, all followed by fresh-baked pud-
dings and pies for dessert, with jugs of country cream to pour
over them. He considered the Washington restaurants provincial backwaters compared to the cooking he'd grown up with,
not to mention the famous kitchens he liked to patronize on
his reporting excursions to Hong Kong, London, and Paris.
Over the years, he hired a series of cooks whom he trained to
produce the old-fashioned Anglo-American classics he loved:
poached eggs on triangles of toast buttered with anchovy paste
for breakfast; deviled rib bones with Yorkshire pudding for a

stout weekend lunch; and classic Virginia country hams, which he sometimes brined in rock salt and spices in the bathtub upstairs.

Alsop was related to the Roosevelts through his mother—Eleanor was a cousin and Teddy was his great-uncle—and although he was well aware of the snobbery and parochialism of the world of privilege in which he'd been raised, he was sentimental about his "greatest generation" and their strange, vanished rituals, and puzzled by errant baby boomers like me who seemed to spend more time complaining about life than enjoying it. In an attempt to improve my frumpy appearance, he would sometimes present me with silk ties from his wardrobe and boxes of faded silver cufflinks. Once, after a long, tedious interview session, I asked his advice on a birthday gift for one of my brothers. "A pot of caviar!" cried Mr. Alsop. "After this damned book, you and your brother should take an apartment in New York together. Between the two of you, you should be able to afford decent rooms. With the savings, you should be able to afford a not-too-grand manservant. Without one, the apartment is sure to be uninhabitable!"

Alsop was aware that listening to an opinionated gentleman drone on about his life was not the most exciting job for a young journalist, and he would try to boost my morale with lunchtime leftovers from elaborate dinners the night before: chilled crab, bowls of vichyssoise, warmed-over braised sweetbreads, plates of rolled chicken and mayonnaise sandwiches with their crusts carefully cut off. In the evenings he'd bribe me with glasses of whiskey and large, frosty gin-and-tonic cocktails, which he usually began imbibing at around five in the afternoon, and sometimes he invited me to his dinners, which were served downstairs in the townhouse dining room. His guests included prominent journalists and politicians of the day, along with his oldest friends, like the British philosopher Isaiah Berlin, the historian Arthur Schlesinger Jr., and the very formidable owner of the *Washington Post*, Katharine Graham, who usually arrived with a stern look on her face that softened into a smile as the friends traded stories and gossip around the dinner table. There was the time when Alsop gave a party for the young King Hussein of Jordan. Guests were not permitted, by protocol, to leave before the king, so as he danced with one woman after another, they crept quietly out the bathroom window. Another time, back in the not-so-distant '60s, the powerful columnist's pet toucan, which he kept in one of his Georgetown homes, vomited on Defense Secretary Robert McNamara's head during an interview. Dinner, when it arrived, might be puréed peas and tube-shaped cutlets of chicken Kiev that popped with pools of melted butter when you tweaked them with your fork, or slices of cold beef flecked with consommé jelly, followed by lemon soufflés for dessert and more champagne. Later I'd stagger home to my cluttered little apartment, and tap out my diary and tasting notes late into the evening, before falling into bed for a fitful, slightly drunken night of sleep, much the way, it later occurred to me, a bilious food critic might do after a glamorous, but overlarge, restaurant meal.

7

The Birth of a Critic, Part 2

One of the characters I met during my time at Mr. Alsop's house was a merry, disheveled Englishman named Alexander Chancellor, who'd made his reputation in London writing columns for the Fleet Street papers and editing the *Spectator* magazine during its heyday in the 1970s and early '80s. When Tina Brown hired Alexander to run the "Talk of the Town" section at *The New Yorker*, he gave me an assignment or two, and eventually offered me a contract to come up to New York and write for the magazine full-time. One of my first pieces was a sketch of the mess hall dining room in the White House, where I unlimbered the old chestnut descriptive phrases about dining rooms ("The little space looked like the state room of a ship") and food (the pickles accompanying my club sandwich were a green "irradiated" color) that I would end up using in my next professional life again and again. My assignment was to pay a call on the great gourmand R. W. "Johnny" Apple, who was the Washington bureau chief of the *New York Times* and already a legendary figure at the paper for his extravagant, Rabelaisian appetites. The barrel-chested Apple had rose-colored cheeks and effected the brusque manners of the swaggering, macho newspaperman type that I'd observed during short unhappy tours in other big-time newsrooms. Apple was famously the only reporter at the *Times* to be issued his own personal company credit card, on which he happily rang up huge sums over the decades at his favorite trencherman dining establishments, like L'Ami Louis in Paris, which A. A. Gill of the *Sunday Times* would so merrily pan in a legendary review for *Vanity Fair*, and Wiltons on Jermyn Street in London, where he advised me to order half a dozen oysters, followed, if I could afford it, by the famous Dover sole, which the kitchen always brushed with gouts of melted country butter. The wall of Apple's corner office was decorated with antique maps of the brandy-producing provinces of France, Armagnac and Cognac, and his favorite dish, he told me with evident satisfaction, was a heaping platter of sausage- and sauerkraut-laced choucroute garnie from Alsace, which was A. J. Liebling's favorite dish too. Apple told me that he always wore brightly colored tailored shirts from London because they cheered him up on gloomy days, and when he traveled, he habitually carried a pepper mill in his suitcase because like Mr. Alsop, he felt that most restaurants, especially in Washington, DC, couldn't be trusted to properly season their food.

Like lots of journalists who find themselves on the other end of an interview, Apple hated the little story I wrote about him and complained bitterly that I'd gotten everything wrong, including the name of his London tailor, which I'd pulled from one of his books and had been rechecked several times by the *New Yorker* fact checkers. But after the piece was published, I got Alexander's official job offer and moved back up to New York, and into a small cubicle at the *New Yorker's* posh new offices on Forty-Third Street, where the magazine had recently moved after being purchased by the Condé Nast Newhouse empire for a cool $200 million. I spent my few brief, happy months at *The New Yorker* passing my old literary heroes (Brendan Gill, Roger Angell, Lillian Ross, and the great Joseph Mitchell, who appeared at the office every morning dressed in his gray fedora) in the silent halls and venturing out into the city to find the kind of classic "Talk of the Town" characters I'd grown up reading about in the magazine. I contrived to cover boxing matches at Madison Square Garden, as the great Liebling had done, and for a series of baseball stories I took the train up to Yankee Stadium, where I ate large numbers of the ballpark hot dogs, available to beat reporters up in the press box for less than a dollar apiece, and called my brothers to tell them that I'd finally attained a state of nirvana. I interviewed Jesus Christ impersonators, Japanese baseball interpreters, and virtuoso violinists, and spent a happy afternoon with the longest-serving bellhop at the Algonquin Hotel, who told me that he once dissuaded Thelonious Monk from jumping off the hotel roof ("What Mr. Monk was doing up there, I have no idea") and that William Faulkner used to check into the hotel, disappear into his room, and not emerge until he'd consumed a bottle or two of gin.

NOT LONG AFTER I ARRIVED AT MY NEW JOB, HOWEVER, A FLUS-tered Alexander would depart back to London, and not long after that, his replacement invited me to lunch at the Oyster Bar, where, over a bowl of richly simmered oyster pan roast, he fired me too. Like all of my failed, star-crossed dream jobs, however, this one had a silver lining: the atmospheric, closely observed writing style I attempted to practice at *The New Yorker* would be useful later when it was my job to sit in a

thousand different dining rooms—not just the glittering upscale dining rooms of the past but the ever smaller and noisier
rooms, decorated in the same mind-numbingly spare, utilitarian style, of the present—trying to come up with a new way to
describe the same cookie-cutter style of decor again and again.

It would turn out, in fact, that I was more qualified for the
strange business of restaurant writing than I imagined when I
sat down for lunch with Gael Greene at Monsieur Ducasse's
restaurant years later. The knack of writing to a compressed
space—a required skill at *Newsweek*—would be helpful too,
and so would the exercise of taking a tired formula, like obituary writing at the *Boston Globe*, and making it sound fresh and
vaguely new. After *The New Yorker*, I would write travel stories, magazine profiles, and a diary column for the *New York
Observer* in which eccentric family characters kept popping up
and being quoted—just as they would, for better or worse, in
my restaurant reviews. I wrote about all kinds of food during
my journalistic travels, and the best way to do this, I would
gradually discover, was to avoid flowery adjectives and just let
the dish—whether it was fried chicken or a pot of cassoulet or
a cool glass of milk—describe itself. And when I finally became a professional critic and began to roam around the city on
my daily rounds, I would also discover, to my happy surprise,
that I'd finally found a kind of calling. The restaurant critic's
job turned out to be the perfect vehicle for a rambling, inquisi-
tive, dyspeptic personality who wasn't a classic company man
or much of a team player at all but had a healthy appetite and a
taste for what my iron-stomached compatriot Ed Levine calls
"deliciousness." I would discover that the actual review—part
cultural essay, part personal diary, part service journalism, and
part travel and cultural commentary—involved bits and pieces
of all the various styles of writing I'd attempted or failed at over
the years. And I would discover, as time went on, that the job

had a unique kind of magic to it, especially in a great dining metropolis like New York City, where it's possible, if you have a little money in your pocket, to sit in a newly opened mixology bar in the Bushwick neighborhood of Brooklyn, say, or at the bar of an ancient, steamy noodle stand or deli somewhere downtown, or at a grand linen-covered table at the latest gilded new Indian or French restaurant in a midtown hotel, and watch the whole world unfold before your eyes.

8

Eating with My Family

Like families who grow up in circus troupes, or behind the scenes with actor parents, or in the strange, slightly cockeyed orbit of other glamorous-seeming professions, my own family has always had a blasé, even slightly jaundiced view of the work-aday professional eating life. During the early years of food and travel, Mrs. Platt did her best Alice Trillin imitation, knocking back daiquiris in Havana when I went on assignment there and gamely staring down toppling platters of choucroute garnie and steak frites when I went on an extended wild ramble through the bistros of Paris. But over the decades the pace of the job ground her down, and as my girth and appetite expanded, hers seemed to shrink, to the point where she now subsists on a reasonable, increasingly modest diet of grains, vegetables, and a few scraps of protein, and often she'll go months without ever visiting a restaurant at all.

Our two daughters, Jane and Penelope, were adopted three

years apart from different orphanages in the neighboring provinces of Jiangsu and Anhui in eastern China. Compared to my wandering childhood, however, theirs has been a settled existence, attending the same neighborhood school in New York City all the way from kindergarten to high school, patronizing the same local diners and bagel shops, and living in the same apartment in the central part of New York's Greenwich Village for their entire young lives. At first, of course, adoption was a great passage, and one thing the experts tell adoptive parents to look for during that turbulent period of trauma and adjustment as the infant leaves one life and enters another, experiencing separation and then rebonding, is how he or she accepts their first tiny morsel of food.

Both of the girls have the palates they were born with: they like noodles of any kind, umami-laced ramens and soups, and dumplings dressed in the traditional northerly, non-Cantonese way with black vinegar, instead of sweetened soy sauce, the way the kitchens of New York's various Chinatowns tend to serve them. For the most part, they've inherited their mother's measured, rational style of eating, but when we picked them up from their orphanages in China years ago, each girl had a unique way of taking that first little bite of dinner from her strange new family. Deliberate, observant, careful Jane regarded a shred of fish at the end of her new mother's chopsticks for what seemed like hours in a kind of silent trance before taking one tiny bite, and then another. By contrast, Penelope, her voluble, opinionated, animated younger sister, who has always had a focused, singular quality toward the foods she enjoys (chicken soup, ramen, BLTs, sweet glasses of orange juice), clamored for one comforting helping of wonton soup after another in a haze of knocked-over bowls and noisy tears.

Except for a few favored neighborhood joints, Joe Jr.'s on Sixth Avenue, the ramen shop around the corner, and Bob's Bagels down on University Place—where we would go Saturday mornings to watch the shiny fat bagels being shuffled from the oven on hot wooden palettes into the silver wire bins—the Platt girls didn't have favorite fancy places to eat. What they saw instead was a dad who was often napping on the couch when they arrived home from school in the afternoon, or coming back to the apartment late at night with stacks of elaborate leftovers packed in plastic boxes, which would pile up in the refrigerator for a week or two before being quietly thrown away. For the most part, they were unimpressed by glamorous big-city restaurants, with their complicated recipes and carefully staged sense of intimacy, and thought of them as simply the places where their dad worked. On off nights, Dad usually preferred eating at home—or more likely, if he was on a diet, returning to his place on the couch to digest the previous night's dinner and try, for one night that week at least, to eat nothing at all.

Now and then, however, Dad does manage to awaken from his prolonged, low-grade food coma for long enough to prepare the occasional home-cooked meal. I'm often asked whether I cook at home, usually with the expectation that I will answer yes and then describe in intimate detail the shelves of well-thumbed cookbooks and the collection of seasoned pots and pans that I put to use twirling out exotic ragùs and creoles night after night. But in our household, Dad is usually given simpler tasks—he's the breakfast short-order cook ("Two eggs over easy please, Dad!"), the roaster of Sunday chickens, the procurer of bags of frozen dumplings for only a few bucks down in Chinatown, and the chef who's called upon to prepare large, gently simmered stews when the weather turns cold outside.

When I first moved to Greenwich Village, the neighborhood was filled with family-owned markets and food shops, like the original Jefferson Market on the west side of Sixth Avenue, with its low-raftered ceiling and sawdust-covered floors, and across the street that original New York prepared food destination, Balducci's, where the glittering glass displays were filled with tall, brightly frosted cakes, sugared holiday hams, and tubs of fried chicken or baked lasagna. For the most part these days, only the venerable neighborhood butcher shops remain, like Ottomanelli's and Faicco's on Bleecker Street, and the slightly less traveled Florence Prime Meat Market around the corner on Jones Street, where you'll still find handfuls of sawdust scattered over the floor and, on occasion, a lazy cat sitting in the window, just like at the butcher shops in Rome.

I buy the eggs I cook for the girls during the morning rush before school at the Union Square Greenmarket. From there I make the rounds to either Florence or Ottomanelli's for cubes of stew meat or the occasional family roast chicken on a Sunday. I dress the chicken with a little olive oil, in the Mediterranean style, bulbs of husked fresh garlic from the market if it's garlic season, and the juice of a lemon before putting the bird in the oven to cook for a few hours at close to 400 degrees. Sometimes for Sunday dinner I turn the chicken into a curry or Filipino adobo stew laced with soy and plenty of vinegar, or I simmer chunks of beef rolled in a little flour in some beef stock, a bottle of red wine, and chopped carrots, onions, and bacon in a quick approximation of boeuf bourguignon. The girls' favorite Sunday dish of all, however, is a version of the red cooked pork that Mr. Wong made for us back in Hong Kong, with pork ribs, chunks of belly, and sugar, soy, star anise, and choppings of ginger all stirred together with splashes of Shaoxing wine. As with most of my winter stews, I usually make too much of it for the Platt ladies to finish and keep sneaking back for a taste of the leftovers, the way dads often do, until all of the delicious gravy has disappeared and the last bit of soft, fatty pork is gone.

I sometimes compare my predicament as the only slow-moving, oversized male in a household of energetic, fast-moving, petite women to being like a hippo with a flock of birds on his back. The birds carry on chirping to each other, and flying off on their endless errands and excursions, and the only time they tend to notice the great hippo is when he's gone. But now and then the hippo manages to lure the birds into his natural habitat. In my professional world of restaurants and food, I've used Mrs. Platt and the girls as props over the years in my writing, or as commentators in reviews or in videos, or simply as welcome company during the long hours whiling away time in these settings, as I look for new ways to describe the same entrées and desserts, the same service, the same numbingly familiar dining room décor again and again.

Over the years the Platt girls have developed their own culinary specialties in Dad's writing, most of which they rarely comment on or even bother to read. Jane's expertise lies in elevated tasting menus and French and Continental cooking, while Penelope has been quoted extensively in different articles and videos on the styles of cheesecake and doughnuts she prefers, her favorite style of ramen (any style, for the record), and the most crucial ingredient for her beloved chicken noodle soups (plenty of salt). Over the years, my daughters and I have gone on excursions together around the city to find the best ice cream, visited pizza museums and other venues for a video series, and worked on taking better photos for my drab Instagram feed. We've traveled around Paris together sampling fancy vegetable dishes and debated the merits of different styles of regional noodle dishes in Chinese restaurants. Once, in London, where I was writing a story about the famously powerful martini served at Duke's, a bar in Mayfair, dutiful eldest daughter Jane took over the note-taking as her jet-lagged, increasingly woozy father started slowly nodding off to sleep.

WHEN JANE WAS MUCH YOUNGER, I HAD THE RASH, SLIGHTLY loony idea of organizing a dinner for a gaggle of nursery school children at one of the city's exceptionally posh establishments, one of those places you wouldn't normally associate with children of any age. I thought it would make an amusing story to put children in the comically stilted and overserious world of a gourmet restaurant and see how they reacted. I wondered what policies and rules of engagement the finest restaurants in town had, if any, when it came to accommodating younger guests. Would they welcome our unruly little party with open arms? Would they politely banish us to some distant, noise-proof Siberia section of the room? Or would they block the door and usher us down the street to the nearest McDonald's?

Before embarking on this mad adventure, I'd posed these questions to various members of the dining community. The chef and co-owner of the excellent midtown seafood restaurant Le Bernardin, Éric Ripert, told me diplomatically that when children did appear, the staff did their best to accommodate them. They prepared bowls of buttered pasta, and Ripert himself sometimes conducted tours of the kitchen. The Union Square restaurateur Danny Meyer said that he offered classes for children on table manners and etiquette at some of his famously hospitable establishments ("We have customers who had their diapers changed in our restaurants and are now coming back for their first bottle of wine!"). But like Ripert, when I mentioned I was planning to take a whole party of four-year-olds out for a fine haute cuisine meal, he sounded bemused, then downright horrified: "I hope you're not coming to any of my restaurants," he said.

The venue I ended up choosing for my little party was Le Cirque, which in those days was located in a sprawling series of rooms in the Villard Houses on Madison Avenue. When I called up, a little nervously, to book a table, the proprietor, Sirio Maccioni, came on the line to officially welcome the critic from *New York* magazine and to profess his love of children of all ages. "Children are the future," said Sirio in his most flowery, effusively flattering Sirio kind of voice. "Bring ten if you like, bring twenty—we will take care of them all." In the end, we settled on five as a manageable number. Along with Jane and her friend Willa, and to create as much challenging chaos as possible, we invited three boys from her nursery school class: Linus with his plastic dinosaur; the quiet, exceptionally well-behaved Alex; and Adrian, who would arrive for his dinner at Le Cirque dressed in a tiny jacket and tie and clutching a black plastic replica of Spider-Man.

On the evening before my rash experiment, several of the children's parents called with words of comfort and advice. They spoke in hushed, concerned, slightly amazed tones, as though I were contemplating skydiving for the first time, or an expedition up Mount Everest, or some other unimaginable, slightly rash, totally loony act. "Alex should be okay," said Alex's mom, "but if the other kids get antsy and start moving around, I can't guarantee anything." Linus's mother wanted me to know that if Linus began to misbehave (a likely possibility, she thought), I should threaten to take away the little plastic dinosaur he carried with him at all times. Willa's mom, Vicki, tactfully suggested that I seat the boys and girls separately. Then Jane's mom chimed in, a little less tactfully, with her own down-to-earth advice.

"Be sure to get the food coming fast," said Mrs. Platt, who had plenty of battle-hardened experience in this field. "If you don't, there'll be anarchy." She wondered whether I could explain the menu to all the children in stern, fatherly tones. "Run things like you're at a military camp," she suggested. "If you don't get the kids to focus, you'll be doomed."

At precisely 5:30 p.m. (no self-respecting restaurateur would contemplate giving us a table any later), I gathered the children in the foyer of the restaurant, while their parents and babysitters snuck off to calm themselves with a round of stiff cocktails at the bar. Sirio Maccioni was conveniently out of town and had left his trusted maître d', an elegant European hospitality professional of the old school named Mario Wainer, to orchestrate the festivities the best he could. Mario was dressed for the evening in his tuxedo, and as the children began squealing and scampering around the room, he smiled gamely and motioned us toward our table, which was in a corner of one of the restaurant's two large dining rooms, with tall chairs covered in aqua-colored linen and a high-backed, curving banquette made of crushed blue velvet.

Rows of empty tables had been set in a protective ring around our little private Siberia, although at the far end of the room I could see groups of adult diners watching us with looks of not very well concealed suspicion and alarm. I tried, as one mother had suggested, to seat the boys next to the girls, just like at an adult dinner party, but the boys gravitated to the chairs while the girls sat primly on the banquette. The boys ordered lemonade and the girls ordered Shirley Temples. The drinks came quickly, and Linus asked for two straws, one for him and one for his dinosaur. I'd been told that short, stumpy glasses are best for kids (they don't spill so easily), but these glasses were tall, and when I made the mistake of distributing menus just as the drinks arrived, Adrian knocked his lemonade all over the table. Despite the mess, we managed to order spaghetti, and then, as we waited for our food, Linus held an empty wineglass to each ear and began emitting high-pitched squeaking sounds.

"I can do lots of animal noises," Linus cheerfully cried to his assembled friends.

"I can do them too," said Adrian.

"Woof, woof," said Alex.

"Let's all be animals," screamed the girls in their sweet, giddy voices.

Chaos would be briefly forestalled by the arrival of two stacks of pommes soufflés, folded in white napkins. I described these delicious little treats (they're lightly fried potatoes filled with air) as "French-fry balloons" to the children, and soon they were calling them "balloonies" and stuffing them into their mouths at a frightening clip. Linus devoured ten balloonies (or maybe thirty), and my daughter, who weighed barely twenty-five pounds, had eight. As the children stuffed the balloonies into their craws, a sympathetic waiter sidled up and asked if I'd like something stiff to drink. "No, thank you," I heard myself say, "but could you please bring us some more balloonies?"

Unfortunately, the balloonies didn't arrive soon enough, and neither did the pasta. When the children sensed a lull in the proceedings (when dining out with kids, I later calculated, a lull is about forty-five seconds), they began clamoring for their parents. The boys bolted from the table first, running off through the crowd, zigzagging around the waiters' knees. The girls looked at me, and I looked at them, my face contorted in a faux scowl of disapproval. But our little standoff quickly ended when my daughter whispered, "I'm sorry, Daddy, I just want to go tell Mommy that I love her."

So off she went, and by the time I'd rounded them all up, the pasta was on the table. Everyone liked the pasta, so much so that a couple of the kids (Linus and Willa) began eating with two forks. A wise parent told me that it was better to let children play with their food than with each other, and with this in mind, I organized a spaghetti-sucking contest (won by Willa). But the spaghetti-sucking contest led to a round of communal animal calls, which led to more glowering from the grown-ups at the distant tables, and so, as our main course was cleared away ("But, Daddy," said Jane, "there's still lots of spaghetti on the floor"), I brought out the crayons and paper.

Crayons and paper are the Kryptonite of the children's restaurant world, I would later write, invaluable tools that render even the most obnoxiously empowered four-year-old momentarily passive and mute. In our case, the relative calm lasted for about four minutes, which was too bad, since it took ten minutes for the desserts to arrive from the Le Cirque kitchens. In the delicate interim, the waiters distributed little chef's hats, which some of the kids wore and some didn't. (Linus put his on top of his dinosaur.) Then, when the desserts arrived, a few of the kids didn't know what to make of them. Alex stared blankly at a multilayered napoleon dusted with powdered sugar, and Adrian continued to draw quietly, clutching a handful of crayons in his tiny fist ("I'm making scrambled eggs," he said). Willa received an entire miniature stove made all of chocolate, one of the restaurant's signatures, and she and my daughter took it apart and then ate it, piece by piece, in their precise, feminine way. Linus appropriated Alex's napoleon (causing Alex to spill his lemonade), and soon clouds of powdered sugar covered Linus's jacket and face.

My notes on the rest of the meal are messy and imprecise, as if they were jotted in the middle of a windstorm. At one point, bowls of ice cream arrived, and after a period of intense, lip-smacking silence, the table was buffeted by a collective sugar rush. According to my notes, Linus pointed to me and said, "Mr. Platt, there's a big lizard on your head." Shortly afterward, dinner ended. Danny Meyer said his biggest worry when serving young children in his restaurants is to keep the parents from losing their heads, and so it was at Le Cirque. The table looked like a bomb had hit it, but the waiters buzzed around with merry smiles on their faces, picking through the layers of debris. As the children rushed to and fro, the parents emerged from the bar to survey the wreckage.

"How was it?" Mrs. Platt wanted to know.

"It was fun," I said, which was more or less the truth.

Then Mario appeared, looking unruffled in his tuxedo, grinning his stiff, professional grin.

"What a lovely party," he said, giving a little bow.

"You must be kidding, Mario."

"Oh, this was fine. It was very amusing to watch."

Then he handed me a gift pack, which contained a set of crayons, neatly packed, and boxes of leftover cookies and chocolates.

"A little something for the children," said Mario. "Please come again."

THE PLATTS NEVER MADE IT BACK TO LE CIRQUE FOR ANOTHER family meal before the restaurant moved from that gilded Madison Avenue space to a slightly more corporate, antiseptic venue looking out on the circular courtyard at the bottom of the Bloomberg Building on Lexington Avenue. We took the in-laws from Michigan to this new venue for one of my review dinners when they were visiting town, and the famous circuslike desserts made of stalks of twirling candy and giant walls of chocolate, followed by a ritual papal greeting from Sirio himself, dressed in starched cuffs and a coffee-colored suit, caused almost as much excitement at the table as when Jane and her friends had visited years before. But Maccioni was frail by then, and after three iterations of the restaurant, his loyal old regulars began to fade away one by one. A couple of years after our visit, the family would close the New York City branch of the restaurant forever after a long and prosperous run.

My children have very presentable manners at restaurants around the city these days, although we still don't tend to visit them with the avid, manic regularity that the Platts did years ago, when my brothers and I fought over platters of chive dumplings or for a taste of the last shred of Peking duck. Like her sensible midwestern mother, who served up her ritual blue-plate specials each day of the week back in Michigan, the head of our household is a stickler for routine and for the soothing rhythms of a steady rotation of reliable, home-cooked meals. Every once in a while, however, when the family gets tired of the endless diet of Dad's Sunday roast chicken and the vats of heavily flavored pork stews, I'll persuade everyone to get in the car or on the subway train and rumble around the city looking for something interesting to eat.

We have a favorite place down in Chinatown for carryout dumplings and packets of chopped roast pork dressed with ginger and scallion sauce in the Cantonese style. We have a favorite place for bowls of steaming wonton soup, and a favorite place for the kind of noodles I enjoyed when my brothers and I haunted the ramen and soba stands of Tokyo. We have a favorite place for Peking duck downtown, and every once in a while the family gets into the car on a weekend afternoon and drives out into the suburbs for a taste of the kind of Mongolian barbecue my brothers and I enjoyed a half-century ago in Taichung.

Khan's Mongolian Garden, across the Hudson River in Rockland County, isn't quite like the place we used to visit, near the Japanese house back in Taiwan, set among the palm trees and rice paddies. There are no water buffaloes in sight (the place is down the street from a Dunkin' Donuts), and the cooks use enormous curved grills heated with gas instead of braziers filled with smoldering charcoal. The meat is frozen, not fresh, and laid out on a buffet tray under the glare of fluorescent lights. But the proprietors of Khan's come from Taiwan, and although there are no fireworks at the end, the meal unfolds in the traditional way: once you've mixed the lamb and pork with Asian-style vegetables like raw scallions, chopped cabbage, and coriander, you give your bowl to a grill man, who speaks Mandarin in a singsong northern accent and who fires your dinner up with squirts of "special sauce" on a sizzling range. The shaobing sesame seed buns are made fresh every morning by the staff and served in toasty stacks with your meal. My family and I stuff them with the savory meat, like hamburgers, the way my brother and I used to do, and we wash them down with mugs of ginger ale. With the whiff of coriander and the crunch of sesame seeds, the dish still tastes the way it did fifty years ago—exotic and magical and strangely soothing. It still tastes to me, come to think of it, like the comforts of home.

9

The Showdown at ZZ's Clam Bar

wasn't expecting very much to happen when I booked my table for two, under the usual randomly contrived name, at a small, lavishly expensive, slightly ridiculous-sounding tasting room called ZZ's Clam Bar, in the West Village, several years ago. I can't say I wasn't surprised, however, when a large linebacker-sized gentleman loomed up next to my table, halfway through what up to that point had been a surprisingly enjoyable meal, and asked my guest and me, in a polite, dispassionate bouncer kind of way, to get the hell out of the restaurant.

"I'm sorry, but you guys are done here," said the bouncer, still wearing his thick, winter bouncer's coat. He had been stationed outside by the door the last time I'd seen him on my way into the restaurant.

ZZ's Clam Bar was run by two popular young chefs named Rich Torrisi and Mario Carbone, following the model of young cooks like David Chang, at his seminal East Village noodle bar, and Gabrielle Hamilton, at her fine little East Village restaurant called Prune. Torrisi and Carbone had trained together in top Continental-style kitchens in New York and then opened a small, deceptively simple Italian-style deli on Mulberry Street, on the fringes of Little Italy, called Torrisi Italian Specialties. Like Chang and Hamilton, they applied the knowledge about sourcing and technique that they'd mastered uptown to the kind of everyday cooking they'd grown up with—vegetable antipasti, bricks of gooey home-style lasagna, fat veal parmesan sandwiches made with fresh-baked rolls and the finest veal, all carefully sourced and of the highest quality, unlike the usual packaged bread rolls and desiccated, leathery cutlets found at many of the corner Italian delis around town. In the evening, the corner space was turned into an inventive, modestly priced tasting room, which had received breathless and rhapsodic review treatment from critics like me, and from the ever-growing rabble of bloggers and informed, next-generation, postmillennial diners who'd bull-rushed the place in the months after it opened.

With success, however, came a certain amount of brassy swagger and attitude. The original Torrisi restaurant would close not very long after its smashing success as new money began to flow in from high-finance investors and boldface names from Wall Street and the entertainment world. The chefs' next project was a noisy, ambitious, extravagantly expensive Italian restaurant called Carbone, which was designed to summon up the convivial, theatrical world of the traditional Italian red sauce establishment, complete with heaping platters of linguini vongole and stuffed clams, and bow-tie-wearing waiters dressed in glimmering yellow jackets, some of whom looked like they were about to burst into song. In the circus world of big-money restaurants, as in any fashion-conscious business, new trends and styles are endlessly manufactured, trumpeted, and breathlessly parroted; it was one of the ironies of those early postmillennial days around the city that just as the appetite and audience for everything about the food and dining culture was exploding, the style and quality of what used to be called "fine dining" in New York was becoming simpler and arguably less sophisticated than the days when haughty Frenchmen were setting the styles around town. This new venture was greeted with the same praise that had been showered on the first restaurant—with the exception of one grumpy, overfed critic who groused, in his grudging, one-star review, that the rooms were noisy to the point of unpleasantness, the saucer-sized pasta portions were of various quality, and the prices bordered on the insane. Moreover, although some dishes seemed to work well enough, and others were generally below the lofty bar the talented young cooks had set for themselves in their debut restaurant, one creation in particular—an unfortunate experiment called "Chinese Chicken"—tasted like it had been "slathered with a mix of Chinese mustard and crankcase oil."

Most restaurants I review tend not to have bouncers stationed outside the door, and if a towering "doorman" does happen to be looming behind a set of cheap red velvet ropes set up on the sidewalk, it's usually not a fortuitous sign. It means the owners are more interested in creating a nightclub-style sense of scene and pageantry than in serving decent food, although with their flair for theatrics, the Torrisi Boys, as the blogs now breathlessly called them, were specialists at both. It was months after my Carbone write-up, and I hadn't planned on a proper review of ZZ's Clam Bar, which is why I'd booked only a table for two. Maybe I would mention the antic, tropically themed cocktails in a drinks roundup, or write about how the ambitious high-end operations, with rents in the city continuing to climb, were retreating to the smaller, ever more discreet (and expensive) tasting rooms around town. There were only a few tables in the small room, all of which were filled, and the bar was manned by a bewhiskered mixologist dressed in a pressed white jacket who looked like he'd been beamed in from one of the trendier dive bars in Brooklyn by way of the original Ritz Hotel. My guest and I had enjoyed our drinks, a selection of clams on the half shell, and other seafood creations designed to summon up memories of summertime Coney Island clam bars by the beach. But the room had fallen quiet, a few courses we ordered didn't appear, and suddenly the bouncer was looming over our table like the heavy in a Bugs Bunny cartoon.

"I'm sorry, but you guys are done here," the very large gentleman said, still dressed in his outdoor coat, with an implacable dead-eyed Bouncer Expression on his face.

My guest, who had worked with many of the top chefs and restaurateurs in New York and was accustomed to being treated with the highest levels of simpering deference when he dined out around town, began to sputter at the bouncer, and as he talked his face slowly turned a boiling shade of red.

"What do you mean? We haven't done anything," he said, doing his best to muster his own Loudly Aggrieved VIP Voice.

"This guy is done here, you can stay if you like," said the bouncer, looking down at me as I peered into the dregs of my second, quite excellent rum cocktail, still not quite able to believe my luck. I'd heard of critics having drinks thrown in their faces by members of the irate restaurant community. In one notorious incident, the hotheaded, perpetually apoplectic future reality TV demigod Gordon Ramsay emerged from his London kitchen in a rage, overturned the table where the *Sunday Times* critic A. A. Gill and his guest were sitting and ordered them both out of the house. Private business owners are within their legal rights to take this kind of rash action, of course, but the timeless, carefully scripted rituals between the chefs and restaurateurs who open restaurants and the writers whose job it is to critique them have evolved over the decades for all kinds of practical reasons. In taking up space at a corner table while surreptitiously tapping notes, dressed perhaps in an ill-fitting wig, the weary, self-important critic, like the large jungle elephant some of us resemble, contributes to the delicate fine-dining ecosystem in all sorts of subtle and unseen ways. We create stars and nurture careers, and over the course of our long lives we provide coordinates for the herds of paying public, who thunder up and down the vast restaurant savanna, looking for their next meal. Critics have long, elephantine memories and tend to herd together during times of trouble, and we're capable of irrational and unpredictable fits of destruction on the rare occasions when we're pushed too far.

"You guys are done here," the bouncer said for the third or fourth time in his insistent, vaguely ominous bouncer voice, the tone of which never rose or wavered. It was clear that the old elephant would be leaving this overpriced, high-tone clam bar shortly and against his will; the only question was how much of a scene we wanted to create. The chatter around the room had suddenly gone quiet, the way birds do out on the savanna when there's trouble afoot, and our formerly friendly and attentive waitperson was nowhere to be seen. The whiskered barkeep had stopped shaking his drinks behind the bar and was watching us quietly, while the rest of the witnesses to the Showdown at ZZ's Clam Bar were ducking behind doors and desperately trying to melt into the scenery, like comic characters in the gunslinger saloon of a Western movie.

"Let's go, they're kicking us out," I muttered quietly to my guest, who looked like he was about to start throwing crockery around the room.

"This meal is on the owner," said the bouncer.

"Really, I should pay the bill," I replied, trying to summon my most dignified May I Have the Check Please voice.

"No, this is on us," said the bouncer, beginning to show the faintest hint of irritation.

The company expense account is the one tenuous weapon

that separates the professional critic from the other loudly yapping voices in the jungle, and so I asked for our check three more times, my voice getting lower and more monotone until I sounded, it later occurred to me, like a comic version of the bouncer himself. Finally, after several more implacable replies, we rose unsteadily from our seats, awkwardly gathered up our coats, and were escorted by the bouncer through the still saloon, while my red-faced friend sputtered indignantly to himself. Outside on the sidewalk, before going around the corner to calm my friend with several excellent slices of Village pizza, I attached a photo of one of the dishes that we'd been enjoying—four slivers of oily sardine crudo on an aqua-green plate—to a post on my new, dimly understood Twitter account and then sent the news out into the world: "Platty's last dish at the enjoyable (though insanely pricey) ZZ's Clam Bar before a vy large bouncer kicks us out."

No one from the Torrisi empire ever explained why I was removed from their overpriced clam bar. There was no public statement the next day when the righteous Twitter mob of fellow critics—aggrieved diners who'd been snubbed or overcharged at their other restaurants around the city and even a few jealous, vengeful, competitive chefs—accused them of disrupting the carefully calibrated laws of the restaurant jungle and generally acting like touchy and high-handed young millennials who'd let success go to their heads. Maybe they thought that the adage about there being no such thing as bad publicity was true, or maybe they calculated that in the brave new world of overheated, breathless online coverage no one cared about the random musings of a single, dyspeptic, increasingly toothless critic anyway. One or two rumors circulated that Platt had been drinking loudly and disturbing customers. I heard my own rumor—much later, via the jungle telegram—that the chefs and a few business partners were in the basement of Carbone down the street, smoking a fierce industrial-strength strain of weed, when a breathless runner appeared with the news that grumpy Platt was happily grazing at the Clam Bar, and in a merry, stoned haze they gave the Henry VIII–style command to throw him out onto the street. The eternal laws of the jungle, however, have a way of sorting things out eventually. Several months later, when I arrived at the door of Torrisi and Carbone's next venture—a moody, Paris-meets-New-Orleans concept on the Lower East Side called Dirty French—Jeff Zelaznick, who was their business partner and front man, greeted me at the door with a large, possibly forced smile on his face and led us to a banquette in the back of the room. "Thank you for joining us," he said with an elaborate, almost comic politeness, bowing slightly from the waist and presenting the menus, which were printed, in the operatic Carbone-Torrisi style, on paper mortarboards in a large, cartoonishly exaggerated script. He may have even called me by the false name under which I'd booked our table that evening, as any experienced, traditional maître d' in the New York dining world is taught to do. When the wine list arrived, I pretended to study the trophy Burgundys and Bordeaux with the intensity that a large, self-important gourmand of my station is supposed to bring to the task, and as the meal progressed we both slipped back, with quiet relief, into our familiar roles in the timeless, ritual dance between restaurant and critic, like practiced, weary actors in a long-running Broadway play.

My only surprise about the Showdown at ZZ's Clam Bar, as I said at the time—and as I think most experienced critics would agree—is that similar fatwas and controversies didn't erupt much more often, especially in the personal, highly subjective world of restaurants back in those days. More than most kinds of critics, restaurant critics tend to be cast in the public imagination—in movies like the classic Pixar production *Ratatouille*, and in Jon

Favreau's *Chef,* in which Oliver Platt plays Ramsey Michel, a much-feared critic, modeled in part on his brother—as the ultimate, snooty arbiters of decorum and taste. But the reality is that we have our own quirky opinions and tastes; whether we're enjoying a scrambled egg breakfast at a local diner or forking over thousands of dollars for the most expensive kaiseki feast in Kyoto, there's nothing more personal and subjective than the experience of a good (or bad) meal. Book reviewers reach their quirky opinions by reading the same book, and art and movie critics all see the same movies and gallery shows. But like the theatrical plays they're always being compared to, especially in New York, restaurants are elaborate circus productions, with hundreds of moving parts that can vary depending on the time of a particular performance or the actors who happen to be onstage. A diner's experience of a particular lunch or dinner can be affected by whether the haughty hostess decides to seat him or her at a cramped, noisy little table by the kitchen or in a comfortable, quiet space with a glamorous view of the city skyline. Maybe the chef has a cold that evening and decided to call in sick, or maybe the critic doesn't enjoy eating garden vegetables, which happen to be the specialty of the house. Thousands of little variables like these go into the experience of a very good or a very lousy meal, and they keep on changing as the staff turns over, the seasons and menus change, and, especially during the early stages of a restaurant's life, the stressed-out owners make frantic adjustments, the way crew members do on the shakedown cruise of an expensive, oceangoing ship.

To the horror of chefs and restaurateurs, critics come parachuting into this refined operation, with their blasé attitudes and their jaded, blowtorched palates. With the help of their randomly chosen guests and self-appointed "experts," they often attempt to order and consume the entire menu, which is a ridiculous endeavor for any civilized person. With a few noble exceptions, most of them tend to base their lofty judgments on just one or two visits to a restaurant, and they rarely if ever come back, which, as any experienced kitchen hand will tell you, is a little like trying to divine the personality of a grown adult by interviewing a seven-year-old child. To which the critic will respond, sometimes in a meek voice, that the dining public is already spending hundreds, sometimes thousands, of dollars at restaurants the minute the doors open, let alone during the first six weeks of business, especially in a hothouse dining environment like New York City. A critic's first duty is to make a case for how the paying public should (or should not) spend their hard-earned cash in a certain restaurant. It's even possible on rare occasions that the crew on board this shakedown cruise might glean a few things from the write-up. At the end of the day, they point out, the cooks in the kitchen, the team in the front of the house, and even the critic conspicuously taking notes under the VIP table in the corner are all simply trying to do a difficult job as well as we all can.

10

"Adam Platt Is a Miserable Fuck,"
Part 1

The harried, hardworking chefs and restaurateurs who find themselves on the wrong end of a harsh review are under no obligation to believe that the overfed critic in the corner is just doing his or her job, of course. There's a scene in Jon Favreau's movie *Chef* where Favreau's character, a talented, beleaguered cook named Carl Casper, emerges from the kitchen in a rage to confront the glowering, all-powerful restaurant critic, who happens to be played, with a kind of delicious, charismatic menace, by my brother Oliver. I've taken my brother out to restaurants many times in the real world, although, like me, he's sometimes on a diet, and having him sitting at the table of a popular, just-opened restaurant in New York is a little like posting a large sign above us on the wall announcing in giant letters that ADAM PLATT DINES HERE. Sometimes chefs who recognize his face from the movies and television will send out complimentary side dishes and slices of pie, and as a creative soul who sympathizes much more with the talent in the kitchen than with appraising, nitpicking critics like his older brother, he'll often accept these illicit gifts happily and gobble them down whole.

Like all great theater, Jon Favreau's movie is filled with moments of hyperbole and also moments of absolute truth. When the director was working on his script, trying to summon up the most horrible things a critic could possibly write about a restaurant chef's cooking, Oliver asked me to send lines from my own most viciously negative reviews and from other inspired takedowns, like A. A. Gill's famous carpet-bombing in *Vanity Fair* of Johnny Apple's favorite Parisian bistro L'Ami Louis, with its "dung brown" walls and livery, vein-covered lobes of foie gras, which Gill described as tasting "faintly of gut-scented butter or pressed liposuction." My pathetic efforts didn't sound vicious at all compared to Gill's, of course, but even his were tame compared to the thunderbolts that Oliver's Ramsey Michel ended up letting loose on the unfortunate Carl Casper in the movie, which, as the title indicates, is written from the cook's point of view.

In the excellent showdown scene between critic and chef, which takes place early in the film, the glowering, imperious Ramsey Michel is tracked by the camera from behind as he makes his slow, grand entrance into the comically named "Gauloise" restaurant like a villainous professional wrestler entering the ring. Never mind that this villain critic's stylish, tailored brown silk jacket isn't rumpled or stained with streaks of A.1. sauce the way mine often is, or that Mr. Michel is dining alone this evening, which most working critics don't do very often. Never mind that the owner of the restaurant, a fevered, slightly overblown caricature culled from the collective kitchen slave imagination and played by Dustin Hoffman, has unaccountably commanded the chef to scrap that night's trendy, cutting-edge tasting menu in favor, among other things, of a tired molten chocolate lava cake dating from many decades before, which the arch villain critic has already described as "overcooked, needy, and yet, by some miracle, also irrelevant." The critic's grand entrance into the dining room, however, is an inspired and accurate bit of theater, and so is the chef's anger when, after years of pent-up frustration and rage, he bursts into the dining room, to the horror of Dustin Hoffman and all the other actors on that carefully orchestrated stage, and finally gives this haughty critic a piece of his mind.

If a transcript existed of Rich Torrisi and Mario Carbone's muttered dialogue from deep in the Carbone basement just before the Showdown at ZZ's Clam Bar, it might not sound very different from the one Favreau wrote for his aggravated hero, Carl Casper, in *Chef*. He calls his tormentor an asshole "who just sits there and eats and vomits these words back," and he accuses him, not without reason, of having no idea how a molten chocolate lava cake is actually prepared (hint: it's the timing). "It hurts, it fucking hurts when you write this shit!" he cries, before doing what countless chefs have probably fantasized about doing, which is to grab the offending chocolate cake, squeeze it in his fist, and throw the remains back down on Ramsey Michel's plate. Meanwhile, Oliver sits still and says nothing as the chef rages on, with an impassive look on his face. Maybe he was aided in this portrayal by memories of his poor brother sitting impassively on the job, pushing around servings of stale desserts, like molten chocolate lava cake, with his fork. Another inspiration could have been our own father, who as an ambassador in countries that had long, tortured histories with the United States, like Pakistan and the Philippines, used to cultivate what he called "the boiled-owl look" when irate officials criticized him in public. He didn't take their anger personally; he was only the messenger, and just like the critic, who is a consumer, not a cook, and whose job it is to represent the nation of paying customers, not the tortured, hardworking souls in the kitchen, he was sometimes the bearer of unwelcome news.

This caricatured role—the glowering pro wrestler–style villain—comes with the territory when you sign up to be a restaurant critic, of course, although the levels of imagined villainy and supposed influence often depend on the influence of the publication for which the critic is writing. Friends of mine who ascended to top critic jobs at papers in New York and London have told me that it takes some time to get accustomed to the tsunami of scrutiny, insults, ill will, and petty criticism that comes your way if you've spent relatively peaceful years writing for less influential publications. No one experienced more vitriol apparently than Gill, who was famously dyslexic and a recovering alcoholic; he was known for dictating his stories and observations over the phone to his editor, who would commit them to paper, then send the piece back to Gill just before deadline to be retouched. Like the antihero in a comic book, Gill drew power from the rage of his imagined enemies, someone at the *Sunday Times* once told me, and he took delight in driving them into mad apoplectic fits of rage and despair. Once, after a particularly savage review, a box arrived at the newspaper offices addressed to the "London Sunday Times Restaurant Critic." When it was opened—no doubt by a team of highly trained specialists—they found a note inside, propped next to a single, mercifully dried-out human turd. "From one Arsehole to Another" read the note in what was, no doubt, a twisted, scraggly script. Gill never saw the offending package, I'm told, but when the note was read to him over the telephone, I like to imagine he let out a long, cackling, slightly villainous-sounding laugh of happy delight.

I never took pleasure in writing a critical review, and although, as far as I know, I've never received a signature A. A. Gill care package in the mail, I've received many letters and had other occasional uncomfortable face-to-face encounters like the one at ZZ's. Such encounters happened more often downtown in SoHo, Tribeca, and Greenwich Village, where many members of the writing and restaurant community lived before the mass exodus of Manhattan's creative freelance culture out to the wilds of Brooklyn and Queens. The sense of aggrievement and occasional outrage directed at me began to increase when the magazine asked me in 2008 to concoct its inaugural star system of rating restaurants. Star systems—like the one invented by the ingenious mandarins at the Michelin Tire Company as a gimmick to entice bourgeois Frenchmen to travel the roads of the country after the war, preferably on sets of their tires, to find a good meal, using their Michelin Guides—have always been a controversial but useful part of the restaurant landscape. For chefs, star ratings are both an object of obsession and good for business; for consumers (and editors), they're a source of endless argument and discussion, as well as an imperfect tool for bringing a sense of objective order to a sprawling, highly subjective world. But ask working critics whether they like star ratings and, depending on how many martinis they've imbibed that evening, you're likely to get plenty of scowling boiled-owl looks, followed by a litany of complaints.

"Boy, are you screwed," a former critic friend of mine had said when I called her to ask for advice on creating my system, which was supposed to be roughly equivalent to the famous *New York Times* system devised by Craig Claiborne, but not exactly the same. There were already too many types of star systems in the crowded firmament, she said, and one more would just add to the confusion. The most venerable systems, like the Michelin and *Times* systems, tended to skew in favor of expensive, Continental-style establishments, leaving restaurants that were also worthy of inclusion but that offered more international styles and cuisines, like Japanese, Italian, or even Chinese cooking, out in the cold. Readers would fixate on the stars instead of my carefully crafted reviews, she cautioned, which was one reason why stylish writers like Gill in London and the great bard of the Los Angeles restaurant scene, Jonathan Gold, never used them. I would become a prisoner of my stars, just as the old white tablecloth dining tradition was being replaced by a more raucous, democratic style. No matter what kind of system I managed to devise, she concluded, the chefs would have one more reason to hate me.

All of these dire prophesies would come to pass during my star-crossed, decade-long career as a haughty, star-giving critic, before the practice was mercifully discontinued by the magazine. My tortured passive-aggressive solution to copying the vaunted four-star *Times* franchise without doing so exactly was to introduce, in a cover story, with much elaborate fanfare, a five-star *New York* magazine system ranging from "good" (one star) to "ethereal" (five stars), although discerning readers (and increasingly irritated chefs) would soon notice that I rarely ever bestowed the fifth star at all. In ten years, I gave only two restaurants the vaunted five-star prize, and in both cases (Eleven Madison Park, run by the talented Swiss chef Daniel Humm, and a ridiculously priced sushi bar called Masa) I ended up taking that fifth star away in a dramatic huff the following year. I rarely ever gave out four stars (to an "exceptional" restaurant, according to the tortured Platt system), and three-star reviews became increasingly rare as the tectonic leveling of the dining world, which was already under way when our system was introduced, continued to accelerate. The stately Continental fine-dining culture would disappear under a blizzard of comfort food fads, noisy *No Reservations* bar-restaurants, and trendy ramshackle pizza destinations like Roberta's, which opened in 2008 among the truck docks of Bushwick in Brooklyn, a place that snooty

Manhattan gourmets would never have dreamed of visiting in the not-so-distant past when lofty, Alain Ducasse–style palaces in midtown were the gold standard of the French-centric, star-obsessed restaurant era.

Over the years, as I tapped out a steady stream of one- and two-star reviews, I would find myself endlessly repeating the restaurant critic's mantra ("One star means good!") while trying to dream up catchy new buzzwords to describe this shift from what used to be called "le haute cuisine" to a more democratic, less formal style of dining. "Haute Barnyard" was a phrase I attempted to popularize as more and more decorated, accomplished chefs like Dan Barber at Blue Hill and Tom Colicchio at his hit restaurant, Craft, began to highlight locally grown chickens and other boutique barnyard products on their stripped-down (though still expensive) big-city menus. The "Kitchen Slave Revolution" was the term I used to describe the culture of tattooed backroom cooks who were moving from the shadows of the closed, Continental-style kitchens where they'd resided for decades out into a casual, open kitchen, which in this new world would become a glamorous kind of stage, and then from there, thanks to the wildfire popularity of the internet and the charisma of cooks like Tony Bourdain and David Chang, out into the buzzing popular culture at large.

Still, the most ambitious New York chefs tended to fixate on the stars, and now and then their outrage would bubble up, like the Carl Casper scene in Jon Favreau's movie, into public view. One of the few three-star ("excellent") reviews I did write back in those early days was for an extravagant Italian venture called Del Posto, which Mario Batali and his business partner Joe Bastianich, whose West Village establishment, Babbo, was the enormously influential hit restaurant of its era, opened in a tall, slightly drafty space in Manhattan's Meatpacking District, by the Hudson River. "Vegas on the Hudson" was the title of my generally favorable review, although Batali, who was more notorious in those days for his undoubted skills as a cook and for his cheerful "Molto Mario" personality than for the abusive and crude sexual behavior that later would sink his career, was not amused. "Platt's a miserable fuck," he told a writer for *Grub Street*, shortly after sending out for a bottle of vodka and some tonic. "He can't help himself," he explained to Tony Bourdain, who had accompanied his friend Mario to a book signing for one of the early heroes and inspirations of the Kitchen Slave movement, the wild man London chef Marco Pierre White. "His understanding about the star system is misguided," huffed Mario, presumably as he chugged one vodka tonic after another. "He's not about awarding stars, he's about taking them away, you know?"

As it zipped around what was still a relatively modest online restaurant community back in those days, the "miserable fuck" line was happily repeated to me by amused editors, friends, and slightly startled members of my family, including my mother, who wondered out loud what her son had done to make this chef person so horribly upset. I told her that I'd just been doing my job, and as usual, I maintained the signature Platt boiled-owl look in public and never responded to Batali. At the end of the year, however, when it came time to compose that other unhappy burden carried by most working restaurant writers, especially in the world of service magazines, the annual end-of-the-year wrap-up of all the new and trendy places to eat around town, I took my quiet revenge.

My long-suffering editor at the time, Jon Gluck, and I used to call this yearly restaurant cover package "the monster," because it covered hundreds of restaurants and took thousands of words and several weeks of labor-intensive eating to research and write. That year when I handed in the seven-thousand-word monster, I quietly deleted Batali's name everywhere in the text and referred to all of his restaurants, including Del Posto, as "Bastianich establishments," in reference to his partners, Joe Bastianich and the first lady of Italian cooking in New York, Lidia Bastianich. When the monster was published just after the new year, no one noticed, of course, except for the sensitive, bloviating, image-conscious chef himself. "Tell Platt that I can see what he's doing," Batali told one of the food editors with what I like to imagine was a tone of aggrieved, menacing outrage in his voice when they called about another story on one of his restaurants. "And tell him that I don't like it."

11

"Adam Platt Is a Miserable Fuck,"
Part 2

hadn't expected Batali to notice my modestly subversive response to his "miserable fuck" outburst, but in retrospect, why wouldn't he? In today's more egalitarian, digital world, where a negative Yelp review can have as much of an impact on business as the lordly pronouncements of a self-serious critic, superstar cooks tend to cultivate a more studied, user-friendly persona. They aren't just cooks anymore, they're philosopher kings, and with Instagram and Twitter providing a window into top kitchens around the world, they comment on everything from politics, to the environment, to what their children had for breakfast that morning. As writers from Orwell to Bourdain have pointed out, however, there are few tougher, more Darwinian, more dictatorial working environments than the traditional, French-inspired "brigade" in a working restaurant kitchen. Before restaurant kitchens around the country began to mercifully reform thanks to the #MeToo movement, many of the cooks who managed—

either by force of will or talent or both—to fight their way to the
top of this mostly male, testosterone-fueled, high-pressure world
were autocratic, imperious personalities who didn't always take
very kindly to criticism.

The talented Frenchman Daniel Boulud was another member of the beloved star chef pantheon back in my early days as
a critic, who went to extreme lengths to cultivate a polished,
almost cuddly public persona but was a famous martinet in the
kitchen and could be touchy about critics and their misguided
views. "Adam Platt is my bitch," he loudly declared to anyone
who would listen at a hastily convened press party in the fall
of 2009 after his flagship Upper East Side restaurant, Daniel,
was given the predictable three-star treatment by the resolutely
Eurocentric mandarins who put together the bible of bygone dining trends and styles, the Michelin Guides. Never mind that I'd
heaped effusive praise on many Daniel projects over the years,
including his revolutionary foie gras–laced DB Burger, which
was responsible for creating the Great Gourmet Chef Burger
Craze of 2002, from which the dining world still hasn't quite
recovered. Daniel's rage was directed at two reviews I'd written many months before. One was about Bar Boulud, near Lin-
coln Center on the Upper West Side, a modest, perfectly decent
(one star means good!) exercise in the casual-bar dining trend
that was sweeping through town. The other concerned a more
populist, star-crossed, and ultimately doomed gourmet beer
hall–style venture on the Bowery called DBGB Kitchen and
Bar (the name being a slightly tortured reference to the famous
Bowery punk club, which was once down the street) where the
casual menu was filled with patés, Alsatian sausages, and various other less successful examples of the gourmet burger craze.
I dimly recall that I had plenty of complimentary things to say
about both places (the now-shuttered DBGB also received the
dreaded one-star "good" rating), but Daniel was used to receiv-

ing glowing notices from the local press, who in those days had a habit of treating outsiders much more harshly than local heroes like Batali and Boulud. And both restaurants received respectful two-star write-ups from the *Times*, which no doubt added to Daniel's sense of outrage. "We are working so hard to create pleasure, to make people happy," he announced to the slightly bewildered reporters, who were probably hoping to hear about the joys of having achieved the pinnacle of Michelin success. "When you see a guy who is miserable like Platt, it doesn't matter what you do!"

Traditional restaurateurs who learned their trade in the mannered and theatrical hall-of-mirrors region formerly known as "the front of the house" tended to be more diplomatic and discreet in how they went about cajoling and influencing the critics. Like the chefs, they were adept at spotting the critic once he or she entered the dining room and, unlike the eccentric Georges Briguet back at Le Périgord during my first months on the job, would place the critic at the best table, with the best waitstaff, and order up what used to be called the "soignée" treatment: for VIPs, the kitchen would find the fattest, most succulent scallops available if they ordered the scallop entrée, or the tenderest cut of roast duck or prime rib. Daniel and his fellow top chefs were famous for this kind of excessive VIP treatment too, but the front-of-the-house restaurateurs tended, with one or two exceptions, to be less prone to intemperate outbursts and more adept at playing the long game when it came to buttering up susceptible writers, if not for this review, then for the next one.

Early on, before I'd ever visited any of his restaurants, Sirio Maccioni, the charming, tuxedo-wearing owner and front-of-the-house man at Le Cirque, wrote me a perfectly penned letter on his thick personal stationery, asking for advice on how to "adjust" his menu to the tastes of "the younger generation." Danny Meyer, whose children attended the same grade school as mine in downtown New York, would often greet me in the halls of the school—he dressed in his natty suit, I in my usual rumpled trousers and track shoes—with his trademark smile and a firm handshake, no matter what enraging things I'd written about his restaurants the day before. Like many canny professionals, Danny kept track of the critics' reviews and studied their tastes. He had his chefs hold in reserve certain choice trencherman items that the kitchen called "Plattnip"—such as pork chops, or the odd prime cut of fiorentina beefsteak—so that they could quickly shuffle them onto the menu as specials whenever I loomed up at the door of one of his new restaurants, dressed ominously in my flapping black coat.

One morning at school, after I'd attacked the quality of the cooking at what was at the time a much-hyped Danny Meyer barbecue restaurant called Blue Smoke—the baby back ribs were "like Chinese takeout," the chili "tasted like something from the kitchen of a not very reputable sports bar," and the Texas beef ribs had the "texture (and taste) of old pastrami"—I spotted him, to my horror, coming toward me at full speed with his hand out-stretched, like a pastor greeting one of his favorite parishioners on a bright Sunday morning after church.

"Hello, Danny," I said, looking down at my shoes while hastily attempting to pull up my gently sagging sweatpants.

"I just want you to know, that was an excellent review that you wrote. My team read every word, and it was very valuable to them."

"Umm, thank you very much, Danny."

"I also want you to know that, thanks to you, we'll do better next time," he said as I smiled a pained, uncomfortable smile, while clutching at my sweatpants. "The restaurant is a work in progress, and I hope you'll be back to visit soon." I did go back to Blue Smoke, as it happens, and whether it was thanks to Meyer's famous powers of persuasion or my own developing palate, I wrote that I liked the ribs much better the second time. It would be several years before I gave a Danny Meyer restaurant a harsh review again.

One of the exceptions to the general rule about old-school restaurateurs was that mercurial king of the New York brasserie, Keith McNally. His habit of blasting critics with furiously penned letters at all hours of the day and night blossomed into a kind of performance art with the rise of social media and the new crop of competitive, round-the-clock food blogs eager to get story tips (and possibly a free meal or two) in exchange for a steady stream of free and breathlessly favorable publicity. Originally from London, McNally made his reputation by filtering the style and sensibility of the classic Paris bistro, with the smoky mirrors, nickel-topped bars, and platters of boeuf tartare and steak frites, through his own transatlantic sensibility—first at the Odeon, that much-imitated scene restaurant of the '80s, and then at a succession of hit establishments like the popular faux brasserie Balthazar in SoHo and the Minetta Tavern in Greenwich Village. I had taken to describing the carefully staged look of a McNally restaurant—which he, like any good businessman, duplicated again and again in different ventures around the city—as "McNally Land," a name that the great man might not have appreciated.

Every now and then McNally tried to vary his formula, usually by serving Italian bistro food instead of French, and in the spring of 2010 he opened a restaurant called Pulino's Bar and Pizzeria on the corner of Houston Street and the Bowery downtown. In my review, I cataloged the features of the familiar McNally style—"The faux bistro bar clad in distressed metal," the "walls lined with glimmering backlit bottles of booze," the "magazine rack in the corner," and, in the evenings, a room "filled with that trademark of all McNally venues: a carefully calibrated, golden light." The difference between this McNally Land outlet and others, however, was the casual Italian menu prepared by a young, award-winning chef from San Francisco named Nate

Appleman, whom the British restaurateur had somehow cajoled into leaving the comforts of his small, laid-back, seasonal restaurant kitchen on the West Coast for the shark tank of high-pressure New York dining. Six weeks after the opening, it was apparent that the transition was not going smoothly. The menu was overcrowded and confused; the locavore theme was noble (Appleman and his team made their own charcuterie and even broke down whole hogs in the basement) but nothing seemed to taste very good, even the pizzas, which were dressed with an "almost toothpastelike tomato sauce" and had brittle crusts that tasted, according to one of my guests, like stale matzo crackers. "In fairness to Appleman," I wrote, "he's not in Kansas anymore. Serving carefully wrought escarole salads to sun-splashed foodies in San Francisco is not the same as feeding a roiling piranha tank of New York scenesters pretty much around the clock."

I was sitting down to work one bright morning not long after the review came out, feeling bloated and fuzzy brained from dinner the night before, and dressed in my usual writer's attire of rumpled socks and gym clothes, when an email popped up from my friend Ben Leventhal, who had cofounded the restaurant blog *Eater* just a few short years earlier, asking if I had any comment on Keith McNally's letter.

"What Keith McNally letter?"

"He wrote an open letter about your Pulino review, which we're going to run."

"Oh shit," I muttered, or something to that effect.

"I don't think Keith liked your Pulino review, Platty," said Ben with the quietly suppressed glee of a writer who knows he has a good scoop on his hands.

Eater's amusingly malicious headline, which went up within seconds after I typed out my conciliatory reply, read: "McNally Calls Adam Platt Bald [which was true], Overweight [sadly, also true], Out of Touch [debatable]." In his letter, McNally had protested, as aggrieved recipients of a tough write-up are prone to do, that I'd reviewed the restaurant way too early. The more respectful two-star write-up in the *Times* was published two weeks before mine, however, and although six weeks is early in the life of any restaurant, it's not egregiously early for a print critic working at the relative dawn of the Yelp era. McNally accused me of having a bias against "less formal restaurants" like Pulino, and of mistakenly identifying the blue sweater I described him wearing one of the nights I dropped in as a "cardigan." "I may not be a paragon of fashion," wrote the indignant restaurateur, possibly while waving a clenched fist in the air, "but I haven't worn a cardigan since 1965. (The year Dylan went Electric!)" I replied that I'd admired Mr. McNally and his restaurants (which was true); "as always, in these cases," I added, "he is entitled to his opinion and I, as a bald, middle aged and, alas (slightly) overweight professional restaurant critic, am entitled to mine."

In the end, things did not go well for Nate Appleman in the big city. The San Francisco chef would be out of a job within six months, and a few months later, after more futile tinkering, McNally brought in weathered veteran bistro chefs from elsewhere in his empire, remodeled the space in the mold of the other prosperous McNally Lands around town, and installed a French menu heavy on the beefy chops and frites that his New York audience (and the New York critics) were sure to love. Except for my allies at *Grub Street* and Steve Cuozzo in his *New York Post* column, the reaction from other corners of the internet had been swift and amusingly slanted toward the celebrity restaurateur. "Platt Acknowledges He Is Overweight, Stands by His Bad Review of Pulino's" was the headline on *Gawker*, then run by the Balthazar regular, and fellow expat Englishman, Nick Denton. And then, just as predictably, the buzzing locust horde forgot about the incident and moved on to other momentary crises and events.

The doomed Pulino was replaced, in time, by a more familiar French concept called Cherche Midi, which I reviewed respectfully ("Two stars means 'very good'"!) and without incident, reserving special praise for the very fine Plattnip-style cut of English rib roast. That restaurant has also closed, however, and the cursed space on the corner of Bowery and Houston stands empty these days, although after all these years, if you Google the names "Adam Platt" and "Keith McNally" together, the immortal words that pop up below my name are "Bald, Overweight, Out of Touch."

12

Travels, Part 1

There's a difference, of course, between happily grazing off the fat of the land, as I did during my rambling, overfed childhood, and the slightly more exhausting and perilous life of the professional food tourist. I don't know when it was exactly during my whirlwind, champagne-soaked junket to Ferran Adrià's famous restaurant El Bulli on Spain's Costa Brava that I felt the first slight tinglings of discomfort in my big toe. Maybe it was late that first night, tossing and turning in my fluffy bed back at the hotel, after the first-class flight from JFK to Barcelona, and the chauffeured drive up the coast to a Catalonian castle in the town of Vulpellac. The friendly people there from Dom Pérignon—the sponsor of what one of my woozy companions was already calling "the Mother of All Boondoggles"—served us platters of goat confit, among other things, washed down with so many magnums of rare vintage champagne from the company's private cellars that my notes on the evening faded into a series of delirious half-sentences and exclamations before disappearing altogether. Maybe it was the next day, after another bountiful, booze-filled luncheon, or maybe it was during my carefully allotted twenty minutes with the chef himself later that afternoon. There were magazine editors from Shanghai in our boisterous little party, and a restaurant critic from Parma, who had a silk handkerchief blooming from the pocket of his neatly tailored suit. Before meeting the most famous chef in the world, I limped along behind this motley group of poseurs, professional aesthetes, and food hacks on a tour of the restaurant's famous state-of-the-art atelier-style kitchens, where a small army of cooks were busy chopping mushrooms, shucking oysters, and feeding esoteric ingredients into giant, gleaming blenders. A young chef showed us a translucent wafer made of clarified potatoes. It would be used, he said in the hushed, slightly reverent tone of a young scientist discussing the latest rocket ship innovation, to create a "never before seen" mushroom tart.

After the kitchen tour, the assembled junketeers lined up for our interviews with the most famous chef in the world, who received us at strictly allotted twenty-minute intervals on the terrace of a nearby hotel. Adrià was a short, intense man, dressed in his military whites, with the pale complexion common to all hardworking cooks and teeth stained from cigarette smoke. He had a frowning, expressive look on his face, which reminded me of pictures I'd seen of Napoleon, and he examined his phone and stared politely into the middle distance as the same questions were translated for him again and again.

"How does it feel to be leaving the kitchen after all these years?" I asked him, fighting the urge to take off my shoe and rub my gently throbbing toe on a nearby chair.

"I feel a sense of lightness and relief. Maybe you can run a restaurant for forty years, but to run a truly fantastic restaurant for that long, I think it is impossible, the pressure is too intense."

"If you had one last meal to eat on earth, what would it be?"

"The best Iberian ham and a bottle of Dom Pérignon, of course," he said with a weary smile, being sure to name-check the sponsor of the evening's festivities.

It wasn't my idea to fly over to Spain to write another canned "I Ate Dinner at El Bulli" story, which leading up to the closing of Adrià's famously remote restaurant at the end of a winding dirt road up the coast from Barcelona had already become a kind of parody of itself. By now, everyone in the food world and beyond knew the legend of El Bulli, and many of us could recite it by heart like nuns chanting the Stations of the Cross: how in the '70s a modest German couple had purchased a whitewashed, mission-style house in a small beach town called Rojas, in between the moon-shaped blue-green bay and a palisade of cliffs. How they'd named it after their pet bulldogs, and how in the mid-'80s they'd hired Adrià, an anonymous former cook in the Spanish navy, to work in their kitchen. How over the next few years, and more or less out of nowhere, he'd begun to spin out little miracles: glasses of sea smoke scented with salt, tinctures of tomato foam that captured the essence of the best tomato you'd ever tasted, the yolks of raw quail eggs encased, by some wonder of gastro-physics, in pouches of golden sugar that slowly dissolved like spun candy on the tip of your tongue. Cooks and writers had made pilgrimages from around the world to marvel at these creations and to study his radical techniques, which were upending the stuffy, staid world of haute cuisine. Adrià was compared to Dalí, Picasso, and Le Corbusier, and his impossibly complex (and generally impossible to replicate) recipes were collected, with religious care, in a series of giant, glossy volumes.

But now the most famous chef in the world had had enough, and in the spring of 2011, leading up to the restaurant's final service in late July, a cavalcade of big-foot food writers and nattering TV hosts were making one last pilgrimage up the coast to Rojas, over the famously winding dirt road, to pay their final respects. Jay McInerney had penned his own elegiac, rose-tinted farewell in *Vanity Fair*. Tony Bourdain was devoting a whole episode of his show to his last dinner at El Bulli, and before the show aired, he tweeted out every one of the fifty courses to his eager, salivating public. Big-money trophy diners were flying in on their jets that spring and summer from around the world ("It's the sanctum sanctorum, Platty," one of them told me. "It's the impossible get"), and corporations, like Dom Pérignon, were bringing in clients, with Adrià's happy blessing, on an endless series of elaborate junkets and publicity stunts.

Serious restaurant critics, at least those of us still operating under the ancient, slightly tattered rituals of the trade, with our ironic faux reservation names, our dwindling expense accounts, and our discreet though mostly useless disguises, were supposed to be above this sort of thing, of course. We were supposed to righteously turn down the cases of champagne and Premier Cru wines, though they mostly didn't come our way, and when the representatives of tourism boards from the city of Istanbul, say, or the beer-fed, beef-producing prefectures around Kobe, Japan, called with enticing offers to tour their facilities and sample their delicious products in exchange for a little publicity, we were supposed to politely hang up the telephone.

The editor of *New York* magazine, Adam Moss, was familiar with this high-minded code, of course. Being a trim, perpetually energetic person who didn't seem to drink more than a sip or two of wine a week, however, or eat much more than the occasional bran muffin and a few cups of green tea, he'd never been tempted himself by an elaborate junket like this. Which is probably why, when he'd called me into his office a few days earlier, he greeted me with a happy, mischievous grin. The owners of Dom Pérignon champagne had invited him to their version of Ferran Adrià's last supper, but he had better things to do. Why didn't I go? When I attempted to protest, he only got more excited about the idea, the way editors often do. It would be a story about the ultimate junket—a satire of the ultimate junket even—and he wanted me to write it that way, while also stealthily producing a fly-by summation of Adrià and his restaurant for New Yorkers who were, of course, desperate for this kind of inside information. It would just be a short weekend trip. The first-class seats were already paid for, along with the Relais & Chateaux–approved hotel along with, according to rumor, a scenic helicopter trip to the restaurant itself, which was designed to generate a maximum amount of publicity (and Instagram hits) from the assembled press, and also to spare the pampered VIPs from having to drive in a convoy up and down the twisting mountain roads of the Costa Brava.

"Helicopters?"

"You'll love it. It's the trip of a lifetime!"

"I'm not crazy about champagne."

"That's even better!"

"When do you need the story?"

"As soon as you get back. You can start writing on the plane!"

NOT MANY THINGS CAPTURE THE CONTRADICTIONS OF THE PRO-fessional eating life—the work obligations in an endless stream of luxurious holiday settings, the relentlessly delicious foods, the weirdly seductive combination of happy anticipation (I'm going on an all-expenses-paid trip to Naples to eat pizza!) and quiet horror (how am I supposed to eat all that fucking pizza in three days!)—than the all-you-can-eat, all-expenses-paid road trip. Making the normal gastronomic rounds at home as an eating professional, it's possible to halfway manage the workaday cavalcade of luncheons and banquets and restaurant tastings with restorative naps, the occasional skipped meal, and the tactic, at a particularly challenging dinner, of having other, nonprofessional eaters happily gorge themselves on your behalf. But there is no escape on the road: time is limited, every market and noodle shop you visit feels momentarily new and exciting, and most of the time it's only you doing the tasting. "Food-fucked" is the term I've heard chefs use when they visit a friend's restaurant and the kitchen sends out the entire menu, and the same applies to a critic or writer on a working trip through the street food markets of Saigon, say, or the venerable sausage parlors of Lyon. Food-fucked is more or less your permanent condition from the time you wake up bright and early for your sausage breakfast until you stagger into bed late that night.

Many years ago, I visited a famous auberge restaurant run by an eccentric French genius named Marc Veyrat, who'd achieved fame, like Ferran Adrià, for mingling the particular terroir of his home region in the French Alps—wildflowers, indigenous herbs, high-altitude cheeses—with the Adrià-style high-angle molecular gastronomic tricks that were all the rage in the posh dining circles of the early 2000s. His original chalet inn on the shores of Lake Annecy, near the Swiss border, has since, tragically, burned down, but in those days it was a magical place, with soft feather beds and double-sized bathrooms and balconies you could sit out on in the evenings, with your glass of chilled Savoy wine, to watch the ferries and motorboats cut back and forth across the wide green lake. An eccentric figure, Veyrat effected the style of a reclusive rock star who rarely emerged from his state-of-the-art studio, although sometimes guests would see him wearing his trademark John Lennon–style acid-trip dark glasses and tall, conical peasant's hat, foraging for flowers and herbs in the fields above the hotel.

I was writing a story for a travel magazine on the gourmet inns of Europe, and when I arrived with Mrs. Platt at Veyrat's three-star Michelin auberge, I'd already dined on roast beef with all the trimmings, among many other delicious things, at a luxury inn in the Lake District of northern England, and on the more classic specialties of the Savoie at another well-known auberge farther down the lake. Mrs. Platt had sensibly stopped eating on the trip long before, but, sadly, I still had a job to do. She'd snapped a picture of me that morning at breakfast, surrounded by crocks of truffled scrambled eggs and cutting boards strewn with local hams, jamming a large croissant into my mouth and looking, it later occurred to me, like a bloated contestant trapped in a nightmare gourmet eating contest. We ordered a full lunch of Veyrat's richly inventive cooking on the terrace after that supersized breakfast, and I interviewed the chef later that afternoon, after a fitful nap. He spoke in strange, whispering riddles, which were even more confusing when translated into English. When I told him about our delicious breakfast and luncheon and mentioned we'd be staying for dinner too, he regarded me over the top of his spectacles as if I were slightly mad, before saying something to his interpreter, and then, after a polite interval, wandering off into the garden sunlight squinting under the brim of his peasant's hat. Later when I called to reconfirm my dinner reservation, the kind woman on the other end of the line said, "Our food here is very rich. I don't know if another meal is a good idea for you, Monsieur Platt."

During the course of my professional food travels, I've contracted a severe case of what one wise barbecue pit master described as "pork bloat" during a short, woozy tour of the famous barbecue joints of North Carolina, a trip that turns out to be as you eat your way slowly westward an anthropological study of the history of American barbecue itself. I've had a near-death experience sampling the sperm sac of the deadly fugu fish at the end of a weeklong eating binge in Tokyo, and suffered blurred vision in one of my eyes for weeks after someone who was commenting excitedly on the quality of a soup dumpling down in Chinatown spat a tiny speck of gristle into my eye. One day, in preparation for spending a week in one of the famed pizza academies of Naples, I rode around the crooked cobblestone streets of Naples for a day with a voluble cabdriver named Salvatore who was practicing his English for an upcoming trip to New York. Like all Neapolitans, Salvatore considered himself an expert on the local marinara pies—the particular crispiness (or noncrispiness) of the crust, the sacred ratio of olive oil to tomatoes to cheese. His little cab was decorated with miniature shrines to the Virgin Mary and the Argentinian soccer star Diego Maradona, who spent his glory years playing in Naples. By the end of the day, after we'd visited our fifth pizza joint, he was cheering me on, like I was one of the exhausted players on his beloved Napoli football team, and also a little horrified. "This is a crazy job you have!" he cried as we careened home through the afternoon traffic.

Seeking the culinary wisdom of loquacious cabdrivers is something I used to do on my trips abroad. In Singapore, for instance, the learned cabbies are street food experts who can speak at length on the intricacies of the famous hawker markets and food halls which dot that city like a network of bustling piazzas in a sprawling Renaissance town. Early on as a critic, I thought it would make a fun story to spend the day hailing taxicabs around New York City, politely asking one driver, and then another, to take me to their favorite restaurant. I met Alphonso Compoverde from Ecuador, who took me for breakfast to his favorite Cuban restaurant, on Eighth Avenue, where we sat at the counter with several gentlemen dressed in guayabera shirts, eating braised short ribs and flat, toasty slices of a Cubano sandwich filled with pickles and melted cheese and bountiful pieces of pork. Later I sampled plates of wet, Haitian conch stew, and then a Ghanaian stew called egusi at the African Food Temple, a noble but long-since closed dining establishment on Webster Avenue in the Bronx, where the bathroom was strung with brightly colored tropical flowers and the waiters brought bowls filled with warm water to wash your hands after the meal. Of course, I ate many samosas that day, and I watched real Punjabi roadside tea being poured into paper cups from a great height at a long-vanished gas station on Houston Street, which was torn down many years ago to make room for a glittering condo.

The trip lasted only five hours but felt like a whirligig gastronomic tour of the world, and when it was over, I lay on the couch describing the highlights of the day to my daughters, while crunching horse-pill-sized tablets of antacid. They listened to my strange bedtime story politely, and when I was finished, they digested it in silence for a while. Finally, one of them said, "I don't think you should eat any more food this week, Daddy."

13

Travels, Part 2

When you're not passed out on the couch or gasping for breath on the floor of your hotel room, the traveling food life is filled with all sorts of little wonders, of course. Before starting to write about food full-time, I had a travel column in *Elle* magazine, and I also spent years contributing work to travel magazines of every kind. I'd taken train trips across India wedged into compartments filled with jolly groups of gentlemen from Bombay, camped out in the Kalahari Desert under the twisting branches of giant baobab trees, and written columns on what it was like to visit Paris for a long weekend without ever leaving your luxury hotel. I spent a week shooting rapids down the Grand Canyon with a group of Texas cowboys in the kind of tippy wooden dory boats in which the original pioneers explored the river. When the boats flipped, which was quite often, the guides told you to calm yourself as you got sucked deep down under the whirling rapids by looking upward toward the sun shining through the bottle-green water. And sleeping out on the sandy banks in the evening, after being tumbled through the rapids, you could see satellites tumbling across the canyon sky.

Contract magazine writers tend to find one niche and stick to it forever: my specialty was the serendipitous, helter-skelter road trip. Before taking up the sedentary life of an overfed restaurant critic, I'd driven on assignment across the western deserts of the United States and traveled from the northern forests of Oregon to the top of Mexico. I'd meandered in a small Volkswagen through the beautiful hobbit landscape of New Zealand's South Island, and I'd contrived, with my deep-pocketed editors in New York, to come up with the ideal road trip across America. This journey involved choosing the perfect time of year (early October, because fall is the best tourist season wherever you travel), the perfect longitudinal, food-friendly route (to circumvent the industrial wastelands of the Midwest and the scrubby desert scenery of Texas and Arizona, begin in Charleston, South Carolina, and head due west), and the perfect car (a wide-body silver Cadillac that I picked up at the airport in Charleston and eventually delivered, mud-splattered, with a pair of fuzzy pink dice hanging from the mirror, to the Hertz rental counter at the airport in Los Angeles).

On that two-week trip, I poked through the Carolinas, up over the Smoky Mountains, and then detoured through the Deep South and out onto the wide spaces of the open prairie. I played bingo in Tupelo, Mississippi, near the famous shotgun shack where Elvis was born, and enjoyed a frosty-glass beer at the Victory Bar on the square of a lovely little town called Las Vegas, New Mexico, which had an antique, perfectly sprung dance floor dating back to the days of Billy the Kid. I interviewed a Cherokee Indian chief on his reservation in the Smoky Mountains and a lama named Karma Dorje, who'd been born in the village of Gangtok in the Himalayan state of Sikkim in India, but now found himself running a Tibetan Buddhist center, somewhat uneasily, among the glitzy mansions of Santa Fe, New Mexico.

As I traveled slowly west, living off the fat of the land, the back of the Cadillac filled up with paper cups and discarded sandwich wrappers. I enjoyed a platter or two of the famous country ham at the Loveless Hotel on Route 101 outside of Nashville, Tennessee, where, for an extra $1.10, you could complement your stolid breakfast with fried chicken gizzards and glasses of buttermilk. I had a delicious poached egg breakfast on the lip of the Grand Canyon, grazed on cheeseburgers and avocado turkey burgers and different regional barbecues, and became an expert at unfurling giant bomb-shaped burritos from their silver wrappers as I drove down the empty country highways at eighty miles an hour.

By the time I reached the lama in Santa Fe, I'd taken to asking people I met on the road about their favorite places to eat, the way I would later do as a full-time professional glutton, but when I put this question to Lama Dorje, he let out a small sigh. A dignified-looking gentleman, dressed in cascading red robes, he was sipping a glass of tea in his favorite rocking chair while mountain birds rioted around in the trees outside. He hadn't wanted to come to the United States in the first place, he told me, but his own lama back in the Himalayas had commanded him to go. Being Buddhist, he was vegetarian, and so not very familiar with the local cuisine, let alone the idea of the bloated, Bourdain-style culinary road trip. "In this country everything is pleasure, pleasure, pleasure, money, money, money," the lama said. "I'm afraid I don't even know how to drive."

Maybe the lama, sensing something from the slightly manic, overfed aura I was giving off, was trying to tell me something? Who knows? But later on, when I started incorporating my affinity for road trips into the world of food writing, I tried to search out curious characters like the lama along the way, in an attempt to keep the "pleasure" aspect of the assignment from veering too drastically out of hand.

For the North Carolina barbecue story, which would be published in the *Washington Post* Sunday magazine, I sat down with "Pete Jones," who even back in those days was as famous in barbecue circles as any venerable vintner in the vineyards of Burgundy or Bordeaux. Jones told me that his ancestors around the small town of Ayden, which sits halfway between Interstate 95 and the coast, had been serving their chaste, unreconstructed version of pit-cooked chopped pork since before the Civil War. He was in his seventies ("Hell, I think I'm about seventy-two," he told me) and would die several years later, but he'd managed to catch the very early waves of the coming international barbecue craze by turning the ramshackle establishment called the Skylight Inn, which he owned with other members of the family, into a world-famous hog-cooking destination. Mr. Jones traced his Spartan cooking methods back to his great-great-grandfather Skilton Dennis, who began roasting pigs for church gatherings in the 1830s; at the Skylight Inn, they still cooked their whole hogs more or less the same way as his ancestor—for up to fourteen hours in the brick pits out behind the little restaurant, over a mixture of smoldering oak and hickory wood. Over the years, dignitaries had come from around the world for a taste of his famous pork sandwich, including several presidents, and when a magazine named the Skylight Inn the best barbecue joint in the country back in 1979, he'd slapped a large plywood replica of the Capitol rotunda up in Washington, DC, on the roof to celebrate.

"This is known to be the barbecue capital of the world, so I figured I had to put up a dome," said Jones, who looked more like a hardscrabble pig farmer than the kind of bluff, burly, and bearded barbecue pit master who would become a staple on the food cable TV shows. As I wrote in the story, he received me in his cluttered office, wearing a beat-up pair of work boots and a faded red Coca-Cola cap propped on his head. He took me out behind the restaurant to tour the barbecue pits, which still operated more or less the way they had back in the days of Skilton Dennis, whose own ancestors, living in the Tidewater region of the Carolinas and Virginia, learned the coal pit technique from the local Indians.

After the tour, I had a taste of the chopped pork for the first time. It was finely diced, interspersed with smoky, salty, barely visible cracklings of pork fat, and already seasoned by the cooks in the chaste lowlands Carolina style—with just a splash of vinegar and some salt and pepper. When Jones saw me reach for some more sauce, he gave me the same disapproving look I'd gotten from the lordly sushi chefs in Tokyo when I asked for a little extra soy sauce to go on their perfectly flavored fatty tuna belly. In the low country by the coast, the base for the barbecue sauce is vinegar, and as you travel west through the state the familiar sugary red tomato ketchup tinge slowly begins to appear. Jones regarded these newfangled developments with the same suspicious contempt reserved for slices of previously frozen American pizza by the Neapolitan pizza masters I would meet years later on another story. The chopped pork at the Skylight Inn was served between two simple slices of white bread, or piled, unadorned, on little paper "trays." Except for the crackling bits, the fat had been slow-cooked off the soft, finely chopped meat, and the faint umami taste of vinegar made you want to come back for another deliciously addictive sandwich almost immediately after you'd finished the first one. "If it's pure barbecue, it's barbecue before the sauce goes into it, no way of saying nothing but that!" Jones exclaimed, as he watched me head back to the counter for seconds with my pork tray.

I MET OTHER GRAND BARBECUE PERSONALITIES ON THAT TRIP, LIKE Keith Allen of the famous Allen & Son barbecue restaurant outside of Chapel Hill, who was shoveling coals around his cooking pit when I found him, wreathed in blue hickory smoke. Allen used only hickory in his cooking, gathering the wood from fallen trees in the forests and neighborhoods around town, and every day he woke up at 3:30 a.m. to tend his fire. Like French vintners tasting wine, he took a taste of pork only now and then and went about his work with a deliberate slowness. "I can cook a rib eye steak in fifteen minutes," he said, "but it will take me half a day to cook you a proper barbecue sandwich." Wayne Monk, in the famous barbecue city of Lexington, maintained that good barbecue, like anything else, is predicated on freshness. He cut me a taste of crispy-skinned "brown" shoulder, which was baby pink and succulent to the point of sweetness, and told me that discerning locals knew when one of his brown pork shoulders was perfectly cooked and in a state of peak deliciousness and would begin to line up outside his restaurant, Lexington Barbecue, a half hour ahead of time, in their pickup trucks and wide-body cars, to wait for a taste.

I introduced myself to William McLawhorn, a former cotton and corn farmer who operated B's Barbecue and Grill. This ramshackle establishment at a country crossroads near the town of Greenville was famous for the addictive quality of McLawhorn's barbecued chicken. "Cook 'em low and slow and keep watching 'em, that's my secret," said McLawhorn, who cooked three hundred birds per day over hot coals for two hours, bathed them in a warm vinegar sauce of his own design, and then closed up shop when they were gone. McLawhorn's chicken was the best chicken I've had before or since—the skin was parchment thin, and even the little bones disappeared to nothing on the back of your tongue. I ate one of McLawhorn's chickens at a picnic table under the shade of a spreading oak tree, chatting about the finer points of regional Carolina barbecue with a county judge who was a regular at McLawhorn's; and for a taste of the best chicken in the world, with corn bread, coleslaw, and a tall sweet iced tea, I remember we paid a grand total of $3.95.

On that trip, I also visited with a genial gentleman named Martell Scott in the town of Goldsboro, who told me he'd earned an accounting degree from Howard University before going into the family business, which his grandfather, a minister, had started back in 1917. The Scotts were famous for their barbecue sauce, which was patented and sold by mail in every state of the Union. It was the ribs that grabbed my attention, however; when I got a second order, along with a tray of lean chopped pork, for the road, the waitress cried, "Go for it, baby, it ain't gonna kill ya!" as I waddled out the door.

That trip didn't quite kill me, but over the years several of these madcap excursions almost did. The awkward gout flare-up during my visit to El Bulli would be cured by a few pills, once I tapped out my farcical deadline story in a hungover frenzy (yes, there was a helicopter ride to the restaurant at sunset) and hobbled off to the doctor when I got back home. The closest I've ever come to an actual near-death experience on the job, however, was at the end of another long eating excursion to Tokyo. I'd already spent a week in the city, recording the strange food manias that took hold in Japan during the early part of the millennium and spread from there around the world. I'd visited the sets of the frenetic, *Iron Chef*–style cooking shows and stood in line with legions of young girls waiting for a taste of the latest social media pastry sensation. I'd roamed again through the department store food halls from my high school days, interviewed diffident sushi masters and tempura chefs, and taken the train up the coast to wander around the wonderful ramen museum in Yokohama, which was built during the 1990s by an eccentric developer to celebrate the favorite comfort food of his youth. The developer had spent years turning a large subterranean space in a nondescript Yokohama office building into a ramen geek fantasia, designed to look like his childhood neighborhood back in 1958, the year instant noodles were invented by the great Momofuku Ando in his small workshop in Osaka. All of the different styles of ramen from around Japan were collected under one roof at the museum and sold at little street stalls and stands by cooks dressed in full costume. In that uniquely obsessive Japanese way, replicas of vintage Godzilla movie posters were plastered on the fake building walls, and hidden stereo boxes filled the space with clattering subway sounds and street noises. There was even a diorama on the ceiling, lit up with orange and purple colors, designed to look like the early evening sky.

The day before I was about to leave town to fly home, my editors in New York called and asked if their wandering restaurant critic could locate a fugu restaurant on short notice and write about the experience. I knew all about the dreaded puffer fish, having been living in Tokyo in 1975, when one of the biggest stories of the year was the death of a famous Kabuki actor named Bandō Mistugorō, whose organs shut down after he ingested too many deadly fish livers at a restaurant in Kyoto. The emperor of Japan was forbidden by law to eat the fish, which fed on a deadly shellfish common in the waters around Japan. The poison, called tetrodotoxin, collected in the liver, eyeballs, and ovaries of the fish, and if you ate too much of it, you would slowly become paralyzed and suffocate to death. There was no cure for the poison, and its effect was so slow and insidious that victims in the fishing villages, I'd read, were laid beside their open caskets for several days to ensure that they were not being buried alive by mistake. Once certified fugu chefs passed an exam, they were given an official government certificate to display in their restaurant. Because people had died foraging in garbage cans behind fugu restaurants, and because toxic fugu entrails were occasionally used by enterprising murderers as poison, the fugu chefs, by law, had to keep the poisonous entrails in a metal container under lock and key, then deliver it every week to Tokyo hazmat officials stationed at the fish markets, who disposed of the poisonous remains in sealed toxic waste cannisters.

"I don't want to write about the goddamned fugu," I told my editor.

"See what you can find!" was his cheery reply.

My guide on that trip was Shinji Nohara, a writer and former law student who had developed a specialty leading jet-lagged foreign journalists and other fat-cat food adventurers on culinary pilgrimages around the city. It was a Sunday afternoon in early spring—the end of the fugu dining season, Shinji said—and my flight out of town was the next day. When I told him about this new assignment, he smiled happily and started making calls.

"You've never had fugu?! You will love it! I'm a big fan!"

After ten minutes or so, Shinji had found us a fugu restaurant, one of the few that could open on a rainy Sunday evening. We piled into his battered Jeep Wagoneer and rumbled through a spattering of springtime rain to a lonely little restaurant in the working-class district of Tokyo called Sumida. When we arrived, a TV was flickering on the wall of the empty little room. A food show was on—starlets were learning to cook a dish from a dour chef wearing a tall white toque. Our chef, Mr. Hashimoto, was hacking at a fugu carcass behind the bar when we arrived. There were speckles of blood on his apron, and I remember thinking, as I wrote in my story, that he had a striking, not very confidence-inspiring resemblance to the famously bug-eyed, twentieth-century American comedian Don Knotts.

Like lots of cooks in Tokyo, Mr. Hashimoto lived above his restaurant, although there was no evidence of a Mrs. Hashimoto on this stormy Tokyo evening: no shoes were lined up neatly by the stairway leading up to his apartment, and the pitter-patter of children's feet could not be heard from the floors above. There was no one in the dining room; in fact, there were no chef's assistants, no waiters, and no busboys to clean the tables and wash the dishes. As I scanned the walls nervously for the chef's government-approved fugu certificate, Shinji asked him about the evening's menu. He was preparing the usual smoked fugu fins, he said, slices of raw fugu sashimi, and delicate helpings of Kara-age fugu ribs rolled in flour and sizzled in oil. But the chef excitedly reported that he'd also procured some very fine shirako, which, according to Shinji, was one of the ultimate seasonal delicacies in the fugu canon. It appeared only briefly in the spring, the way white truffles from Alba filled the grand New York restaurants every fall.

"Shirako?"

"The literal translation is 'white babies.'"

"You mean fugu eggs?"

"No, the ovaries are deadly poisonous! This is the fugu's sperm sac," said Shinji with a look of barely suppressed glee on his face.

"I'm not eating the engorged sperm sac of a deadly fugu fish."

"We're not eating the whole sac, just a little."

"I'm not eating even a little bit of sperm sac."

"It's a famous delicacy, like the smoothest brie cheese from France!"

"I don't like brie cheese."

"I've already ordered it, so we'll just take a little taste. Your editors will be happy!"

"So where the hell is everybody in this restaurant?" I whispered to Shinji, looking around nervously at the empty tables in the deserted dining room and at the chef, who had returned behind the bar, where he commenced hacking at the fish again in his blood- and guts-stained apron.

"Maybe it's the rain," he replied. "Or maybe Sunday is not a big day for fugu eaters. Or maybe Chef Hashimoto has killed everybody."

Shinji was a prankster and also something of a fugu promoter, having introduced the dish to Anthony Bourdain when he came through town. Like most local diners, he considered fugu to be generally safe, and he liked to poke fun at what he considered the hysterical foreign caricature of the dish. "We don't think about the poison," he said. Fugu's appeal, he believed, stemmed from a different kind of primal force. "It's seasonal, it's ceremonial, and it's expensive, so you can impress the girls." When I asked him how Bourdain handled his fugu ordeal, he said that Bourdain had handled it well, although there had been some suspicion that the producers and crew substituted a "caged," farm-raised, nonpoisonous fugu for the actual wild-caught fish so as not to jeopardize the health or fragile psyche of the talent.

As we sat down to dinner in the empty restaurant, the only sounds were the pattering of rain on the windows and the clattering of plates as the chef prepared dinner behind the bar, interspersed with occasional, ominous rumblings of thunder outside on the deserted street. Presently, the food began to arrive—miso soup first, with shreds of pale fugu flesh that, in color and texture, looked like pale candle wax. Then fugu sashimi, which Shinji enjoyed more than I did. As he gobbled my portion, he showed me how the pieces of fish had been arranged in the shape of a chrysanthemum—the traditional funeral flower of Japan, he merrily reported.

We tasted the small, crunchy fugu ribs, which had been rolled in flour and fried, and then Chef Hashimoto emerged from behind the bar to proudly display the engorged sperm sacs before preparing them, the way waiters in grand restaurants bring out the whole roasted duck or prime rib for everyone to admire before returning to the kitchen to carve it or fire it on the grill. The sacs of shirako looked pale and glistening, like two wet plastic bags filled with condensed milk; they were a little slippery and bouncy to the touch, like water balloons, and as I examined them, I began to feel the first faint tingling sensation around my lips and the tip of my tongue.

"Do your lips feel numb?" I asked Shinji.

"My lips don't feel numb!" he cried, gobbling more sashimi and looking at the engorged sperm sacs the way a hungry cowboy looks at a well-cooked steak.

To settle my nerves, I ordered a glass of beer, then another, and then excused myself to visit the tiny bathroom before the shirako arrived. The small, faintly creepy dining room felt even smaller and creepier when I returned. A sheen of flop sweat had collected on my forehead, and my heart began racing like a baboon's. Trying not to act like the terror-stricken foreigner undergoing the classic fugu near-death experience, I took out my notebook and started scribbling random things about Chef Hashimoto's apron, the waxy nastiness of the raw fugu, and the sounds of the weather outside. Presently, more sake was served, followed by more beer, followed by a few more fugu ribs, which had the nice meaty texture of monkfish and were actually sort of delicious. I ate several of them, trying not to focus on the faint numbing sensation that now seemed to be creeping, inexorably, from my tingling lips, down the back of my throat, toward my lungs and heart. I was moved, between bites, to ask Hashimoto whether there had ever been a fugu "accident" in his restaurant. Shinji translated my question, and the chef said something that caused them to burst into what, for two dignified Japanese gentlemen, was the equivalent of riotous laughter.

"Chef Hashimoto says if someone had an accident in his restaurant, he wouldn't tell you, because it would be bad for business," said Shinji. "But don't worry. There was an American in here a few weeks ago, and he didn't have an accident."

"That's good."

"But Mr. Hashimoto thinks you should know something."

"What's that?"

"That other American, he didn't eat the sperm sac."

"ACCIDENTS" IS THE POLITE EUPHEMISM THAT FUGU ENTHUSIASTS like Shinji tended to use when discussing the perils of fugu fish dining, and despite all the precautions, they can still happen. I would report in my story that, according to the Bureau of Social

Welfare and Public Health in Tokyo, 315 cases of poison by fugu were reported between 1996 and 2005 in Japan, 31 of them fatal. Most victims were fishermen engaging in Russian roulette–style bouts of fugu consumption, or amateur cooks who were trying to duplicate cooking demonstrations they'd seen on TV. There was also the experience of shibireru, a much-debated, slightly alarming numbing sensation, which some thrill-seeking fugu enthusiasts described as one of the addictive pleasures of the fugu experience (the word means "to become numb" in Japanese) but others considered to be an urban myth.

Chef Hashimoto had prepared two varieties of Shinji's favorite delicacy for our enjoyment—one raw, tipped with a lime-flavored ponzu sauce; and the other grilled and chopped into little bite-sized nuggets. I dabbed at the raw fugu with my chopsticks and put a little of it on the tip of my tongue. It had a creamy consistency and tasted icy cool, but the real pleasure aside from the buzzy, thrill-seeking aspect, it would strike me later on, was in the complete absence of flavor. It was like tasting the ultimate palate cleanser, albeit one that might or might not lead to slow paralysis and a certain, highly unpleasant death. The grilled shirako was just the opposite—piping hot and grimly unpleasant, like warm, fishy curds of milk. I swallowed one little chunk, and while Shinji merrily devoured the rest, I excused myself and retreated again to the coffin-sized restroom, where I examined my tingly, possibly lifeless tongue in the mirror. I'd read that fugu victims get their stomachs pumped and are force-fed charcoal to absorb the poison, and I had images of doctors waving long green tubes over my paralyzed body, my face seized in a black, charcoal-covered grin. I flipped through my notes, which read "feeling disoriented, a little panicky," before trailing off into a series of illegible scrawls.

When I returned to the table, I was in the midst of a full-on paranoid fugu meltdown, and Shinji, now a little drunk on sake and sperm sac, could barely contain his glee, having seen this condition in sensitive, overfed foreigners before. He asked if I wanted to try some pickled fugu ovaries—which would also lead to certain death if they had not been soaked in poison-leaching salt for several days—but mercifully, Chef Hashimoto, who came to the table with more sake, reported, with a sad shake of his head, that he was out of pickled fugu ovaries that night. Instead, we sampled nasty-tasting smoked fugu tails stuck in little cups of tea and a warm, vaguely soothing nabe stew, made with tofu, fish broth, and parts of the fugu carcass, including the spooky, eyeless skull.

Outside in the quiet neighborhood, the rain had stopped, and after we finished our nabe stew, the chef came out to clear our dishes away. "Mr. Hashimoto wants to know how you have enjoyed your dinner," Shinji said as I nervously poured the dregs of my third sake carafe into a bowl of ponzu sauce. I told him that the grilled shirako was not one of the best things I'd ever tasted but the ribs and nabe stew were excellent, and that all in all it had been a very interesting experience. Chef Hashimoto nodded politely and said that shirako in all its forms was an acquired taste.

Then, gently feeling my tingling lips, I asked again about the numbing shibireru sensation, which I thought I could still feel tingling down the back of my throat, although now that my fugu experience had mercifully ended, the tingling was not quite as extreme as before. According to Mr. Hashimoto, some chefs said that they purposely left a trace of poison to create the sensation, and some people said that they could actually feel the sensation, but he was a member of the urban myth school. Maybe in my excitement I had experienced a phantom-shibireru, which he said he'd seen many times before, especially in people who were trying the dish for the first time. "Don't worry," he said, as I paid the check and we got up to leave as quickly and politely as we could. "It is your mind playing tricks. If your lips are really numb, then nobody can save you. If your lips are really numb, Mr. Platt, then you are already dead."

14

Meditations on Dieting as a Restaurant Critic and Other Ridiculous Pipe Dreams

Working restaurant critics—those of us who eat out at least three times a week and have survived on the publishing savanna with expense accounts large enough to pay for a taxicab or an Uber ride to dinner, or even the occasional plane to our next meal—are always, as I say, being told that we have the best job in the world, and of course it's true. But even the best jobs are fraught with hidden and unexpected perils, and the job of a full-time professional eater can feel more perilous than most. The working life span of even the hardiest full-time critic is not much longer than that of a coal miner or a commercial fisherman, and like miners descending uneasily down into their coal pits or fishermen taking to the seas despite a stormy weather report, the longer we survive, the more we tend to spend the dark midnight hours worrying about all the horrible ways we might expire on the job.

At least, that's what I worry about sometimes when I lie

awake listening to the rumbling of my stomach late at night, or sit down to my fourth tasting menu of the week. Maybe I'll just slowly gorge myself to death, or keep drinking the intoxicating cocktails it's my duty to sample until my kidneys expire. Maybe I'll suffer an allergic reaction to a rare form of shellfish, like the those the fugu ingest in the waters around Japan, or contract a grim, cannibalistic disease after sampling a few too many strange raw meat dishes in a food market far away from home. Maybe I'll be struck down by a sudden thrombotic event, or slowly fall into a diabetic coma, or choke on a piece of pork gristle in a crowded dining room (tabloids blaring "Restaurant Critic's Last Horror Meal!" the next day) and collapse to the floor, taking the linen tablecloth and all the crockery with me, while the guests scream in horror and the waiters rush to perform the Heimlich maneuver on my giant overfed frame.

You could build an impressive monument to all the merry, red-faced professional gourmands who've expired from too much eating or drinking or various horrible afflictions contracted in the line of duty. Eating is an addiction, of course, and like the doomed Augustus Gloop in Roald Dahl's famous parable of excess, professional eaters are tempted more or less around the clock by an endless buffet of delicacies fiendishly designed by master chefs to dazzle their audience and bring them back to the trough again and again. I've seen brave colleagues overdose on pills and bourbon, addle themselves with too much wine and whiskey, or grow so fat and gout-riddled that they had to hobble from meal to meal like war veterans, with the help of a cane. There's A. J. Liebling, of course, who finally ate himself to death at the age of fifty-nine, and Jonathan Gold, who had Liebling's gorgeous prose style as well as his contempt for diets, died suddenly of pancreatic cancer when he was only fifty-seven years old. After decades of feasting (and, in his early years, hard drinking), the enviably trim A. A. Gill announced to his startled *Sunday Times* readers that he'd contracted "an embarrassment of cancer . . . the Full English," and was dead three weeks later at the age of sixty-two. One of my colleagues who also managed to remain remarkably fit and trim during his long, award-winning dining career told me once that the key to his good health was avoiding bread baskets and taking the stairs whenever possible, including walking several times a day up and down the staircase of his large suburban home. Several months after that conversation, however, he also was diagnosed with cancer, although the last I heard, he was doing fine.

Not surprisingly, women seem to navigate the treacherous shoals of the dining life better than men do, although Mimi Sheraton, who is a picture of health well into her eighties, told me once as we were having a large and not very good working dinner at some nameless restaurant in New York that she'd added seventy pounds to her small frame when she was the *New York Times* restaurant critic in the '70s and '80s. Mimi is a steely and disciplined personality, and it took her five years of judicious light eating as a regular civilian to take all the weight off. "Don't let this job kill you," she said as she watched me merrily forking large amounts of food from everyone's plates. "I'm telling you, it's not worth it!"

Mimi's right of course, but I've never heard of a working full-time restaurant critic who actually managed to lose weight over the long term, and if you come to the job with a built-in proclivity for ravenous eating, as many of us do, the results can be depressing. Every once in a while my older food-loving relatives furtively embarked on "cures" or diets, the way Joe Alsop, who repaired every year to the same spa in Switzerland, used to do. More often, when they weren't toasting each other with goblets of martinis or gathering for Sunday roast beef dinners, they were muttering darkly, like Alsop also did, about being afflicted with the dreaded "fat gene," the way other families were afflicted with dementia or alcoholism. To ease their sense of dread, they invented comic family names for different fatso parts of the body—such as "pie wings" for the ridges of paunch dripping over the belt. One of my uncles was so large as a little boy that the family named him "Count Ponty," after the air-filled pontoons you see on the sides of ships. My father developed large pontoons of his own as a hungry young boy, but when he went off to college, he took up rowing, began to weigh himself obsessively every morning, and jotted the results down in a small leather-bound notebook, a practice he continued for most of his life. When we returned from Asia to live in Washington, DC, in the 1970s and my brothers and I began ballooning in size as we gorged nervously on high-calorie American soda pop and grease-bomb cheeseburgers, he developed elaborate diet plans for his lumbering sons and tried to run the calories off us by organizing weekend walks and touch football games.

None of these diet strategies worked very well, at least in my case, because diets rarely ever work, and also because I'm different from my father in crucial ways. I've always tended toward roundness, while he's angular; I'm often as sloppy and disheveled as he is neat; and I approach the world in zigzags and circles, while he tends to go at things in a straight line. He used to peruse high-angle catalogs for newfangled gadgets with which to facilitate a dignified passage through life, and now he spends just as much time collecting these gadgets on the internet; amassing gadgetry has not been my style at all. Well into his eighties, he still maintains a revolving collection of techno wristwatches and ballistic space pens; when they become obsolete, he frequently tries to pawn off these accessories, neatly stacked in boxes on his desk, on his sons, and if we don't want them, he gives them to his grandchildren, who accept them politely, the way my daughters do, and take them home to stow in little boxes of their own.

Mr. Yu in his chef whites in front of the red gate of the Taichung house, Taiwan, 1963.

Adam and Oliver eating a late lunch with Mr. Yu and his family after school, Taiwan, 1963.

The Three Tigers—Adam, Nicholas Jr., and Oliver—one of them dressed uncomfortably in his British boy scout uniform.

Number Three Tiger prepares to board the Trans-Siberian Railway in the fall of 1967.

A family hot pot with Mr. Wong and his children, Hong Kong, 1966.

The Two Tigers, one with a pomelo skin on his head, Hong Kong, 1965.

The Platt family junk, *The Star Elephant*, at anchor in Hong Kong.

My mother and her camera,
Hong Kong, 1967.

The Platt house, Cornish, New Hampshire.

Cousin Frank, the family gastronome, uncorking a large bottle of wine during a Labor Day goat roast, Cornish, New Hampshire.
Thomas Palmer

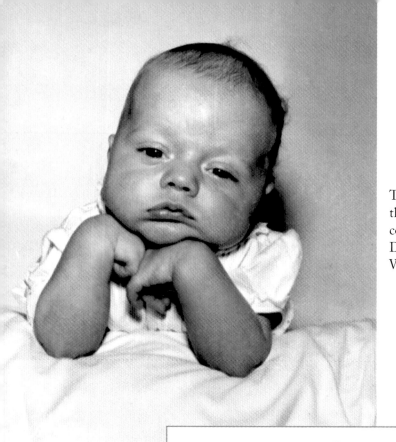

The birth of a critic: the best Young Adam could do for the Di-Dee-Wash Diaper man, Washington, DC, 1959.

Cover boy, January 2014. *Bobby Doherty*

Penelope Platt greets her strange new father on her adoption day, Hefei, China, 2003.

On the job bright and early, beginning with a very big breakfast, Lake Annecy, France.

The Platt family on assignment in Paris, spring 2015. Note the slightly pained look on Dad's face, who will dine at two more restaurants that evening.

Before and after diet photos for yet another paunchy-critic-attempts-to-diet story, September 2016. *Bobby Doherty*

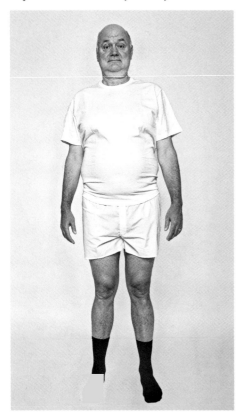

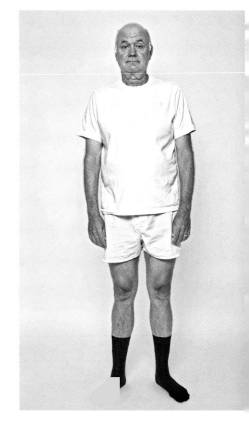

Sometimes the diets our father gave us when we were growing up had motivational names like the "Samurai Program," which was developed for his giant sons as they began happily fattening up on bowls of stir-fried yakisoba noodles and pork ramen when we lived in Tokyo. I have dim memories of intricate exercise charts tacked up on the bedroom doors upstairs, complete with goals for each day of the week in neatly arranged boxes, and young Nick Jr., who began growing to full, fearsome Platt-boy size while in Tokyo, remembers my father exhorting him to do "push aways" from the table during his ravenous noodle feasts, rather than eating that second, or third, bowl of ramen. Like all of us, the former Baby Dalai Lama listened to the wisdom of his elders for a while before returning happily to his noodle dinners, and as an adult, I tended to repeat this dynamic when it came to my own diets, of course. One summer I lost twenty or so pounds in a very 1970s way on a regime of cottage cheese and little tubs of Dannon yogurt, but gained it all back when the school year began. My undoing was a long-ago submarine sandwich and future pizza shop on the upper reaches of Connecticut Avenue, in DC, called Armand's, where I first experienced the complicated joys of that ruinous regional delicacy of the mid-Atlantic USA, the steak and cheese hoagie. The countermen knew me by sight and would fire up the onions and Cheez Whiz and shreds of fatty, previously frozen beef as soon as they saw my Godzilla-sized shadow darken the sidewalk outside. "Don't bite yourself," I remember one of them said as I collected my gloomy little afternoon snack and headed out the door.

Despite our father's best efforts, by the time the Platt boys reached young adulthood we had a formidable reputation for devouring everything in our path. Once, when we were coming home to visit from overseas, one of my uncles spotted my grandfather coming back from the grocery store, loaded down with bags of TV dinners and potato chips, and asked him if he was giving a party that night. "No, the boys are coming to stay," he replied, with a wild, apprehensive look in his eye. "They'll eat everything in the refrigerator but the screws and the ice trays." In young adulthood, we were famous for plundering wedding buffets and ransacking entire kitchens together, choreographing our movements precisely, without sound or signal, according to some dim genetic code. My dieting habits during those carefree days tended to be seasonal: I'd consume the most in the summertime, during the frantic family pie- and lobster-eating contests up in New Hampshire and Maine, and then starve like a hibernating bear through the winter months. Despite the stern commands of our father, the Platt boys rarely ever staggered onto a scale, unless threatened at gunpoint, and like many neurotic eaters, I still have an aversion to scales, on the grounds that they always make me gain weight. If the scale says I'm thinner than I thought, I'll usually run out for a celebratory meal. If it says I'm too fat, I'll usually, with glum self-flagellation, do the same thing. Even before I started eating for a living, I preferred to cruise along in a state of vigilant denial, climbing on the exercise bicycle or the StairMaster at symbolic intervals, even as I glanced nervously in the mirrors now and then and watched the notches slowly disappear on my belt.

Since I became a restaurant critic, my exercise habits haven't changed very much, although, like lots of cagey veterans in dangerous occupations, I've attempted to develop strategies over the years for surviving on the job. I never like to have more than four people, including myself, at the table for a working meal, since the number of dishes it's your duty to sample grows exponentially with every guest; and with more than four at the table, a civilized dinner can turn quickly into a chaotic, booze-filled social event. Bread baskets are the devil for any working restaurant critic, especially if you're attempting to diet, and so are sugar-saturated cocktails and extra glasses of wine. Tasting one teaspoon of each dessert is the ideal but rarely achieved goal when eating on the job, and the same goes for the fried foods, steaks and burgers, and butter- and oil-saturated pastas that I snap pictures of, then pass on to my guests. Ideally, I engage in some light, pro forma exercise every morning, have a healthy, non-bagel-and-bacon breakfast, and eat one meal a day, preferably early in the evening, when it's easier to find a reservation at a busy restaurant.

Most critics I know would rather avoid endless, time-wasting tasting menus whenever possible. The preferred time to dine for the weary dining professional is early, and the preferred meal tends to be a leisurely luncheon, because when the dining rooms around the city tend to be quieter and less hectic, you have time to actually consider the food, and once you've finished with your meal, and a glass or two of wine, there's plenty of time for a restorative afternoon nap. Of course, in the real world many of the restaurants I review don't serve lunch anymore and the fatso comfort foods, which any sensible dieter strives to avoid (burgers, fried chicken, pasta in all its relentlessly fattening forms), are more popular than ever and always do best on Instagram. In addition, all sorts of factors—the rise of Japan as the gourmet capital of the world; the obsessive copycat popularity in the social media era and "fifty top restaurants" lists; the brutal economics of fine dining in the post-gourmet, cost-cutting world; the arrival on the scene of a new generation of charismatic Nordic chefs who have embraced the tasting menu form because where they come from there are rarely enough ingredients to fill out a full à la carte menu, especially in wintertime—have conspired to make the expensive, time-consuming, relentlessly gut-busting omakase tasting menu the dominant gourmet dining style of today.

To manage my increasingly tenuous health after nearly two

decades on the job, I now take a battery of daily medications—pills prescribed by Dr. K for my possibly diabetic blood sugar levels, pills prescribed by my long-suffering internist Dr. P to diffuse the frighteningly high levels of cholesterol and fatty lipids that have collected in my veins, and pills for the occasional El Bulli–style flare-ups of gout when the levels of uric acid in my blood reach intemperate levels. I've consulted a cavalcade of dietitians during my long eating career and visited my share of what A. J. Liebling, the patron saint of all whale-sized food writers, contemptuously referred to as slimming prisons, where I've huffed up and down arid desert hillsides, twisted myself into torturous yoga poses, and consumed vats of healing green tea. I've experimented with trendy juice cleanses over the years, choked down buzzy taurine-spiked protein powders, embarked on twice-a-week fasting regimes, and consulted more concerned, wraithlike dietitians and nutritionists than I care to count, before being drawn back, inexorably, to the life of leisurely, booze-filled luncheons, decadent tasting menus, and furtive midnight tubs of ice cream.

15

Further Meditations on Dieting

The grim little secret about diets, of course, is that they usually don't work at all, although I like to think that my repeated doomed forays into sensible eating have had a kind of cleansing, spiritual effect over the years, like forest fires that sweep the overgrown wilderness away, so that greener, more verdant forests can grow up again. The countless number of doctors, dietitians, and witch doctors promoting bizarre powders and juice cleanses whom I've consulted have tended to appear at intervals of two or three years, like prophets rising from the parched desert, speaking in mysterious, barely understood tongues, and promising the salvation of everlasting thinness. One of the first was Anne-Marie, the proprietor of the Ashram, a famous diet boot camp in the hills of the Kardashians' future home, Calabasas, where I bunked with a portly chef from Belgium on leave from his job overseeing the kitchens for a large hotel chain. The Ashram was a Spartan offshoot of the famous Golden Door, a spa outside

San Diego, but instead of pampering skin treatments and delicious low-calorie dinners, guests paid thousands of dollars to get rousted out of bed in the early morning darkness to go on long, half-starved hikes through the parched California wilderness.

The chef and I fantasized about flaky, triple-layer napoleon pastries as we nodded off to sleep at night, and we discussed our favorite braising and sauce techniques as we huffed up and down the windy, sun-splashed hiking trails in the hills above LA. One of the sacred days of the Ashram experience was Toxic Tuesday: after three days of this rigorous, hyper-clean, coffee- and sugar-deprived lifestyle, the impurities began to emerge from the body, giving everyone toxin headaches and causing a strange acid taste in the back of the mouth. With her icy blue eyes and walnut-colored skin, Anne-Marie looked like she'd managed to stay toxin-free for thousands of years on a diet of dried berries and water. She would appear periodically during the course of the week, arriving in her gold Mercedes-Benz, to dispense bits of puritanical dieting wisdom to her half-starved flock of overweight record executives and B-level celebrities. Anne-Marie was famous in West Coast health circles for being an early pioneer in the gold-mine field of "wellness" and weight loss. She was the first person to bring dance music to her exercise classes and the inventor, among other things, of a gadget called the "Thighmaster," and her little compound in the hills was filled with all sorts of early adopter health gadgets like this, going slowly to seed.

When the Belgian chef and I weren't staggering up and down the California hills, we spent time in a crumbling geodesic dome hung with strings of weirdly colored crystals, getting our chakras checked for the first time and meditating fitfully to the canned, mellifluously rumbling chants of Indian healers, and twisting ourselves into painful yoga positions. At the end of the week, we were so suffused with lightness and well-being that I remember we shared a celebratory nonmeat pizza (with salad) before going our separate ways at the airport. I think I lost fifteen pounds at the Ashram on that first week-long visit, and another ten pounds when I went back for a second torturous visit ("Maybe don't eat too many almonds next time," Anne-Marie said), and when my brothers heard about my adventures, they lumbered out to the Ashram too.

I lost hundreds of pounds on similar boondoggle excursions that I contrived to write about over the years, including a slightly hair-raising survivalist program in the wilds of southern Utah designed to replicate the wanderings of the early Mormons in the wilderness. During the course of a long, desperate week, my fellow campers and I slept on the cold ground and subsisted miserably on cans of beans warmed up over sad little fires, which we attempted to start, caveman style, by rubbing sticks together. We fell into creeks and got lost in the hills, and our efforts at fire starting became increasingly futile as we slowly starved to death. Those who lasted into the second week (I didn't) were treated to a live, bleating goat led out to the campfire by the instructors, who directed the group to figure out how to butcher it, then cook it for dinner, before disappearing back into the wilderness to eat their bountiful campfire supper.

These occasional, biblical starvation regimes can become a kind of addiction, of course, and back in New York, I consulted a series of madcap diet shamans, many of whom would force me, in comically humiliating fashion, to keep a meticulous food diary of my nightly restaurant visits, which I would write out in my tiny, largely indecipherable big man's handwriting. One year, after noting an alarming twenty-pound weight gain during my annual checkup, my increasingly perplexed internist, Dr. P, sent me to a spectrally slender nutritionist in my neighborhood whose tiny office looked out onto the back of an elevator shaft. She gave me cups of laxative tea to promote what she called "intestinal well-being" and a powder that made my ears ring so loudly that I stopped showing up after several visits.

I did much better with a good-natured tag team of nutrition-ists named Vinny and Diana, who cajoled me into losing almost fifty pounds over the course of several months for an article I'd been assigned by the magazine. The piece was never published, however, and I would end up gaining all of the weight back over the course of a happy year of eating. Rummaging around in my desk drawers not long ago, I found a few sections of one of my long-ago food diaries, which gives a snapshot of the manic life of the dieting restaurant critic:

MAY 16: Breakfast shake, apple. Lunch, too dizzy to re-member. Maybe a chicken breast or some goat cheese and a diet Coke. Took daughter to birthday party—abstained from chocolate cake. Dinner—2 chicken cutlets, salad w. to-matoes, almonds, goat cheese. Popsicle for dessert. Piece of salmon before bed and a handful of peanuts.

MAY 22: Wake up weak and woozy. Walking at half speed. Protein shake for breakfast. Eat an apple and some almonds and feel marginally better. Lunch at Macrobiotic restaurant, filled w. "the slightly cadaverous mien of the severely health conscious." Wild salmon, scrambled tofu, hijiki (seaweed). Observing me feed among the pale faced folk clutching their yogi pamphlets, my friend says "this is an absurd spectacle." Dinner—two diet pops preceded by more salads. In bed that night, Mrs. Platt whispers, "good night, Shamu."

MAY 23: Feeling light headed, a little befuddled. Find my-self staring blankly at the computer screen. Stomach crying for grub. Pad over to the refrigerator. Gnaw on a piece of fat-less swiss cheese. It tastes like old candle wax.

MAY 24:   Breakfast shake mixed w. frozen raspberries. One apple for snack. Lunch at Mexican restaurant, chicken salad w. pico de gallo. Dinner at Italian restaurant—taste of swordfish, eggplant, salad w. octopus, piece of prosciutto, mushrooms, half a glass of wine. Popsicle for dessert. I ask Mrs. Platt if I'm smelling strange recently because Vinny has said the toxins are now being released—"No more than usual." She smells my breath. "Come to think of it, your breath smells like animal by-products."

MAY 25:   Breakfast shake mixed w. frozen raspberries. Two pieces of (salty) tofu for lunch snack. Tasting menu at Per Se, including bites of oyster and [Ossetra] caviar, a taste of foie gras w. pickled white peaches, a bite of crispy skin black bass, a (delicious) bite of lobster and fennel in vermouth sauce, a bite of rabbit w. braised swiss chard, a bite of (delicious) "calotte de boeuf grillee" w. crispy bone marrow on top, followed by a taste of vegetarian cheese made w. whey, a taste of almond sorbet and a (tiny) taste of a milk chocolate "cremeux." All delicious. I am so fucking doomed.

It turned out that I wasn't completely doomed on that particular diet, or while following any of the other crackpot regimes I attempted in the decade of serious and generally unregulated feasting—at least not for the few months of illusory skinniness and good health I briefly enjoyed before the needle on the scale began, inexorably, to quiver upward and I stuffed the offending instrument in the closet and vowed never to weigh myself again.

A few years back, however, as I began to enter the choppy

waters of middle age—a time when many of my portlier colleagues were either leaving the fraternity of professional gluttony for healthier occupations or disappearing slowly under the waves—I began to think about taking a last, gasping lunge at the golden ring of good health. After an absence of three or four years, I made an appointment to see the eternally patient and long-suffering Dr. P. When I waddled sheepishly into his office, gasping for breath and with my shirt untucked and covered, as usual, with random stains from a not-so-modest dinner the night before, he shook his head sadly and gave me his best imitation of a disapproving scowl. Dr. P is a chatty, convivial soul in normal times, and over the years we've developed an elaborate choreography around my weighing phobia. He distracts me with cheerful pleasantries about the weather or questions about the family while gently herding me, like a skittish barn animal, toward the scale in the corner of his office. Once I'm on the scale, he makes pleasantly diplomatic comments ("It could be worse" or "Not as bad as last year!") while I hum nervously and gaze at the ceiling. Once he finishes adjusting the weights, he quickly pushes them back to zero so that I won't see the number and become despondent or overly stressed.

On this visit, however, there were no pleasantries during the ceremonial weigh-in as I looked apprehensively up at the ceiling and hummed to myself. Once Dr. P had made a note of my weight, he pushed the measuring weights back with an authoritative snap, then conducted the rest of the checkup in an ominously perfunctory way. When my blood tests came in later that week, Dr. P called me up with a note of alarm in his voice—sounding, as I later wrote in yet another story about one of my professional dieting adventures, like the engineer of a wallowing, recently stricken ocean liner making a last, desperate call to the bridge. My numbers were spiking, and in all the wrong directions. I weighed close to 280 pounds, up 15 from the last time I'd staggered into his office, and by his calculations, if drastic measures weren't taken soon, I would be drifting past what one of my brothers calls the dreaded, 300-pound "blimp line" by the next year. Once his patients drifted over that line, he said, there was often no return. Dr. P was prescribing cholesterol-lowering statins for the first time and horse-sized pills to control my blood sugar levels, which had suddenly gone haywire too. He would be introducing me to my new diabetes specialist, a strict, no-nonsense gentleman named Dr. K with a cool, appraising manner, along with my new eye specialist, with whom I should check in at least twice a year for the rest of my increasingly tenuous-sounding life, since people who eat themselves into ravenous diabetic comas, like I was doing, sometimes tended to go blind. And finally, Dr. P said, I should try one last time to lose a little weight and bring some kind of order to my unchecked grazing over the long run, or consider making a change in what he diplomatically, and a little darkly, called my "professional routine."

16

Meditations on Dieting,
Final Thoughts

Which is how, two weeks after this fateful doctor visit, and consulting my editor, Noreen, about another diet story, and after doing a little research on the newest crop of both prominent snake-oil conjurers and nutritionists and the zany foolproof plans they were peddling around town, I found myself getting weighed once again, this time high up among the skyscrapers of midtown Manhattan, in the office of my last-chance weight loss savior, Tanya Zuckerbrot. Tanya was dressed, as usual, in a sleek black pants outfit by Chanel and a pair of red-bottomed shoes by Christian Louboutin. Her office, with its soothing pale tones of gray and white, a long leather designer couch on one side of the room, and a glass coffee table stacked with large art books, felt less like a medical consultation room than a thousand-dollar-an-hour psychiatrist's office or something you'd see on the set of a morning television chat show. A statue of meditating Buddha stood in one corner of the room, as well as a yellowish, juddering piece of translucent rubber, which she liked to use as a motivational tool to demonstrate to her patients exactly how large a five-pound piece of fat can be. Tanya was famous in nutrition circles for her fiber-heavy "F-Factor" diet. She charged her flock of corpulent Wall Street brokers, weight-conscious TV anchors, and gilded big-city housewives thousands of dollars for various F-Factor plans, which included the initial consultation and a "twenty-four-hour availability platform"—a special number to text for advice and counsel during moments of existential panic while loitering guiltily in the Shake Shack line, say, or scanning the menu before ordering dinner at Nobu or Le Bernardin. There was a dreaded doctor's scale in one corner of the room—recalibrated every day, she assured me, to the exact ounce—and framed on the wall among her many first-class dietitian medical degrees was a signed poster of the toothy, grinning Houston televangelist Joel Osteen. Tanya had a toothy, telegenic smile too, and moonlike eyes that she fixed on me in a mesmerizing, vaguely unsettling way. I'd discover that she often liked to quote bits of Osteen's self-help scripture to her prominent clients and had even seen him in person at least three times, which she happily told me on that first visit was "a lot of times to see Joel Osteen for a nice Jewish girl like me."

Tanya assures me in her messianic, motivational, Joel Osteen way that it's actually not such a crazy idea to try to lose weight while working as a full-time restaurant critic. I can drink alcohol on her diet (although not too much, and no sugar mixed with your spirits please), and I won't be punishing myself with endless sweaty workouts, which are good for morale and general psychic well-being but tend to actually increase appetite and burn off only negligible calories anyway. Proteins are fine too, although not the overly fatty kind ("Those British banger sausages you eat for breakfast are going away, Adam!"), and because I'll be taking my carbohydrates, not in the normal white, processed pasta and bread basket form but in the complex, distressingly taste-less Scandinavian oat crackers that F-Factor devotees devour like crazed bunny rabbits on an almost hourly basis, I'll actually feel full over time without tipping too far into the zombie, carb-starved state of longing and regret I've experienced on thousands of diets before.

During this first visit, she weighs me in on her carefully calibrated scale at a hefty 273 pounds ("You're afraid of scales—some people would call that denial, Adam!") and measures my body fat, which, at 31.3 percent, puts me just south of the vast, morbidly obese population beyond the Hudson who whir up and down the grocery aisles of America on their golf carts, grab-bing bags of potato chips from the shelves ("In America now, being thin is an abnormality, Adam! In America now, everyone is fat like you!"). She gives me cheerful tips on how to avoid the temptations of the several Peking duck dinners it's my happy professional duty to devour that week ("Forget those pancakes, Adam, and just *taste* the skin"). She instructs me to ban that fat man's delusion, the Caesar salad, from my diet forever ("You might as well eat a hamburger, Adam!") and gives me a quick primer on how to behave at the cocktail function I'm about to attend ("Anything on a skewer is your best friend, Adam"). She diplomatically pretends to find glimmers of hope in my comi-cal food diary, which includes, on this first day of the rest of my healthy eating life, carefully recorded visits to Sparks Steak-house to dine on dainty slabs of New York strip (for a list of the best steakhouses in New York City) and a vegetarian meal at a restaurant called Nix, where my dinner the night before featured an unfortunate gut-busting creation called Fried Potato Bread, accompanied by a few healthful sprigs of greenery.

After our fifteen-minute debriefing session, Tanya hands

this offending document off to one of her many distressingly slim assistants, who tend to have blinding white smiles, speak in punchy, motivational sentences the way she does, and wear designer shoes on their perfect tiny feet. I'm subjected to the F-Factor "beware of sushi" lecture ("Did you know the rice in a dragon roll has the carbs of three slices of bread, Adam?!") and the F-Factor "beware of beans" lecture ("Hummus is a gateway drug, Adam!"). I'm also informed that trendy foods like hummus, quinoa, and avocado may be healthy and good for me, but carb- and calorie-wise, I might as well be jamming sticks of salted butter down my throat ("If I see another avocado toast on my Instagram feed, Adam, I might puke!"). I'm cagily asked to describe my ideal "fantasy cheat day" ("My whole life's a fantasy cheat day" is my mournful reply) and subjected to slide presentations depicting the endless horrors of the fatso lifestyle. "Let's get you educated, sir!" cries Shana, whose fervent tone and bright, unblinking eyes remind me of the pictures I saw back in Hong Kong during the 1960s of Chairman Mao's youthful Red Guards, chanting slogans and waving their Little Red Books.

Shana shows me a photograph of a much larger, unhappy-looking Shana, snapped just before she gave herself over to the Life of Fiber ("Everyone is definitely in a cult here, Adam. Welcome to the Cult of Tanya!"). Then, for several minutes, I'm shown a series of cartoon-sized bar graphs illustrating the remorseless correlation between obesity and certain death ("Cancer loves your fat, Adam!"). Like everyone inside the petite, impeccably coiffed Tanya circle of trust, Shana says, in her friendly, remorselessly positive voice, that she loves food and eats out at fattening restaurants all the time, just like me. That very evening she'll be meeting her husband at Keith McNally's West Village restaurant, Minetta Tavern, to enjoy one of the famous Black Label Burgers, which are laced with deposits of fatty, high-grade brisket and served with a stack of French fries the size of a small lapdog.

"You'll be eating the whole Black Label Burger?" I ask hopefully.

"The key to survival in restaurants is tasting and sharing, Adam!"

"Your husband doesn't want his own Black Label Burger?"

"My husband is a healthy eater, Adam! Do you think I'd ever marry a fat guy?!"

Shana's voice is still ringing in my ears the next morning as I whirr up a breakfast smoothie made of swamp-colored hemp protein powder, frozen blueberries, and almond milk. The gray-green concoction looks like a glass of gently dissolved plasterboard and is so thick that I end up eating it with a spoon. Lunch that first day (according to the tiny, unsteady entry in my new food diary) is two lox sandwiches made with a scrim of yogurt and four of Tanya's compressed, Brillo-pad-like F-Factor crackers. She'd discovered them, she told me, on a dusty bottom shelf of a store across from her apartment, while looking for ways to cut the carbohydrates from the diets of the diabetes and heart patients she was working with after she finished her master's in food and nutrition at NYU. After months of ingesting industrial amounts of mostly indigestible (and also calorie-burning) fiber while following the usual low-sugar, modest-carb diets, her patients were not only losing weight but also lowering their blood sugar. Soon nondiabetic fat people were coming to her for diet tips, and as the bits and pieces of her holistic, high-fashion, motivational program came together, the Cult of Tanya began to take off.

That evening I visit not one but two steakhouses in search of the city's finest cut of New York strip for another one of the treacherous "top ten best in category" lists I've been assigned to write. I've been briefed by my new diet consultants on the difference between "hunger," which is a physiological state (your stomach grumbles, you feel irritable and light-headed), and "appetite," which is a murky, psychological state, susceptible to all kinds of imaginary and inherited cues. In addition to her health reeducation lectures, Shana has also given a short lecture on the funhouse world of restaurants, where the size of your plate (larger ones make you eat more), the height of your cocktail glass (taller is not better), where you happen to sit (anyone on a diet should choose one by the window, far away from the buffet), and even the menu descriptions ("succulent," "fresh baked") are all carefully manipulated to seduce customers into gobbling down the maximum possible number of calories like hogs at a trough. I call for the haunches of beef with the usual sense of ceremony and expectation, but then, as the waiters and my guests look on with slightly stunned expressions on their faces, I cut off one or two slices of delicious red meat and chew each morsel the way I imagine Shana would, in a thousand tiny little bites. We order all of the usual trimmings too—ruinous potato dishes, butter-soaked carrots, boatloads of onion rings, and creamed spinach—and when they arrive, I take a few dainty spoonfuls and push the rest around on my plate.

I repeat my new smoothie and cracker routine the next day, and the day after that. I visit a few more steakhouses and enjoy several Peking duck dinners, which I'm researching for another top ten list on that beloved delicacy of my youth. Noting that these meals consist mostly of scallions, hoisin sauce, and delectably crispy skin, I avoid indulging in the soft, steamy shaobing pancakes, as Tanya has instructed me to do. I begin work on a new article on the sudden appearance of fiber-rich veggie burgers on the menus of trendy establishments around town, and as the days click by I can feel my giant stomach slowly contracting, like a hot-air balloon leaking gas and gradually crashing to the ground. "I'm beginning to notice a strange change in your eating habits," Mrs. Platt says suspiciously when she comes home one afternoon for lunch to find me sitting at the kitchen table eating my salad and crackers instead of standing over the sink, devouring last night's congealed restaurant leftovers, along with the remnants of the girls' macaroni and cheese dinner, as I sometimes do. The girls also express their concern ("What's wrong with Dad? If he stops eating, does that mean he'll lose his job?") as they rush in and out of the apartment on their busy daily routines.

Eight days after beginning the last diet of my life, I return to the F-Factor offices. Tanya is dressed in a slim blue suit today and sporting a golden Rolex that looks as big as a toaster. She seems a little shocked that I've actually even bothered to return, considering my dire circumstances, and as I sit on the couch she attempts politely to decipher my handwritten food diaries ("Does this say 'sixteen ounce steak,' Adam? That's only ten ounces above the ideal portion!"). Prior to herding me nervously onto the scale, she explains, in her cheery, staccato style, the concept of "thermogenesis" (an F-Factor nirvana state achieved when the body is burning more calories than it can absorb in order to digest all the complex fiber you've been consuming) and tells me about how much she hates the word "diet" ("It means 'a pattern of eating,' not a temporary weight loss regime. Japanese sumo wrestlers are all on diets, Adam!"). When I finally lumber onto the scale, she instructs me to look out the window and hum to myself while she adjusts the weights. She adjusts them once, then a second time, and as I keep humming to myself and peering out the window at the rows of marathon-running, zero-body-fat traders hunched over their terminals in the glass box next door, she lets out a little gasp. "Would you believe it, Adam?" she finally says, in an awed, slightly shaky way, like someone experiencing an out-of-body experience at a Joel Osteen event. "You've lost fourteen pounds."

Supersized people are apparently subject to a condition called "rapid weight loss syndrome," mostly because they have more weight to lose than anyone else. Usually this happens at the beginning of their weight loss regime when their shocked and shuddering system purges unsettling amounts of watery impurities, like the squeezing of a dirty, water-soaked sponge, although the actual number of pounds lost sounds a little less impressive when you look at it as a percentage of body weight. Today the other members of the Cult of Tanya clap their hands when she tells them about my miracle ("Adam, that's so crazy!"), and as a reward, and also as a kind of benediction, Tanya presents me with a new honey-flavored style of cracker, which I enjoy that afternoon, spread with some yogurt and fig jam.

Over the next several days, I begin to experience other little miracles. I have bizarre surges of energy and good cheer, and instead of slouching off to the coffee bar for my usual post-lunch pick-me-up, I begin taking jaunty afternoon power walks around the block. I've always considered myself to be an unfussy, no-nonsense eater, but as I drop three pounds the next week, and three more pounds the week after that, I begin regaling my startled fresser colleagues with the kind of obsessively flowery, taste-oriented descriptions that I rarely use at the table or in my writing life.

"Now this is what's called 'depth of flavor,'" I hear myself loudly proclaim one evening at a bistro somewhere in SoHo, after luxuriating in the brininess of several oysters on the half shell, followed by some smoked gnocchi and a forkful of fatty, crackly-skinned duck breast—dishes that a few short weeks ago I would have hoovered into my whale-sized maw without expression or comment. After being carpet-bombed with Nordic oat bran for a few weeks, however, my taste buds are suddenly reacting like they're experiencing the flavors and buttery soft textures of the food for the first time. Even after years of practiced, public grumpiness, it doesn't take long for this bizarrely optimistic new tone to creep into my work. "You're getting soft, Platty," one cranky editor says as he reads the draft of one of the three-star reviews I've begun to tap out with an unsettling regularity that spring and summer. After that miracle fifteen-pound weight loss the first month and another ten pounds the month after that, the pounds start falling off in smaller and smaller fractions. I continue to amble slowly around town on my gastronomic rounds, furtively ingesting fiber cracker snacks in the back of taxicabs and primly pushing bread baskets and desserts away night after night, but as the weeks tick by the magic goal of losing 20 percent of my body fat—which I've been told again and again is the US Surgeon General's benchmark for shedding the dreaded "technically obese" definition—seems, paradoxically, like an increasingly Sisyphean task.

When I finally tell Tanya that it's time to take the training wheels off and chart my own wobbly course to good health, she looks at me in silence for a while, her perfectly penciled eyebrows knit in a disapproving frown. She tells me cautionary tales about clients who lost hundreds of pounds, but failed to follow the patented F-Factor Maintenance Program (with a price tag, if supervised, of upward of $50,000) and returned a year later fatter than ever before. She reminds me that although I am still technically a fat person, it's time to throw out all of my large lumberjack pants ("I'm going to come over to your apartment and throw your former fat person clothes out. No safety net, Adam!"). Given my job, I still need "wiggle room" to gain a few pounds, she says, and of course she's right. My rate of weight loss is slowing, not just because my metabolism may be slowing down and there's less weight to lose, but possibly also because I'm feeling pleased with myself, and when portly people feel self-satisfied they tend to reward themselves with buckets of fried chicken and midnight tubs of ice cream. That night at dinner I celebrate my new semi-svelte form with two martinis and an order of an exceptional $48 lamb chop. I take a few sips of a very nice Vouvray ('09 Le Clos de la Mcslerie, for the record), and when a grand flotilla of French desserts arrives at the table,

I manage to restrain myself for a few seconds before choosing a classic Opéra, which has a shiny, round white top and is flecked with gold leaf. I take a bite or two and put down my spoon, enjoying the sugar blast as it washes through my veins. When coffee comes, I take another bite of the Opéra, then another, and before I know it the alluring, delicious, addictively sugary pastry is gone.

"If they ask you to take your shirt off don't do it," my editor Noreen says when I hand in the draft of my diet story, en route to the photo studio to have an after picture shot for the magazine. "You really have lost weight," says the photographer, who takes a hundred shots of me posing in a relatively slim dark jacket and tie before asking politely if I wouldn't mind taking my pants off. The article is titled "Platt vs. Fat" and features a two-page splash of the before and after shots of a slightly trimmer restaurant critic wearing a white undershirt, wrinkled boxer shorts, and a pair of black socks pulled up to his knobby knee-caps. When the girls see the pictures they laugh out loud, and Mrs. Platt shields her eyes, like she's just seen some horrifying apparition from a recurring dream. Tanya will put the magazine proudly on her office table for a while when the article comes out, although after a few more maintenance sessions, my visits slowly taper off, before stopping altogether. I still eat my fiber wafers now and then, although not with the religious fervor I once did, and I'm afraid it will be a long time before I ever step on a scale again.

17

The Best Job of the
Twentieth Century, Part 1

The mannered, front-of-the-house restaurant culture wasn't the only stuffy, anachronistic institution to get turned on its head during my early years as a self-important, and increasingly old-fashioned, big-city restaurant critic. "Your day is over, Platty, the barbarians have stormed the gates," Josh Ozersky would gleefully cry in his strangely lilting, high-pitched voice when I drifted over to his cubicle in the new downtown offices of *New York* magazine on the far western fringes of SoHo, where the company moved when the midtown rents got too oppressively high. Ozersky was the first editor of *Grub Street*, which the magazine launched in the fall of 2006 to compete with the rabble of popular restaurant news and food sites (*Eater, EGullet, ChowHound*) that were sprouting up around the media landscape like pods of fast-growing mushrooms during those early cowboy years of the internet culture. Ozersky was not a natural creature of this glib, ephemeral world—as he liked to endlessly remind me, and anyone else who would listen, he'd earned a PhD in American studies at Notre Dame before washing up in New York, and he'd written learned books on popular culture, including one on the '70s-era sitcom *All in the Family*, and his masterwork, *The Hamburger: A History*, was published by Yale University Press while he was writing for *Grub Street*. Ozersky had dreamed of being a respected public intellectual and historian in the mold of his heroes Samuel Johnson and the Victorian historian Thomas Macaulay—both of whom he liked to quote at length while jamming a steady stream of cheeseburgers down his throat.

Ozersky had the passion and disputatious nature of a natural online journalist, however, and he also had the metabolism of one, although when the pressure of turning out a post every hour of the day, beginning at 8:00 a.m., started to grind him down, he would supplement his resolutely nonvegetarian burger and steak diet with a variety of stimulants, including that favorite drug of jet fighter pilots and manic writers everywhere, Adderall, which he obtained in little wrinkled mail-order envelopes from India. Like lots of people in the business, including me, he'd found his way to the food world in a meandering, circuitous way. When the magazine's online editor, Ben Williams, who had an eye for spotting eccentric talent, hired him to run *Grub Street*, he was living out in the Ditmas Park neighborhood of Brooklyn—a distant exile region he liked to call "Ozerkistan"—churning out food guide books (he was proudest of a beef primer called *Meat Me in Manhattan*) and grainy, low-production videos celebrating the glories of beef and starring himself as an antic, bug-eyed character he called "Mr. Cutlets." When Ben hired Mr. Cutlets, he brought us together for lunch at a steakhouse near the office. Mr. Cutlets, who had an aversion to the heat and was built, he liked to say, like a burly Jewish linebacker, was sweating profusely through his shirt. He ordered a large platter of porterhouse or some other giant cut of beef, and as he devoured it, more or less on his own, he regaled us in his bluff, insecure way with stories about all the chefs he knew (he had a habit of calling them by their first names, like basketball stars, which often left you guessing which one he was talking about). Adding to our general confusion, Mr. Cutlets also quoted liberally from his beloved North American Meat Processors manual, a book of standards for butchers and producers, published by the US Department of Agriculture, which he'd committed to memory with a kind of Talmudic devotion and carried with him during his forays into the field.

Ozersky used to half-jokingly call himself a polymath, and on the topics that interested him—Victorian history and literature, NBA basketball, the richly fatty joys of the "top flap" cut of deckle meat on a well-cured slab of pastrami, the writings of his fellow Adderall-addled literary hero, Philip K. Dick—this was not far from the truth. His parents died at an early age—his father was a failed painter who made his living designing stage sets for the casinos of Atlantic City—and he had no siblings. So like an orphan from a Dickens novel, he was free to invent all sorts of characters for himself as he made his way through the world, and there were many of them—the erudite gourmand with a fondness for cheeseburgers; the conspiracy-obsessed, left-leaning intellectual; the neurotic tummler from the Old Country, always rolling his eyes to the heavens and cursing the fates in Yiddish; and the slightly deviant wiseguy flaneur straight from the pages of Damon Runyon, who wandered the bright avenues of the Emerald City at all hours of the night, wearing his Homburg hat.

Like his literary hero Samuel Johnson, Ozersky cultivated a convivial, almost clubbish sense of community among his equally eccentric, ragtag group of friends, many of whom would gather with him at dive bar hangouts like the old Box Car Lounge in

Alphabet City, where he would regale them with a familiar grab bag of favorite quotes and sayings. Late one evening, I heard him recite Lewis Carroll's poem "The Walrus and the Carpenter," from beginning to end, to a startled group of diners. Having committed James Boswell's famous biography of Johnson more or less to memory, he had an endless supply of Johnsonian quotes on writing (yes, it was true, no one but a "blockhead ever wrote for money") and the joys of a good feed ("A man seldom thinks with more earnestness than he does of his dinner"). The one he liked best was the famous Johnsonian prescription for fame and notoriety, which the scholar compared to the endless batting back and forth of a feathered badminton shuttlecock. "It must be struck at both ends; if struck only at one end of the room, it will soon fall to the floor," Ozersky would declaim in a loud baritone voice from his cluttered office cubicle—a predictably chaotic space filled with freebie bottles of bourbon, stained, half-read cookbooks, and piles of sandwich wrappers and desiccated sandwich ends—as he monitored the shuttlecocks zinging to and fro via this new medium called the internet.

The Ozersky cubicle sat in those days next to the magazine's fashion desk, a land of slimming salad lunches and rows of neatly ordered Post-it notes, whose occupants regarded the new *Grub Street* restaurant blogger with a mixture of amusement, fascination, and quiet horror. As Ozersky raved away across from her well-ordered desk, a young reporter named Sharon Clott Kanter began quietly jotting down a diary of "Josh-isms." She noted his frequent cries of "Oy vey ist mir!" when he was beaten on a scoop or otherwise exasperated, which was often; "Do me a Mitzvah" when he wanted a favor (which was often); and the much-used "She gave me the Mitten!" when his invitation to dinner, or for a drink, or to return to his surprisingly fastidious apartment across the East River in the wilds of the distant outer borough he called "Ozerkistan" was rebuffed. She recorded his quirky names for people and places—"Manahatty" was the favored Joshism for "Manhattan"—and his endless hectic, increasingly fraught conversations with sources as he attempted to wheedle information for his hourly posts. Ozersky occasionally used the communal office refrigerator to store the vanity meat products he obtained during his wanderings, and a heated office drama ensued one afternoon after an artisanal Ossabaw hog jowl, which he was saving for one of his pork dinners, disappeared from the fridge. "What kind of nut steals a man's jowl?!" the meat aficionado asked in a loud, pained voice, before sending out an irate staff email that read: "Somebody took an Ossabaw pork jowl which I left in the refrigerator for a few hours today. I acquired it at great personal expense and difficulty and need it for a special meal I'm preparing this weekend. Please return it to the refrigerator; there will be no questions asked."

As the Ossabaw incident shows, Ozersky wasn't a traditional company man. He belonged to that early pioneer generation of writers who'd grown up in a more discursive and settled world of letters and had to adapt on the fly to the relentless burnout blizzard of posts, retweets, and digital hot takes. "I've been in a bad marriage, survived a doctoral program, suffered obsessive episodes requiring medication, lived with a girlfriend who worked as an escort, struggled to keep a business afloat, been in tax trouble and written nine books," he wrote, long after he'd left New York, "and I never felt the kind of pressure I did when I was helming *Grub Street*." But he recognized early on that the Johnsonian batting back and forth of the shuttlecock was a perfect metaphor for this emerging world of online journalism, where "conversation" and "engagement" were already replacing the statelier, less immediate, more "objective" brand of magazine journalism that we were both used to. During the manic early years of *Grub Street*, he would compete in a desperate frenzy for hourly scoops with his sworn enemies at sites like *Strong*

Buzz, *Eater*, and *Serious Eats* over the kinds of stories—outer borough bar and pizza joint openings, obscure menu changes, the comings and goings of talented but temperamental cooks— that just months before traditional print food writers like myself would have filed away for possible use in some distant, carefully composed essay, or more likely would have just ignored altogether. But from his new perch, Mr. Cutlets could also see that these endless incremental crumbs of minutiae and the ever growing, ever more informed, ever more passionate audience that fed on them hour by hour, and even minute by minute, like roving, jittery, endlessly distracted schools of fish, were changing not just the news cycle and the way people processed information but the very nature of the restaurant business itself.

Like the rest of the United States, New York's dining community had traditionally taken most of its fashion cues from elsewhere during the twentieth century—from German cooks during the early part of the twentieth century; from Paris in the 1950s and '60s; from Italy in the '70s and '80s, when Sirio Maccioni infused classic French cuisine with a dose of Tuscan conviviality at his midtown restaurant, Le Cirque; and from California and points east during the '90s, when chefs like Nobu Matsuhisa and Jean-Georges Vongerichten arrived in town with their impressive bag of fusion tricks. But with the coming of the *No Reservations* generation early in the next century and the opening of influential restaurants like Tom Colicchio's chef-centric venture, Craft, in the Flatiron District in 2001, the heat emanating from New York's kitchens began to have a vibrant, original quality all its own. Later on, I would compare this new sensibility—brassy, heavily flavored, accessible in the utilitarian way most iconic New York dishes tend to be (the pizza slice, the bagel, the Porterhouse), but filtered, like the Torrisi Italian deli, Roberta's out in Bushwick, and

Chang's noodle bar, through a certain sophisticated big-city swagger and style—to a loud, new, distinctive big-city sound. It was the online writers who heard the music first, however, and gave it a local audience; eventually it was picked up by the slower-moving mainstream writers, like myself, and broadcast through the usual ponderously slow official channels, out into the large and expanding universe of food fashion and culture to be dissected, reworked, and imitated again and again.

Several months into my new career as a restaurant critic, I'd reviewed Craft for the magazine, and looking back, I can see that, like most people, I didn't quite know what to make of it. I wrote about the menu, which was framed around ingredients instead of elaborate recipes, and described the polished, wood-paneled room with its bare, linen-free tables and pods of filament bulbs, which would soon appear in trendy restaurants around the globe. I quoted someone at the table saying, "It's as if they've rearranged the way traffic works," although just how radically Colicchio and his cooks—who would go on, like the Frenchman at Le Pavilion a generation ago, to spread their gospel far and wide—had rearranged things wasn't entirely clear. The culinary theme wasn't faux French, or crypto-brasserie, or even haute Californian (that would be Thomas Keller's specialty at his Napa Valley restaurants and later at his New York restaurant Per Se); the theme was the purity of those twin chefs' obsessions—ingredients and technique. Sixty-five ingredients were listed on the first menu (Colicchio's original radical idea was to have no actual recipes at all). Although several new restaurants around town, and, indeed, around the country, were peddling a similar bucolic version of farm-to-table haute cuisine (Savoy in SoHo, for instance, or Blue Hill, the restaurant near Washington Square Park that a pale, intense, young chef-owner named Dan Barber had named after his family farm in the Berkshires), no one had articulated the new cult of simplicity and unpretentiousness in quite such a fashionable, immaculately pretentious New York City way.

The same would be true of Colicchio's little spin-off establishment, Craftbar, when it opened shortly afterward in a small space next door to the mother ship, on East Nineteenth Street. The idea for the casual, counter-style operation had been popularized by the chef's former business partner Danny Meyer, at the Union Square Café and Gramercy Tavern, where Colicchio was part owner and executive chef. When I got around to reviewing this afterthought of a restaurant, I commented politely on the small plates menu, which featured fried oysters and a variety of fine dishes that appeared to have been culled from the chef's red sauce youth out in New Jersey, like soft veal meatballs dressed with shingles of parmesan and the most delicious bread sticks I'd ever tasted. I had no idea, however, that this modest operation, which closed after a year or two and ultimately failed as a larger franchise concept, would help spawn a whole new generation of small, nimble, out-of-the-way, endlessly imitated bar restaurants—like the modest ramen shop that opened a couple of years later, in the fall of 2004, by a former Craft employee and line cook named David Chang.

I heard about an innocuous little Japanese-style noodle bar, down on First Avenue in the East Village and named for the famous inventor of instant ramen noodles, Momofuku Ando, from my underground gourmet colleagues at the magazine, Rob Patronite and Robin Raisfeld, who'd given the ramen, and the gently simmered pork and chicken broth in particular, a short but glowing review in the magazine. I was putting together my usual year-end monster package and hunting for material, so I wandered into the Momofuku Noodle Bar alone early one weeknight off the street and bellied up to the bar, behind which the chef and a few of his cooks were at work in a cloud of steam.

The narrow space was surrounded by the usual collection of tattoo parlors and bodegas I remember, and it had the temporary, just-decorated quality you would see later on around town, when pop-up restaurants were all the rage. Rap tunes played from little speakers attached to an early-generation iPod stuck above the bar. The cooks on the line worked with their backs to their customers and delivered my steaming bowl of pork ramen when it was ready in the curt, no-nonsense style I remembered from my high school days haunting noodle bars back in Tokyo. The rich, silky, steamy broth was like nothing I remember tasting back in Japan, however, having been simmered over time—according to Underground Gourmet, with the care of a classic gourmet chef—in a pot filled with bacon, ham hocks, roasted pork bones, and a small mountain of fresh chicken legs.

The menu items that caught my attention, however, were the steamed bun sandwiches, which were made from the kind of plump, white, folded bao dumplings that you could buy by the dozens in shiny cellophane packages in Chinatown. One of these inspired little fusion tea sandwiches was stuffed with a slab of Berkshire pork, with a familiar type of Peking duck–style garnish of cucumbers and hoisin sauce, and the other contained delicious crackly-skinned deposits of the roasted chicken. I remember enjoying the chicken bun much better than the one with pork; in fact, I liked the chicken bun so much that I ordered a second one from the silent, glowering cooks at the anonymous little East Village restaurant and proceeded to extoll its delicious qualities to anyone who would listen.

"A word to the wise, Platty: always write about the pork," Mr. Cutlets liked to say whenever I told this story. Being an Ossabaw connoisseur, Ozersky was partial to pork products, of course, and in those days before they had their famous falling-out, he was one of the earliest and most vociferous disciples of the Cult of David Chang. Because he followed the flurry of shuttlecocks as they batted back and forth in the ever-expanding digital ethosphere, Ozersky knew much better than I did that formerly hidden cooks' pleasures like pork chops and late-night noodles were being jacked directly, via this supercharged new delivery system called the internet, into the cerebral cortex of the culinary mainstream. At that particular moment, in the early aughts, the internet culture was having the same transformative effect on the restaurant industry that the coming of MTV had had on the music industry in the 1980s. As the medium grew, the appetite for story content exploded, going from a few stories and posts each week to dozens and then hundreds every day on all the competing sites, and each post would be replicated and repeated, echoing and expanding forever out into the exploding cyber-universe in an endless twenty-four-hour loop. The opportunity for cooks and chefs and restaurateurs to develop and tell their own narratives—as opposed to, say, waiting for a weary print journalist to come knocking on their door—would expand exponentially too, and over the years, savvy, inventive chefs like Chang and, later on, René Redzepi at Noma would take the opportunity to re-create their own stories again and again. Blog posts were like self-replicating Von Neumann machines, Mr. Cutlets would later write: each one helped to create hundreds and then thousands of others like itself, which is why an ingenious fusion creation that might have been registered, then politely forgotten, by tastemaking critics just a few years before, like the Changian pork bun, could take on a life of its own. Which may also have been why, when I returned to the Momofuku Noodle Bar a few months later for a taste of my beloved crispy roast chicken bun, the item had disappeared from the menu forever.

Ozersky worked at *Grub Street* for only two years, but we became friends, and for a time we would venture out together on our culinary rounds to my review restaurants, or in his case to sample the endless stream of burgers and meat products turned out by the chefs he was always championing, often, I would later learn, in exchange for a free dinner or two. Ozersky liked to inveigh against the preciousness of what he called gourmet "tweezer food," and he had endless euphemisms for kitchens where he was known to the chef ("I'm big here") and for his habit of never picking up a tab ("Platty, I was born with a permanent case of alligator arms"). Sometimes after I'd paid for his large dinner we'd dive into delis and smoke shops to buy a fistful of lotto cards, which he'd scratch out with a big smile on his face, hoping to win a few bucks. Sometimes during his rounds he would drop by the apartment unannounced and spread out on the couch for a restorative nap, and the girls, who were small and impressionable at the time, would come to me in my office on their tiptoes and whisper, "Daddy, who's that big fat man snoring on the couch?" It was Mr. Cutlets who gave me the name "Platty" and recommended that I check out the comically named online messaging service called Twitter, which went live the same year *Grub Street* did, in the winter of 2006. I eventually got around to signing up under the Cutlets-inspired name "Plattypants" because a doppelgänger restaurant critic in Minneapolis named Adam Platt had taken my name, and who would ever take this "social media" business seriously anyways. Then I watched in bemused horror as within seconds schools of strangers began lighting up my newly purchased smartphone.

Ozersky and one of his eccentric cronies from the online underworld, a genial former nightclub bouncer and reformed skinhead turned meat blogger and food photographer named Nick "English Nick" Solares, would amuse themselves by calling my traditional restaurant critic's job "the last great job of the twentieth century," which even back in those early days wasn't far from the truth. In the fast disappearing pre-digital world I'd been inhabiting for years, restaurant critics were like miners, searching around a mostly hidden landscape for nuggets of gold, shining our creaky headlamps on carefully curated discoveries, many of which took weeks and sometimes months to find, and then sending the news back to a small, captive group of readers in carefully curated articles and magazine spreads. But with the new juiced-up, interactive news cycle, the old hidden mysteries of the restaurant kitchen—which strange and delicious recipes the best cutting-edge chefs were conjuring up, where to find them, how to order them—suddenly weren't so mysterious anymore. Online services like Yelp would soon allow the crowds of formerly docile, captive diners to voice their critical opinions on everything from the quality of the French fries to the cleanliness of a restaurant's toilets. When that game-changing Godzilla of the dining world, Instagram, arrived a few years later, cooks (and diners) were suddenly able to peer into restaurant kitchens and dining rooms all over the world, in real time, and it became increasingly clear that ponderous "legacy media" dinosaurs like myself, who'd grown to enormous size over the decades guiding the slow-moving herds from one watering hole to the next, were going to have to adapt to this rapidly evolving new landscape in order to survive.

Mr. Cutlets took pleasure in heckling his new dinosaur friend about the coming apocalypse—about the exhausting number of posts to file, the diminished role of authority in this crowded, noisy world, and the disguises and mannered pageantry of the traditional critics' routine, which he called "mere outmoded mummery," with a Johnsonian wave of his pudgy hand. Like most passionate online personalities in the early days of the web, he preferred the role of booster and bombastic connoisseur to the traditional, dispassionate pose of the critic. He also preferred the company of workaday chefs and line cooks to ironic, self-serious journalists and writers, and when I took him out on review dinners, I often had to restrain him from wandering back to the kitchen in his bluff, Falstaffian way and announcing his presence to the chef in a loud voice. Like his nineteenth-century heroes back on London's real Grub Street, he enjoyed playing favorites and picking fights, usually in an attempt to keep the shuttlecock endlessly in the air, and to promote what web writers in those days were already calling "the conversation." He picked fights with the growing myth of Brooklyn dining, a place that he viewed, in the old-world New York way, as a provincial region of exile, full of poor, pretentious souls who couldn't make it among the emerald towers of Manhattan. He picked fights with devotees of M.F.K. Fisher, whom he thought was similarly pretentious and overrated, and as the shuttlecock began to increasingly fly out of hand, he picked fights with his friends, including me.

In the end, we had a falling-out over another modestly critical three-star review I wrote about another elaborately posh Italian restaurant called Marea, in midtown, operated by one of his most loyal favorites, a talented chef named Michael White ("the Sultan of Spaghetti," Ozersky christened him). He had a much more public feud with David Chang, who famously banned Mr. Cutlets for life from his East Village dining empire for what, I'm guessing, was a *Grub Street* story he didn't much like, combined with a few too many Falstaffian visits back to the kitchen looking for a complimentary dinner or two. After the Marea incident, during which I'd assumed my usual boiled-owl expression and said nothing in public, Mr. Cutlets would come around to the apartment with a sad, slightly sheepish look on his face, bearing a bottle of Irish whiskey as a peace offering. He'd left *Grub Street* by then and was desperately churning out content for a short-lived website that he'd christened *The Feed Bag*. The pressures of keeping the shuttlecock in the air had caused things to spin out of control, he said with a sad shake of his head, and he was sorry for what he called his "traitorous deed." I accepted his apology and we shared several stiff afternoon glasses of whiskey before he wandered off again looking, I later imagined, like a bear going off into the woods in search of his next meal. We remained friends after our falling-out, Mr. Cutlets and I, although I began to see less and less of him after that and the girls would notice that he never came back to the apartment again.

18

The Best Job of the
Twentieth Century, Part 2

As the new universe of online journalism mutated and grew
and, in short order, began to devour the quaintly mannered
routines of weekly magazine journalism whole, Josh Ozersky
would be succeeded at *Grub Street* by a series of ever more professional, shipshape, conscientious editors who didn't mutter
ancient Yiddish sayings to themselves in their cubicles, or take
furtive favors from the people they covered, or dabble in addictive mail-order stimulants the way Mr. Cutlets did. They were a
little more expert at navigating this new and clamorously democratic landscape, where swirling digital weather patterns caused
fast-moving trends to pop up in Tokyo or Copenhagen one day,
and in Paris and Brooklyn the next. They were adept at searching out different styles and story lines and scanning the great
spaces of the internet, the way ambitious chefs were increasingly
doing, for that single dish that would catch the imagination of

the viral hordes, the way David Chang and his pork bun had done back in the day.

This was the Era of the Great Crazes in the restaurant world—the craze for high-end "burger blends" perpetuated by Keith McNally's famous Black Label Burger at Minetta Tavern; the craze for eye-catching multicolored cookies and bagels, for pizzas of every shape and size, for kale salads and avocado toast; the craze, most of all, for the kind of ingenious mashup creation that a young former Daniel Boulud pastry chef, Dominique Ansel, would create at the dawn of the Instagram age. Ansel had the brilliant idea of marrying together the buttery lightness of a classic Parisian croissant and the satisfying sugary crunch of an American doughnut, filling it with different-flavored varieties of custard, and calling the final product, which took months of experimentation, a "Cronut."

The Great Cronut Craze of 2013 was a *Grub Street* scoop, as it happened, orchestrated by one of Ozersky's very un-Ozerskian successors, a talented young editor named Alan Sytsma, whose work habits were so orderly, industrious, and above reproach, whose cubicle was so shipshape and spotless, whose manners were so formal and polite that I gave him the nickname "the Admiral." After receiving a tip from Ansel, whose bakery was located, conveniently, only a few blocks from the office, the Admiral dispatched a studious former line cook turned writer named Hugh Merwin to investigate. Merwin wrote a three-hundred-word post on this round, multilayered, strangely delicious object and described the "genius pastry engineering" that went into deep-frying each thin sheet of delicate croissant pastry dough. (During his experiments, Ansel had found that linseed oil bubbles at a certain temperature, giving the dough a perfect crunch without turning it to mush.) The post ran complete with alluring pictures of the first-ever Cronut, coated with a rose-colored glaze and stuffed with a light, technically perfect cream filling made in the classic French style and flavored with Tahitian vanilla. The next morning when they went on sale, there was a line stretching out the door of the little bakery and down the block, and the first batch of Cronuts—always limited to just a few hundred, Ansel coyly claimed, because his small kitchen wouldn't allow the baking of any more—sold out in thirty-eight minutes. That same afternoon videos of people enjoying their Cronuts began popping up online, and it wasn't long before the line became so long and unruly that brokers, for hundreds of dollars, began to offer early same-day Cronuts to people who didn't feel like getting up at 5:00 a.m. or risking being trampled in a Cronut stampede. Ansel officially trademarked the name of his invention just weeks after unleashing it on an unsuspecting public. Years later, despite thousands of imitators and populist Dunkin' Donuts knockoffs, there are Ansel bakeries in Tokyo and Paris, and some mornings the line for the original Cronut in SoHo still stretches around the block.

Even before the Cronut Craze of 2013, however, the professional description for those of us who still clung to our "greatest job of the twentieth century" was changing, just as Ozersky had predicted, in all sorts of strange and unsettling ways. Many of the traditional restaurant critic jobs, which required hefty expense accounts to do properly, had already disappeared outright at money-losing newspapers and magazines as they cut costs, then their staffs, and then began to go out of business altogether. When I'd started tapping out my weekly reviews in the summer of 2000, there were close to a dozen other full-time restaurant scribblers wandering from dining room to dining room, filing their flowery, carefully considered impressions of the trends of the day for newspapers and glossy publications around New York. More than a decade later, that number had shrunk to a small handful, and plans were being made at *New York* magazine to move the print operation, which had been published more or less every week since it was founded by Clay Felker and Milton Glaser in the spring of 1968 as an offshoot of the old *New York Herald Tribune* Sunday magazine, to a biweekly schedule. Grumpy, slow-moving print critics like myself were being told to write fewer actual reviews and more roundups, more top ten lists, more snappy, digestible items about food trends and stunt dishes. Permutations of the now-sainted and much-imitated Cronut were popping up all over the wild foodscape in the form of neon cookies and candied ice cream swirls and giant $100 doughnuts made in the Filipino style with purple-tinged yams; one of those would be delivered to me later on at the office from a local Filipino restaurant, wrapped in crepe paper and encased in a shiny cardboard box, like one of my grandmother's fancy summer hats, and covered entirely in 24-karat gold leaf. The quiet, carefully reasoned murmurings of the lordly old mandarin critic still had some value in the chaotic democracy of the dining world, and thanks to many different factors—the leveling democracy of the internet, the rise of a more accessible style of dining, along with an obsessively informed new generation of consumers—the interest in food and the food culture had never been more popular or widespread. But those of us who were used to the stately routines of the job were beginning to feel less like the judicious arbiters of taste we imagined ourselves to be and more like loud, yammering carnival barkers dressed in spats and top hats, herding the growing crowds of informed and unruly diners from one spangled, ephemeral, short-lived attraction to the next.

Since the arrival of Josh Ozersky and *Grub Street*, I'd been trying to raise my digital profile in various haphazard, slightly awkward ways, like an out-of-shape former track star donning his rumpled and stained college sweatshirt and attempting, at the advanced age of fifty-five, to sprint a few laps with the en-

ergetic young team of his former alma mater. I'd written occasional online musings for *Grub Street*, under the title "The
Gobbler," about behind-the-scenes restaurant critic peeves like
the perils of dieting, the many rules on how to eat out with
your children, the foolishness of the Michelin rankings in New
York (and star systems in general), and the legions of sacred cow
dining institutions around town—like the sainted, consistently
overrated Brooklyn steak palace Peter Luger, which had risen
above what I called "the Shit Line" and drew in crowds of customers day after day no matter how bad the service or the quality
of the beef or what the bilious critics said. But even for much
younger, more energetic writers who weren't spending their
mornings in a calorie-induced daze, the voracious appetite for
online content could turn quickly into a bottomless and terri-
fying black hole. And after a few jaunty early sprints around
this hyper-caffeinated track, the Gobbler's efforts slowed to a
wheezing crawl before petering out altogether. As rocket-fueled
stunt dishes like the Cronut took off and the print magazine ad-
vertising continued its march into oblivion, however, our editor
at *New York*, Adam Moss, had another idea on how to raise the
profile of his ponderous, print-oriented, stubbornly twentieth-
century restaurant critic.

Adam Moss had been an editor at the *Times* during Ruth
Reichl's heyday there and had dined out with her while she was
on the job, possibly when she was dressed in one of her famous
disguises. He knew as well as anyone that, like the myth of objectivity, which the Michelin stars had also been designed to
convey, the myth of anonymity was a powerful marketing tool for
traditional, old-line restaurant critics. It added a sense of magic,
even a touch of lordly, Oz-like mystery, to the popular cartoon
conception of the all-knowing restaurant critic—like Anton Ego
in the Disney movie *Ratatouille*, or Ruth at the height of her
magical costume powers—and enhanced their credentials in the

subjective, constantly evolving, perennially fashion-conscious world of fancy restaurants as the ultimate, dispassionate arbiters of taste. But audience tastes in the participatory, postmodern, increasingly riotous and quirky, crowdsourced age were changing at the usual warp speed. You could find anyone's image online these days with a couple of clicks on the keyboard. In London, star restaurant critics routinely ran their mug shots above their columns, and even in New York, high-profile food writers who sometimes doubled as critics, like Alan Richman of *GQ*, had been out of the proverbial closet for years. With the posts about the lowly Cronut generating more clicks than any restaurant review ever had, and faced with marketing yet another formulaic, end-of-the-year monster print magazine restaurant roundup to an increasingly restive and distracted audience of readers and advertisers, Moss asked me whether I'd like to come out of the closet too.

"We're putting your face on the cover, it will be great!" the editor announced, with one of his mischievous grins, after I'd been summoned from my cubicle for one of my infrequent meetings in the corner office.

"That's not going to be good for newsstand sales," I said, with one of my characteristic Eeyore-like sighs.

"Don't worry, they'll make you look fabulous!" said Mr. Moss, waving his hand in the direction of the photo department, with a happy glint in his eye.

The cover, when it appeared on January 1, 2014, would feature my giant bald head, floating against a white background, above the cutline "Hi, I'm Adam Platt, Your Restaurant Critic." The photo session had been suspiciously short. I'd smiled dutifully for the camera several times and dressed, as instructed, in a clean white shirt. I even put on a series of comic "disguise" props, which I thought would be an amusing touch, including a plastic Groucho Marx nose and mustache. Of course, the one glum, unsmiling, boiled-owl look I gave the camera was the image that Moss and the magazine's great photo director, Jody Quon, immediately chose, I'm sure with a good deal of mischievous laughter and cackling. As my parents happily pointed out, the photo of their glum-looking son bore an uncanny resemblance to the famous Platt family baby picture that the traveling diaper salesman had snapped on that fateful morning back in Alexandria, Virginia, many decades ago.

"I told you it would be fabulous," said the grinning Mr. Moss as we regarded a mock-up of the cover, where a tiny piece of sushi was photoshopped beneath my Gulliver-sized fist, accentuating the suspended, Oz-like roundness of my giant, bald, unsmiling head.

"Oh no, Dad," said my daughters, almost in unison, when they saw the cover, and Mrs. Platt said more or less the same thing, before turning away, like she usually did when photos of her husband the critic loomed up in public, and burying her face in her hands. Out in the wide world, the reaction to *New York* magazine's momentous restaurant critic reveal was what you'd expect—a flurry of nattering comment, followed by an uneasy, gently fizzing silence as the digital hordes moved on to the week's next event. I was coaxed into appearing on a network morning show, along with assorted other media outlets, to explain my reasons for coming out of the closet; the rambling and semi-coherent sound-bite explanations I offered would put my dreams of a TV career permanently on hold. Out on the job in my newly unanonymous state, the familiar cat-and-mouse charade between chef and critic continued like Moss predicted it would, although from my perspective, the routine seemed much less fraught and ridiculously self-conscious than before. I would continue to book tables at odd hours, under a string of randomly contrived names, although the increasing use of online reservation systems helped restaurants collect these pseudonyms more efficiently than before. Nevertheless, I didn't run a photo above my column, the chefs generally left me alone to dine in peace, and many of them still larded their menus with Platt-friendly hungry man specials—pork ribs, roast chicken, veal chops—just as they'd always done.

After he'd gotten over the horrible shock of seeing Platty's giant mug plastered on the cover of a national magazine, Mr. Cutlets called to congratulate me on finally dispensing with all of the dated restaurant critic's mummery and to welcome me to the twenty-first century of food writing and brand building. Ozersky was situated out in Portland, Oregon, by then, working as *Esquire*'s roving restaurant expert and living among the cheerful picklers and cheese-makers of that seminal, post-milennial food town, where he made the rounds of his favorite destinations for Thai food and fried chicken and cheerfully trumpeted the names of his favorite restaurants where he was a made man. After much striving and drama, he'd finally attained a kind of public intellectual status, at least among members of the small, fractious food world intelligentsia that we both inhabited. But in addition to his many addictions and medieval afflictions (like me, he was a veteran of the dreaded gout attack), Cutlets also suffered from epilepsy, and in the end he would die tragically at age forty-seven, when he blacked out in his hotel shower, after a characteristically wild evening of karaoke and carousing at the James Beard Awards in Chicago. I hadn't seen him much lately, but like several of his old friends back in New York, I'd gotten a hectic, breathless message from him the day before. He was coming to town and wanted to go out on one of our Johnsonian rambles, like in the old days, searching for strange and delicious things to eat and dropping into smoke shops and bodegas along the avenues to buy lottery tickets in the hopes of striking it rich.

Instead, I ended up going to his memorial service several weeks later, at a restaurant in Harlem called the Cecil, run by a talented young African American chef named JJ Johnson. Mr. Cutlets, having anticipated the need for a broader, more inclusive restaurant world years before the rest of us, and relishing, as always, a good shuttlecock-worthy story, had crowned the Cecil as *Esquire*'s best restaurant in the United States just months before. On the night of his memorial, the room was filled with a weird, slightly disjointed energy as a rogues' gallery of characters from the many different lives, eras, and realms that Ozersky inhabited during his short, eventful career mingled hesitantly together. There were big-name chefs in the crowded room, like Michael White (the Sultan of Spaghetti was looking a little gaunt on his new diet) and assorted meat cooks and members of the kitchen slave revolution, some of whom would soon be swept up in a different kind of earth-shaking kitchen revolution, which was looming just over the horizon. There were raffish downtown barkeeps from his old haunts in Alphabet City, rumpled print writers from the *Times* and *Esquire*, and former food and restaurant bloggers from the early cowboy days of the internet who had moved into the profitable mainstream and were now dressed in their newly pressed suits. There were wiseguy restaurateurs and celebrity butchers, like Pat LaFrieda, whose upmarket blends of prime beef and fatty brisket Josh had vigorously championed as the burger mania spread from its beginnings in LA to Keith McNally's Black Label Burger in New York, and then out and around the globe from there thanks to Danny Meyer's Shake Shack empire.

As all of these enemies, allies, and frenemies of the Great Ozersky clustered around the bar that evening, drinking bourbon and eating sliders and ribs, a Harlem church choir sang gospel songs out on the sidewalk. There were no tearful speeches or memorials, although at one point a friend of Josh's, an eccentric spice expert with a twirling wax-tipped mustache named Aaron Isaacson, burst out in a tearful rendition of the

Irish song "Danny Boy," substituting "Joshy" for "Danny." Plenty of bourbon was poured at the crowded bar after that, and I remember that as the strange, mournful celebration went on into the evening, a few of the oldest Cutlets friends and veterans sidled up to me and asked quietly who I thought was footing the bill.

19

Faking It: The Imperfect Art of the Perfect Review, Part 1

Like most grizzled professionals, traditional restaurant crit-ics tend to develop their own quirky routines over time. Many of these strange little rituals are established early on in our careers and tend to be repeated again and again, often as a matter more of comfort than of convenience, until we are re-placed, retire from the field, or expire on the job, clutching our knife and fork with a rictus grip, a rumpled, grease-streaked napkin still stuck under our collar. The bartender at a beauti-ful little castle hotel on the west coast of Ireland told me once that the staff could usually spot the Michelin "inspectors" who regularly came through their little dining room because they tended to be middle-aged men who ordered many more des-serts than most gentlemen of their age, drank at least a bottle of wine with their dinner, and almost always dined alone. Crit-ics have their own tastes, of course—some are partial to Italian food, others consider themselves to be French scholars; because of my time in Asia I fancied myself a Chinese and Japanese food scholar, and tended to judge those places in a lordly, high-handed way. Some critics like to ambush kitchens, instructing their guests to sit down and order dinner before they make a grand, hurried entrance into the dining room. Some scribble their notes under the table, some run microphones up under their shirts and blouses to record their whispered impressions, while others run off to the restroom periodically to tap furiously on their cell phones. Some critics bring large parties to dinner, especially if they're visiting a restaurant only once, and instruct their guests to take a single bite, then pass the dish on to their neighbor, with a kind of comically choreographed precision. Some critics like a party atmosphere when they eat, especially in the early days, when expense accounts could accommodate several bottles of wine, while others cultivate a serious, almost priestly air while on the job. The latter send around emails to their guests ahead of time, the way one of my colleagues told me he used to do, with carefully notated bullet points on how to comport themselves during a proper review dinner; raise their hands for silence if the conversation grows too loud; and go around the table to ask their slightly terrified guests to offer short murmuring tasting notes on the silky texture of their freshly grilled turbot, say, or the pleasing floral qualities of their possibly oversalted early spring vegetable soup.

A self-serious air of priestliness is one of the classic perks of the restaurant critic's job, of course, although I quickly found that this pose didn't work for a disheveled, non–type A personality like me. The first restaurant I ever reviewed for *New York* magazine was a polished, progressive little establishment on Barrow Street in the West Village called Annisa, which was opened in the late summer of 2000 by a talented young chef from Detroit named Anita Lo. She had studied with Guy Savoy, among others, and worked in many of the finest kitchens around the city. I booked an early 6:00 table because, as I soon discovered, the very early or very late tables were the easier ones to get on short notice, especially at a popular new restaurant in New York City. I'd also learned, as a young father, that if I sat down to eat around 8:00, I tended to nod off to sleep shortly after the entrées arrived. I reserved a table for four people under the comical name of "Mr. A. Duffy," not because I thought four people would be the perfect number of guests for a proper review, but because the dining room at Annisa was a tiny-sized West Village space and the polite woman on the other end of the telephone line said they couldn't accommodate a larger party. I would also discover, through a process of trial and error, that a table for four was the optimum number for a civilized review dinner. Like a small platoon in battle, a table of only two or three diners risked being overwhelmed by the waves of ridiculously rich food, especially at a large Chinese restaurant or pasta-heavy Italian joint. If there were more than four people, however, dinner could quickly devolve into a party, and it was difficult to keep track of the blizzard of dishes, let alone how they tasted, or what your guests thought of them, and which unruly guests might order a second round of drinks for the table (one drink per person was the hard and fast early rule) or even a third expensive bottle of wine.

Another one of the restaurants I reviewed in those very early days was a sturdy, short-lived French establishment called D'Artagnan, which Ariane Daguin, one of New York's famous purveyors of classic French foie gras, among other rusticated barnyard delicacies, opened in midtown to showcase her products. Daguin's family comes from Gascony, home of the Three Musketeers, and the waiters wore Musketeer-style outfits, I dimly recall, as they hoisted platters of game sausages, roast duck, and other stout delicacies famous to the region around to sturdy banquet-sized tables. There were six of us at dinner, including a young gentleman from Paris, who appeared at the last minute, dressed for a refined dinner, in his business jacket and silk tie. Speaking French, I also dimly recall, the Parisian merrily instructed his slightly puzzled, faux Musketeer waiter to bring a glass of sweet Alsatian wine to go with his foie gras appetizer, and then an expensive red, possibly a bottle of Bordeaux, to go with that Gascony specialty, cassoulet, which Madame Daguin served in the traditional way—with sausages, shreds of roast duck, and white tarbais beans, all mingled together under a crust of bread crumbs. The merry young Frenchman devoured his crock of cassoulet, followed by a cheese course, a spoonful of dessert or two, and then, despite my stern looks and quiet pleadings, an after-dinner Sauterne followed by a snifter or two of Gascony's favorite post-meal digestive, Armagnac. "Thank you so much for the lovely dinner," the young Frenchman said, a little woozily, after I'd paid the substantial bill and we'd staggered together out onto the sidewalk. Then he bent over and, with the dignity that comes only with experience and practice, threw up in the gutter just an inch or two away from my shiny new restaurant critic shoes.

Mercifully, nothing like that happened during that first, relatively sedate visit to Annisa, or to a Spanish restaurant called Meigas, which I visited next. Looking back, however, I'm aware of some quirky, unexpected discoveries on those very first dining excursions, about the imperfect art of the restaurant review, that would gradually turn into general rules of operation and that I would use again and again. The culture of food writing and criticism has moved into all sorts of different styles and mediums in the clamorous, post-print digital age, and these days the title "restaurant critic" encompasses an ever-wider collection of video artists, cultural anthropologists, and antic online "influencers." Back in those days, however, I always thought that the quaint little backwater world of food journalism could be divided into two broad schools of learning and operation. There were the traditionalists, led by towering figures like James Beard, Julia Child, and Craig Claiborne, who tended to write about recipes and cooking and mostly focused on what was in front of them on the kitchen range or the restaurant plate. Then there were the reporters and bon vivants like Calvin Trillin, Joe Liebling, and Joseph Wechsberg of *The New Yorker* and Johnny Apple, who were given to a more atmospheric style of writing. Members of the traditional school focused on the intricacies of cooking and taste; their counterparts wrote about the pleasures of a good meal, and the curious culture of dining and food, the way Trillin chronicled his beloved Kansas City barbecue, for instance, or Wechsberg wrote about the foie gras geese farmers of Toulouse and the eccentric habits of the ancient waiters he'd known at the Tafelspitz restaurant back in prewar Vienna. Occasionally these two styles would come together, say, in Elizabeth David's atmospheric writing about the food of Provence, or the culinary cultural ruminations of Ruth Reichl or Jonathan Gold. But as I looked around the little dining room and tasted Chef Lo's elaborate fusion creations—which included an ingenious gourmet version of Taiwanese soup dumpling filled not with pork but with little nuggets of foie gras—it was clear that if I was going to survive for more than a few months in my strange new occupation, it would be as a junior, bumbling member of the reportorial, flaneur school of food writing.

Reporters always ask questions, take notes, and find it useful to obtain hard documents, like menus—which I asked Mrs. Platt to furtively slide into her handbag during that first dinner at Annisa. Back in those pre-smartphone days, I kept boxes of crumpled little pocket notebooks that I'd fill up with my pinched, handwritten scrawl on my non-food-related travel and reporting excursions. As the first courses arrived that night, I took out a shiny new notebook from my jacket and began scribbling away. "You don't look like a restaurant critic anymore," Mrs.

Platt would sadly remark years later, when I had stopped scribbling obsessively under the table in my crumpled little notebooks and started tapping out notes on my newly purchased iPhone, like every other distracted diner in the house. But so what? The lordly objectivity that traditional Michelin-style critics did their best to convey in their reviews seemed faintly ridiculous to me in this swirling, changeable, highly subjective world where the experience of your lunch or dinner tended to change dramatically depending on all sorts of factors—where you sat, what time of day you visited, whether or not the chef happened to have a cold—and it would keep changing, often for the better, long after your review was published. The best you could do in this fluid situation, I concluded, was to make an argument and to paint a composite picture of dinner for your readers, many of whom would never find the money or the time to visit a restaurant like Annisa and sample the wonders of Anita Lo's famous foie gras soup dumpling.

Making my rounds in those early days, I'd try to sit with my back to the wall so I could take in the scene; I'd look for bizarre dishes on the menu because failed experiments often made better copy than good ones; and I'd attempt to tell readers the story of a particular meal, in a particular time, and at a particular place in the strange, spangled world of New York restaurants the way a reporter would who covered horse racings, say, or the British royal family or a succession of Broadway shows. I'd try to populate this world with a cast of characters to whom the reader could relate, including a few recurring ones, like my Mrs. Platt, or cousin Frank the family gastronome, and the narrator, who had his own settled tastes and a definite point of view. That first review was no literary tour de force, but it did have many of the conventions that I'd repeat again and again: a fondness for words like "dainty" and "natter"; an opening setting of the restaurant scene; a description of the meal as it progressed in three classic theatrical acts, from the appetizers to the main course and finally to dessert; and the sense that the writer, like most of his readers, was less of a stuffy, know-it-all gourmet than a curious, affable stranger adrift in a strange, curious land.

"I'm someone of extended culinary appetites, the kind of eater the writer A. J. Liebling used to call a feeder," I wrote in that first, introductory review of Annisa, an influential restaurant in its own right, which I would revisit and review with pleasure several more times.

Feeders are discerning omnivores of the old school. They favor hearty dishes over subtle ones, and lots of food over just a little. Faced with a choice between a robust veal chop, say, or a tidbit of carefully articulated quail, a feeder chooses the veal chop every time. So, it was with mild trepidation that I made my way to Annisa, the sleek new restaurant at 13 Barrow Street, in the clamorous center of the West Village. The storefront space is one of those Zelig-like addresses where chefs and their clientele come and go over the years, always more or less approximating the spirit of the times. It housed chef John Tesar's One/3 not long ago, and the stolid neighborhood joint Rizzolio's for years before that. Now it has been redone, by co-owners Jennifer Scism and Anita Lo, in a blaze of clean minimalism, with an array of dainty fusion items on the menu and two garden benches outside (plus a potted-fern garden), so patrons can natter on their cell phones in the peace of the great outdoors.

As with the name (it means "women" in Arabic), there was a tangible feminine brightness to the proceedings at Annisa. After picking my way among the seedy trinket joints around Sheridan Square, I was pleased to find Ms. Scism herself mixing cocktails in a bubblegum-pink dress. An orchid decorated one corner of the honey-colored bar, near a jar of spindly garlic, fresh from the Greenmarket in Union Square. A pair of women sat at the bar sipping flamingo-colored cosmopolitans in perfect unison. Ms. Scism suggested a martini made with Lillet, the sugary aperitif from the south of France. A bowl of speckled eggs (salted duck as well as chicken) were on display at the bar, and when I lunged for one, she nabbed it first, cut it in half, and placed it delicately on a plate. "It's purely a nibble," she said.

"Nibble" was the operative term at Annisa, where the dining area was the size of a commodious suburban garage. Grand restaurants often peddle the illusion of intimacy; it is rare, however, to find an intimate restaurant that manages, unobtrusively, to appear grand. It's a stylistic trick as well as a culinary one, and Annisa pulled it off. The walls were painted in creamy, outdoor colors, and a variety of architectural tricks—suspended lampshades, a shimmering wall curtain—gave the space an elevated, lofty feel. The bar faced two tall picture windows, and the tables—there were only thirteen—were behind it on a little rise, so diners were lifted above the view of the careering traffic outside. I focused diligently on a nice bowl of vichyssoise larded with iced oysters (after the sweet cocktail, the cool leek flavor had a soothing effect) while glancing furtively around the table at the little towers of lobster salad (leavened with avocado), a helping of grilled squid atop a pedestal of white bean salad, and the plate of zucchini blossoms— golden-fried and stuffed with a North African blend of chickpeas in a tomato sauce with saffron—being fiercely nibbled by my wife.

Chef Lo, who was Chinese American (from Detroit) and had last worked at the doomed pan-Asian restaurant Mirezi, specialized in these cross-cultural tricks. The finicky Japan expert at our table pronounced the tuna appetizer (a sashimi-carpaccio hybrid, brushed with a cod-roe sauce) slightly underwhelming. But everyone fought for a taste of the seared foie gras soup dumplings in an aromatic Chinese broth—reduced from pigs' feet, among other things, Ms. Scism sweetly explained—with a delicate hint of vinegar, plated in a symmetrical pattern. My softshell crab had a tempura lightness and arrived on a bed of corn salad, shot full of creamy Japanese uni. The lamb tenderloin, garnished with minted yogurt and cucumbers, was a successful riff on the classic Greek dish. The saddle of rabbit, wrapped with scallions and sizzly strips of applewood-smoked bacon, was so delicious I ordered it twice. "That Thumper was farm-raised in California," said the waitress when she saw my beatific smile.

More conventional items on Chef Lo's summer menu met with a more conventional response. The roasted fillet of cod tasted chalky despite a pleasingly crunchy pistachio sauce. My friend the Italian snob turned up her nose at the pan-roasted chicken, unmoved by a savory sauce laced with white truffles and sherry. "That's a fatty chicken," she exclaimed. "That chicken hasn't been anywhere. That's an American chicken." Not that we voiced these complaints to Annisa's terminally upbeat staff. The sommelier was dressed like Elvis Costello and announced his recommendations with operatic vigor. I drank a fine Pinot Meunier with my crab one night, and iced organic sake (at $10 per glass, from the temple city of Nara) with my rabbit the next. The sommelier also had poetic opinions about cheese. "It's from the Loire Valley" went his description of one well-known chèvre. "It tastes like a late August afternoon."

Whether other diners at Annisa enjoyed similar Proustian moments is hard to say. The mini-crowd seemed to be an odd mix of boisterous girlfriends and eccentric neighborhood couples. I spied a man with pickle-colored hair one night, next to a claque of aspiring models zipped into airtight hip-huggers. Another evening their places were taken by some startled-looking tourists and an elderly couple dressed in matching safari outfits.

Ms. Scism, who spent a formative year as a hostess at Chante-relle, managed this diverse room with a neighborly touch. On my second visit, she recognized me as the Lillet martini drinker and cheerfully suggested the sweet house cocktail: champagne spiked with pastis, ginger syrup, and cubes of candied ginger. Her malicious pick for dessert was the Chocolate Beggar's Purse, a cholesterol bomb of flourless chocolate cake and port-soaked cherries baked in a feathery North African pastry dough called brique. This confection caused group mayhem at our table, oblit-erating all other sweets in its wake.

Later on, when my jittery taste buds had subsided, I made my methodical way through a perfectly proportioned apple tart drizzled in caramel sauce, then an artful mound of carrot cake, which was light in texture like a madeleine but crispy-cornered like a muffin. After that, I paused, Zen-like, to imbibe a blossom-filled pot of green tea. There are more elaborate spirits on Annisa's menu ($220 for a bottle of the Krug Grande Cuvée), but perhaps I was feeling healthful, even a little demure. A tray of miniature fruit ices appeared after dessert, along with mint truffles and slivers of candied ginger. I took a few rabbit-size bites of a single truffle, then put it back down. It was purely a nibble, after all.

20

The Imperfect Art of the
Perfect Review, Part 2

The food landscape in New York would soon explode into more enthusiasms, crazes, and golden ages than it was possible to count—for cheese-makers and coffee bars, for farm-to-table foraging and "fast casual dining," for pickle-makers and southern comfort foods and ye olde craft brewers who were already setting up shop in abandoned industrial lots across the river in Brooklyn, to name just a few. But those early twilight years when the previous millennium wasn't quite old yet and the new millennium was barely new, turned out to be a kind of golden age for the traditional restaurant critic who wandered the streets looking for strange and interesting things to write about and to eat.

In the summer of 2000, Bill Clinton was still the president of the United States, Danny Meyer had only a few restaurants in his small, neighborly portfolio, and Thomas Keller's famous California import, Per Se, wouldn't arrive in the city for another four years. As I've said, there were no clamorous, yelping bloggers to contend with, the obtrusive glories of Instagram were still years away, and the presumptuous out-of-town inspectors from Michelin were still terrorizing chefs back in Paris, Lyon, and the other bastions of what was still referred to in hushed, respectful tones as "le haute cuisine." New York still occupied its traditional place as the glittering fashion runway for the world's culinary scene, the place where reputations were ruined and made, and where the different styles of the day were chosen and then disseminated out in the hinterlands. Like Czarist Moscow before the revolution, all sorts of exotic characters from different dining eras still mingled together on the runway stage. There were old-world aristocrats like André Soltner at Lutèce and Rita and André Jammet at La Caravelle on Fifty-Fifth Street, whose original owners had named their restaurant after the lines of an elegant style of French sailing ship. There were ambitious young cooks like Anita Lo, whose pint-sized, discreetly chic establishment would be a model for ambitious restaurants around town in the coming stripped-down, post-gourmet era, and Dan Barber and Tom Colicchio, whose radical notions about sustainability and technique would soon combine with other mini-revolutions and movements in the kitchen world to stand the former order on its head. Like one-name rappers and basketball stars, larger-than-life cooks left over from the just-ended super-chef era of the '90s—Nobu, Daniel, Jean-Georges—were still stalking the landscape, and Joe Baum's Windows on the World was at the very end of its long, theatrical, ultimately tragic run atop the World Trade Center.

Baum had died in 1998, but the elaborate, big-box, P. T. Barnum style of dining he'd pioneered for decades at theatrical productions like the Four Seasons, the Roman-themed Forum of the Twelve Caesars, the Tavern on the Green in Central Park, and the Rainbow Room at Rockefeller Center were still being imitated by ambitious, deep-pocketed restaurateurs around the city who could still afford in those days to turn old midtown bank buildings and abandoned downtown dance halls into colorful sushi palaces and fanciful, industrial-sized steak halls, and whose fortunes, like those of other theatrical, fashion-conscious artistic professions around New York, tended to rise and fall with the boom and bust of the stock market. Alan Stillman, who'd built the green-and-white-trimmed Smith & Wollensky steakhouse on East Forty-Ninth Street into an impressive cash machine, was busy opening other concept restaurants around town. So was a real estate financier and former co-owner of Braniff Airways named Jeffrey Chodorow, whose imaginatively crackpot, and sometimes very successful, dining schemes were a constant source of pleasure to the larger, more rambunctious group of dining critics who patrolled the restaurant world back in those days.

Then as today, the dining critic for the *New York Times* reigned supreme over this rabble of sauce-stained scribblers and hacks, although the tastes of the talented writers and reporters who occupied that powerful throne could differ fairly radically from one reign to the next, and some were more hesitant than others to use the powers of the office to upend the star-system status quo that had been so carefully cultivated over the years by Craig Claiborne, Mimi Sheraton, and others. In this much smaller, top-down world, I used to think only the *Times* had the power to actually close a restaurant in the big city or substantially alter its trajectory, although that would also begin to change in the coming years of turmoil and disruption back then and, as today, bad restaurants had a habit of closing themselves. You could wander from one antic, exotically themed production to the next, describing the thousands of samurai swords that dangled menacingly from the ceiling of a Chodorow venture

called Kobe Club, or the strangely oppressive smell of truffle oil mingling with traces of burned beef fat that hung over
the room of another mercifully doomed midtown Chodorow
venture called Tuscan Steak. "It swirls in the air on the sidewalk outside, above the limos and courtesy cars idling two and
three deep," I wrote in an early review titled "Tedium Rare. "It
smells of commerce instead of cooking, like the whiff of cigarette smoke hovering over a busy casino floor."

My rule for tough reviews was the usual one every young
copy assistant or reporter is taught in journalism school or during the first week in a newsroom—to comfort the afflicted
and afflict the comfortable. There could be different shades to
a negative review, however, especially in those days when the
range and styles of dining tended to be more exaggerated than
today. When I grudgingly got around to adopting a star system, I quickly discovered that the respectful one-star review was
considered a cataclysmic disaster by an ambitious three-star restaurant, and that even a vaguely critical three-star review would
provoke howls of displeasure from prominent cooks who were
used to the preening five-star treatment. There was the grudgingly respectful two-star review that read like a one-star review,
and the damning-with-faint-praise one-star review that read
like no stars at all. I also quickly discovered, as any regular week-
to-week reviewer does, that for many restaurants, the ultimate
negative judgment often turns out to be no review at all. Every
working critic has reams of notes that they dutifully compiled
while glumly sitting through entire dinners at an endless series
of mediocre brasseries, steakhouses, and cafés that they visited
only once and never returned to again. One of the worst meals
I ever endured during those early days was at a nameless Japanese place near our apartment in the Village. The kitchen special
on the fateful evening I happened to drop by was squid risotto,
which I imagined would be the usual light, buttery confection

of carefully turned Carnaroli or Arborio rice, mixed with a little squid ink, say, and nuggets of melting, gently cooked calamari. What arrived from the kitchen instead was a yellow, gummy mass of rice and hot cheese, stuffed inside the long, hollowed-out carcass of a grown, rubbery-textured squid. As this grim creation was gamely being hoisted to the table by members of the quietly horrified waitstaff, an unfortunate malfunction in the kitchen caused clouds of greasy back-draft stove fumes to billow out over our heads in the little basement dining room. As we glumly ate our dinner, the chef started to wave his arms around frantically in the smoke and yell at his staff like the captain of a sinking submarine ship, at which point I called for the check and evacuated the dining room as quickly and politely as I possibly could.

Other high-profile disasters were more difficult to ignore, especially back in those days before the explosion of bar restaurants and casual dining and before the gradual erosion of the idea of a Manhattan-centric New York City as the culinary capital of world, when prominent, ambitious productions seemed to open around town week after week, like Broadway shows. Those early reviews are peppered with accounts of blowups and magisterial flameouts that you don't see much anymore in the broader, more democratic, crowdsourced dining era of today. In the first few years on the job, I reviewed an ambitious Italian restaurant in midtown called Barbaluc, where an unfortunate sardine-and-branzino-stuffed ravioli "smelled like it had recently been hauled from some turbid Venetian lagoon." I also visited One C.P.S., a lavish, short-lived production, financed by the steak baron Alan Stillman, in one of the dining rooms at the Plaza Hotel, where David Burke, another talented fabulist chef from the '90s, instructed his legions of cooks to mold piles of lobster meat into the shape of beefsteaks and to stuff fried chicken wings with chunks of crabmeat, an experiment that *New York* magazine would describe as "a gooey, pointless concoction that tasted of mildly fishy chicken fat." During those first months on the job, I also sampled all sorts of delicious things, of course, including what was possibly the finest example of funky, gently simmered tripe I've ever tasted at a wonderful, now-vanished Galician restaurant in Chelsea called Meigas, where the Platt family gastronome cousin Frank, whom I quoted frequently in those early reviews, chattered to the waiters in broken Spanish and toasted the room with several bottles of Spanish wine.

"Tripe is a lunchtime dish at Meigas," I would write in my review for the magazine,

> a tapas-style *primero plato* on a menu crowded with fanciful, traditionalist items like piquillo peppers stuffed with marinated tuna and braised oxtail croquettes rolled in a dusting of crushed pistachios. But my Uncle Frank more or less ignored these delicacies until his tripe arrived. He talked of Galicia (*meigas* means "sorceress" in Galician), the family seat of Francisco Franco and Fidel Castro. "Galicia produces great dictators," he said. "The waiters can be dictatorial, too." Our tripe was served by a grave-looking gentleman wearing a priestly goatee. He watched in silence as the aficionado sniffed the paprika bouquet and stirred the velvety stew with his spoon. Cubes of ham were mingled with the veal belly, which tasted sweet and gamy and evaporated in the mouth, like some strange smokehouse confection. Uncle Frank took one taste, then another. "Mercy," he said, rolling his eyes to the heavens. "Mercy me."

New Chinese restaurants were opening around the city in those days, and new Dutch restaurants that served cool rolls of herring along with trays of *bitterballen* filled with curries and satays from the old spice islands of Indonesia. I reviewed tapas restaurants, restaurants devoted only to French cheeses, and little bunker-style sushi bars in the East Village where the uni was flown in, miraculously, just hours after it was fished from the chilly waters of Hokkaido. For the first time, I tasted hand-foraged wood ear mushrooms at Tom Colicchio's Craft, and I scribbled a few dismissive paragraphs about yet another new Gulliver-sized Asian fusion joint in midtown called Tao, which I failed to predict would soon be the most successful restaurant in the entire United States. I took my mother to a series of lunches—to Monsieur Briguet's restaurant, Le Périgord; to the soon-to-be-shuttered La Caravelle, where she commented politely on the timeless qualities of the perfectly textured pike quenelle; and to a new bistro in midtown where we wondered at the qualities of a stately creation called the DB Burger, which that paragon of big-city Continental gourmet cooking, Daniel Boulud, unleashed on an unsuspecting public in the summer of 2001.

It's difficult to overstate the impact of Boulud's famous dish, which, in retrospect, was a canny acknowledgment of the more casual style of comfort dining beginning to seep into the upper realms of what was still being called the world of "fine dining," as well as a kind of love letter to the more elegant but now slowly vanishing style of haute cuisine on which he'd made his reputation. The DB Burger cost $27, which was an astonishing amount to pay for any burger in those days. The bun was freshly baked and flecked with bits of parmesan and layered in a confectionery way with a smear of freshly whipped mayonnaise, a bouncy sprig of frisée, and a tangy sweet tomato compote instead of ketchup. The ground prime rib beef contained braised short ribs, deposits of truffles, and a melting chunk of foie gras in its soft center. When all of these delicate elements were carefully assembled, the finished dish was brought to our table cut in two fragile halves, alongside a silver cup of round, crisped pommes soufflés.

My mother had arrived for our midtown lunch wearing a summer dress, I remember, and with a napkin spread neatly in her lap, she cut her portion of Boulud's elegant creation in half. She took one delicate bite and then another, and then she put down her fork. "I hope you're not planning to write anything mean about the poor chefs this week," she said.

21

End of Days

Babble as fast as you can, but keep it short!"

This snippet of advice, offered with an amused grin from a longtime veteran of countless TV food shows, rattled around in my brain as the disconcertingly large, Easter Island–sized head of the fearsome chef and TV host Gordon Ramsay loomed up above me, under the harsh lights of a cavernous Burbank studio.

Like most everything that happens when you're being filmed live on a TV set for the first or second time, I had a disorienting sense of time spooling crazily forward, and then freezing again. The little red lights on the four or five giant cameras that moved around the industrial-sized, weirdly hot, weirdly cold studio space, where the hit show *MasterChef* was being filmed, blinked on, then off, then on again.

Ramsay was dressed in an electric blue suit, I dimly recall, and he wore a perpetual, slightly pained smile on his face, which made his teeth seem the size of giant Chiclets as I crouched below him on my little chair. His skin was pale, like candle wax, and caked with trowels of pinkish-orange makeup. Back in the day when he was a working chef in London, the famously volatile Scotsman had been known to toss offending writers out of his restaurants, and I wondered whether he remembered my disparaging description of the precious, over-fussy cooking at one of his now-closed New York establishments, which had left a certain oversized critic "longing in the end for Gordon Ramsay's version of a good old-fashioned cheeseburger." The answer was, probably not: Gordon Ramsay had ascended into the glowing pantheon of TV brands long ago, and like most characters who prosper in that imaginary hothouse world, he radiated a controlled energy that, when experienced in person rather than through a television screen, appeared to be just this side of insane. The eyes in his enormous head looked bright and unblinking, and he spoke in loud forceful sentences, like he was shouting into a rainstorm.

"Adam Platt from *New York* magazine," intoned the Giant Gordon Ramsay Head. "Give us your impressions of the Red Team's roast halibut!"

A herd of other real-life critics, bloggers, and opinion influencers were assembled at tables around the studio set, which had been made up for this segment of the show to look like an actual restaurant dining room. I was at the first table, peering up at Ramsay and the other wildly grinning hosts, whose heads also appeared to be unnaturally huge. Each table was covered with a white linen tablecloth and set with gleaming cutlery, along with leather-bound notebooks for the jotting down of our impressions. Beside each notebook was a bottle of Perrier water, presumably to whet our parched throats and clear our highly attuned palates between the rapidly prepared bites of food.

The critics had been flown in from around the country the evening before from a variety of struggling newspapers, bumptious websites, and glossy, publicity-hungry magazines to judge what would turn out to be a single ten-minute segment of Ramsay's long-running juggernaut series. We'd been put up in a not very fashionable Hollywood hotel the evening before, and then bused to the studio in the morning, like a group of nervously chattering high school students on their first day of school. The award-winning critic from the *Houston Chronicle*, Alison Cook, was in this large, surprisingly accomplished group, her hair dyed a faint, elegant tinge of purple, along with a friend from other crackpot junkets around the globe, Adam Sachs, who was then the editor of the food magazine *Saveur*. Also in attendance was Amanda Hesser, who had wisely left her job at the *Times* years earlier to start her own website empire, called *Food52*. Discerning souls from the food sections of the *Chicago Tribune* and the *Washington Post* were there, and so was the king of the learned traditionalist school of food writers and junketeers, Jeffrey Steingarten from *Vogue* magazine. I knew from dining with him back in New York that the famous "Man Who Ate Everything" liked to cultivate an eccentric, professorial presence. He had a taste for single malt whiskey and the slow, relentless appetite of a true professional, and when he was on the job, he often held his fork down low on the handle, like a lumberjack shoveling in a tall stack of morning pancakes.

The first halibut dish we sampled was baked in big ivory blocks and crusted with some kind of crumbly orange dusting on top (crushed hazelnuts, it turned out). There were strange little decorative dots on the plate, and a streak of beurre blanc flavored with lemons that, like many of the concoctions whipped up in a supposed frenzy by the increasingly competent horde of telegenic, striving personalities who populated the ever-growing world of reality food TV, looked almost shockingly edible.

Once Ramsay and his producers gave the command to taste, the horde of critics began eating and jabbering into the different cameras all at once, taking care, as we intoned our babble of hot-take tasting notes, to maintain glowering, Serious Critic expressions, as the producers had instructed us to do.

"The halibut seems slightly overcooked," I heard myself say, grasping in a random, desperate way for the most obvious kind of intelligent criticism one could offer about any chunk of recently prepared fish. As the cameras approached and zoomed out again, I kept babbling, crouching lower and lower at the table, while looking up hopefully at the huge Head of Ramsay suspended above and jutting my neck out like a giant turtle, in the vain hope that my double chin wouldn't show.

All around, I could hear the gaggle of critics offering what seemed like much more salient and pointed opinions about the fucking halibut: How the colorful dots on the plate looked like some misbegotten birthday decoration. How the flavors weren't meshing quite correctly. How the textural balance of the different elements of the dish was just ever so slightly off. When a second course arrived—a piece of seared duck breast, prepared by the chatty and charismatic Red Team—even I could tell it was quite radically undercooked. The chattering began anew, only to be punctuated, during a pause, by the sound of Steingarten—whose comments would be featured more in the mercifully brief final cut of the segment than those of the rest of us combined—yelling "Fuck" in his forceful TV voice after some kind of incident, possibly a spilled glass of wine, occurred at his table.

When the show finally aired many months later, I sat down with one of my daughters on the couch to watch an actual episode of *MasterChef* for the first time. Refracted through our large TV screen, Ramsay's focused energy seemed normal, well adjusted, almost downright jolly. ("If all these critics came into my restaurant on the same night, I'd be crapping myself," he merrily declared.) My daughter didn't think his head seemed abnormally large at all ("I'm sorry, yours is bigger, Dad"), and she spent most of her brief time in front of the television laughing at his jokes. "Was that all you said?" she politely asked when her father's Oz-shaped visage rose up on the screen to murmur about the possibly overcooked halibut for ten seconds or so before disappearing from the *MasterChef* narrative forever. I told her that most of my restaurant critic colleagues had suffered a similar fate at the hands of the editors and show runners, and that trying to catch people's attention in staccato sound bites, as I was now attempting to do in this new, conspicuously public stage of my professional eating career, was a talent all its own.

"Keep working it, Dad!" she said, with a happy shrug, before disappearing into her room, clutching her pink phone.

I was attempting to work it in my dated, slightly dazed dad way, of course. In those years after the social media meteor obliterated the old ways of doing almost everything, those of us who'd managed, by some divine miracle, to survive the waves of magazine shutterings and print media layoffs, not to mention the clickbait food crazes that seemed to sweep over the landscape like biblical plagues every week, were adapting to our new environment the best we could. Like figures from a Mad Max movie, we wandered here and there in the bleary, post-gourmet twilight, gamely composing top ten listicles of favorite steakhouses and pastrami sandwiches (Katz's Deli, of course!) because a blizzard of scrollable lists and short "hot takes" had long since replaced the measured, haughty thousand-word restaurant review as the coin of the realm in savvy food media circles. We labored to compose pithy posts for our little-used social media feeds ("Nobody reads Twitter, Dad") and posted off-kilter pictures on Instagram of late-night cocktails ("Down the Hatch"!) and dimly lit, out-of-focus images of cheeseburgers and platters of pasta, because, as my daughter (and my editors) kept reminding me, "Everyone likes a good picture of spaghetti and meatballs, Dad!" We talked on podcasts, gamely hosted discussion panels, and loitered nervously in the green rooms of shows like *MasterChef*, where the spectacle of a multitude of critics and influencers, all murmuring and shouting their opinions into the air at once, increasingly resembled the loud, chaotic, helter-skelter state of the food media world itself.

Even the most churlish New York–centric gourmand had to admit, however, that it had been a long, prosperous run for the bloated, overfed—and yes, mostly privileged, white, and male—professionals of our generation. In the glow of that second evening martini or an afternoon cocktail or two, however, we also had to admit that around the country, and indeed around the world, the eating had never been better. It used to be that you had to come to New York, ramble around the vineyards of Napa and the clubby restaurants of San Francisco, or visit LA for a week or two to get a real taste of the American dining scene. But almost decades into the new food-obsessed millennium, the culture of dining and restaurants was much broader, more democratic, and more accessible than ever before. It was the golden age of cheeseburgers and mushroom foragers and artisanal salamis and more craft enthusiasms (for whiskeys, beers, cheeses) than it was possible to count. You could drop into Austin, Texas, or Atlanta, or even the formerly culinarily challenged suburbs of places like Boston and Arlington, Virginia, to sample different styles of Texas, Carolina, or Brooklyn barbecue, Vietnamese pho, fresh-made corn masa tacos stuffed with lamb barbacoa, or platters of carefully sliced Peking duck, all of which tasted uncannily like the real thing. Provided they'd managed to hold on to their jobs in the media whirlwind, restaurant critics in places like Houston and my gourmet-challenged hometown of Washington, DC, were experiencing the kind of restaurant cooking that would have been unimaginable not so long ago, when knowledgeable eaters out in the provinces subsisted, in the fevered imagination of haughty, New York–centric critics like myself, on elevated cuts of beefsteak, vats of Tex-Mex queso, and the occasional lonely French restaurant serving crêpes suzette and wheels of vulcanized mushroom quiche. "I think it's time you came out and visited us," Alison Cook had said in the back of the critics' bus as we inched through the afternoon Burbank traffic after the comical *MasterChef* shoot.

But the shiny, perfumed travel publications that once sent me off on junkets around the globe were reducing their staffs, or cutting their pages, or stopping the presses for good, and no one at my city magazine was interested in dispatching Platt to Houston to cover that city's multitude of new Vietnamese or Indian restaurants, or off to LA to embark on a dumpling ramble through the Chinese restaurants of the San Gabriel Valley. Meanwhile, back in the former center of the culinary universe, where I was still making my weary gastronomic rounds, dressed, after almost two decades on the job, in the same, increasingly frayed, sauce-stained coat, the portents of doom were everywhere. The #MeToo scandals sweeping through the Mario Batali empire and Ken Friedman's notorious gastropub, the Spotted Pig, revealed the seaminess of the restaurant business that had been festering behind the scenes for decades, while portly critics like me obliviously wandered from one lavish expense account dinner to the next. Like New York itself, the dining world seemed increasingly divided between people with too much money and people with too little of it, and for all sorts of reasons—the high cost of doing business, the fast casual dining revolution, the slow erosion of grandiose destination restaurants in favor of a more local, neighborly style—the new restaurants around town were more formulaic and predictable than ever before. At the suggestion of the Admiral, I wrote a story for *Grub Street* lamenting the plague of what he called "Ed Sheeran restaurants," after the pleasing, well-crafted, one-note songs turned out with mind-numbing regularity by the diminutive UK pop star legend. The rooms of the classic Ed Sheeran restaurant tended to be on the small side, both because, in the manner of a soulful folk tune, intimacy in the age of casual, neighborhood bar dining was known to promote bonhomie and good cheer, and because nobody but the huge dining conglomerates and chains could afford to rent the big spaces in the city anymore. The style of cooking at an Ed Sheeran restaurant might be French bistro or classic American bar and grill, although in pasta-mad New York, more often than not, the theme tended to rustic Italian. Their one-page menus were filled with a numbingly familiar selection of raw fish crudos, twirling pastas ritually tossed with crumblings of locally grown pork, and locally procured, midprice black sea-bass and pork chop entrées designed to hit the same comfortably accessible notes again and again. There was nothing wrong with this genial and pleasant style of dining, of course, but like the music critic whose duty it is to listen to an endless stream of saccharine pop hits for twelve hours a day, sitting through these good-natured, narrowly focused meals night after night was enough to drive even the most devoted gourmand slowly insane.

Yes, little miracles, as always, occurred now and then, and thanks to New Yorkers' endless appetite for the next new thing, the rippling, endlessly diverse tapestry of the city's dining scene still survived. But more and more of the fashionable trends that are a critic's duty to curate and popularize tended to come from somewhere else (LA breakfasts! Izakaya comfort food from Tokyo! Spicy hot chicken of Nashville!), and the days when hungry, ambitious cooks came to New York from around the world to make their reputations had been more or less obliterated in the Age of Instagram. Top chefs didn't have to come to the Emerald City to achieve fame and stardom anymore—they could enter antic TV contests, or set up shop back home in Portland, Maine, or Nashville, or Athens, Georgia, where the dining public was less ferociously finicky and the costs of doing business weren't so astronomically high. Why fly off to New York or Copenhagen or the kitchens of Osaka to study the latest gourmet recipes and trends when you could do it digitally, with the touch of your thumb? Many of the venerable dining institutions around town were still in business, like Maguy Le Coze's midtown seafood palace, Le Bernardin, and Daniel Boulud's monuments to "Le Grande Cuisine" on the Upper East Side, but more of the mom-and-pop storefront joints around the city were losing their leases and closing for good, leaving the vacant spaces up and down the avenues to be filled with bank outlets and the deathly fluorescent glow of giant drugstore chains. What was left of the cutting-edge gourmet culture around the city survived, increasingly, in the outer boroughs or in small, exclusive, radically priced "bromakase" tasting rooms patronized by groups of young plutocrats with a taste for diamond-studded watches and thousand-dollar bottles of champagne, who left their trading desks in the evenings to dine on Wagyu and truffle dinners and the dwindling, overfished sushi delicacies, which had replaced steak dinners of long ago as the new status trophy food of the globe-trotting financial set.

Many of the cooks and chefs who'd helped ignite the insurgent culinary revolutions of the last few years, like Colicchio, David Chang, and April Bloomfield, had been swept away by scandal, left the kitchen for the TV studio, or departed for Vegas or LA to pursue the brand-building stages of their careers. Meanwhile, their successors struggled to find some traction in this increasingly challenging and stratified world. I wandered grumpily around the town, writing up learned tasting notes on glorified taco restaurants and vegetable burgers created by former award-winning gourmet cooks. ("This uncannily realistic burger creation tends to get stickier and more dense as you eat it, thanks to the quinoa-and-carrot patty.") I taste-tested a weirdly disagreeable toasted Japanese steak "sando" sandwich made from A5 fatty grade Kobe beef, which cost $185 at a new restaurant down on Wall Street and left an unpleasant, weirdly fishy-tasting slick of fat as it slipped down the back of my throat. My colleagues and I visited gimmicky "fishing" restaurant chains from Japan, where diners hooked lobsters and giant, farm-raised frankenfish "Salmon trout" from glowing blue tanks. I made my weary way to midtown, at the frantic prodding of the Admiral ("You're the last critic not to write anything about this sensation, Platty!"), when the Turkish meat-salting meme phenomenon, Nusret Gökçe, otherwise known as "Salt Bae," took over Jeffrey Chodorow's former China Grill space in the winter of 2018 and began peddling $270 Tomahawk steaks to adoring crowds of sophisticated New Yorkers.

Not so long before, Gökçe had been just another hardworking, T-shirt-wearing meat cook back in Istanbul, until someone had the brilliant idea of posting his signature steak-salting routine online. His comical, strangely hypnotic, praying mantis–like performance—which involved slicing the Tomahawk with his curving scimitar blade, then releasing the salt from up around his ear and having the crystals tumble down his arm to his elbow—turned into the viral sensation of the year, and now Salt Bae presided over a string of Turkish-themed Nusr-Et steakhouses stretching from Dubai to London, and now New York.

My dining partner at Salt Bae's new outlet in midtown was one of the founders of a popular restaurant website and a long-time connoisseur of viral internet food events. We happily noted our suitably horrible table, which was situated between one of the walls near the bar and the trampling herd of waitstaff, who stampeded among the tables dressed in jaunty black jockey caps, attempting to upsell the already ridiculously priced items on the menu. We chuckled smugly at the room's slapdash decor, featuring large decorative fluorescent meat hooks hanging from the rafters, drooping potted palms set here and there, and walls lined with random chunks of glowing pink Himalayan rock salt. We dismissed a comically overcooked $100 creation called "steak spaghetti" and gleefully noted that unlike the classic steak tartare back at the Repulse Bay Hotel in Hong Kong, this house version, which we ordered from a passing meat-themed "dim sum cart," was cartoonishly mixed with spoonfuls of ketchup. But when Gökçe himself suddenly appeared noiselessly before us at the table with his curved, impressively glinting steak blade, we stared at him in silent wonder, looking, it later occurred to me, like a couple of country peasants witnessing Godzilla for the first time as he towered over the crackling power lines in an old Japanese movie. With the exception of a pair of black plastic gloves, which the New York health authorities had commanded him to wear, the live Salt Bae looked uncannily like the viral version we'd seen a thousand times, complete with the same white T-shirt, the same sightless, round John Lennon acid trip spectacles, and the same blank, trancelike expression on his face.

"End of Days, Platty, End of Days," said my friend as we raised our grease-stained phones in the air and filmed the Salt Bae's steak-salting routine, as everyone else in the boisterous room was doing, and then hastily edited and tagged our memes and sent them off into the digital ether to be liked, viewed, and hopefully replicated again and again.

"THE END OF DAYS" HAD BEEN AN IRONIC SAYING OF MINE FOR years, but now it seemed to be coming true in all sorts of strange and formerly unimagined ways. Later that year, as the wet late-spring weather was giving way to summertime in the city, I found myself tapping out obituaries. One was for my mother, who died at the age of eighty-one, in her own bed on a sunny weekday around lunchtime, surrounded by mementos of her family and her travels. Not long after that, news came that Tony Bourdain had hanged himself with the belt of his bathrobe in a hotel room up in the mountains of Alsace, and a week after the Bourdain news, I found myself writing another obituary appreciation late on a Sunday evening, this time for Jonathan Gold. The greatest of all print-era food scribes had called an editor friend of mine just a few weeks before and said, in his usual low-key, phlegmatic way, that he hadn't been feeling well, but would try to complete a chapter of his long-assigned book, the one he'd been laboring on for decades on the culinary glories of Pico Boulevard. No pages ever arrived, and like A. A. Gill, who'd received his fateful "full English" cancer diagnosis the year before, J. Gold was dead a few days later, three years short of his sixtieth birthday, from another cataclysmic cancer event. I wrote my flowery appreciation late at night—about our meeting in Tuscany long ago, and his gifts not just as a critic but as the kind of writer you don't see anymore in the hectic, increasingly digital world of letters at large—and the next morning I called my little battalion of doctors and medical advisers for a hastily arranged series of checkups and precautionary visits.

Later in the week, the doctors received me in their cramped examination rooms, with polite looks of foreboding on their faces. After blasting bright lights into my dilated pupils, the eye doctor announced that I wasn't suffering from diabetes blindness yet, although she wanted to see me again in six months. Dr. P noted that my astronomically high blood sugar levels were still being suppressed by the antidiabetes horse pills he'd been prescribing, although the ominous tingling at the ends of my toes wasn't a wonderful sign. After the usual pleasantries, Dr. P managed to herd me onto the scale, and as I peered up at the ceiling, he snapped the little scale weights back to zero and said, in his most ominous, distressed sea captain's voice, that my weight was ticking back upward toward the dangerous blimp levels, and that radical measures were again in order.

"It might be time for you to write another one of your diet articles."

"There are no more diets for me to try."

"I'm afraid this is the life you've chosen," said Dr. P, before ushering me glumly out the door.

Later that week, I went uptown to have lunch with my father at his favorite neighborhood diner called Neil's, down the block from my parents' apartment on the Upper East Side. Like most of the old diners around town, Neil's had survived thanks to a fortuitous combination of small miracles (the lease, the location next to a breakfast-hungry population of students at Hunter College) for eighty years on the corner of Seventieth Street and Lexington Avenue. It wasn't an elaborate place, but after decades of habitual restaurant-going all over the world, it had become a happy refuge for my father, the way a reliable neighborhood joint in the big city tends to do. He loved the way the waiters at Neil's called out the names of the regulars as they walked through the door, just as Joe the bartender at Giovanni's used to do a few blocks west, over on Madison Avenue. My father loved to banter with the cooks in their ancient short-order patois and he loved to flip through the pages of the huge laminated menu, which he regarded, with its eight varieties of hamburger, platters of Hungarian goulash, and roast turkey with mashed potato blue plate specials, as a living anthropological compendium of the dining trends of his old hometown. He loved the way his poached eggs were cooked perfectly every time he ordered them for breakfast, and how they were served in a little bowl, the way the diners used to do when he was growing up in New York as a child. He loved the democracy of the New York diner, especially compared to other snooty establishments in the neighborhood, and he loved to gather my daughters and the rest of his grandchildren there on weekend mornings to experience the ancient, choreographed ritual of the breakfast rush, the way other elders in the neighborhood dragged their offspring to the Met or the Whitney or any of the city's other grand museums.

"What's good today?" I asked the waiter when he arrived with our menus, sounding, it later occurred to me, the way I'd sounded when Georges Briguet had handed me the menu at Le Périgord at that first review dinner long ago. Since then, Briguet had been arrested, briefly, for tax evasion. He'd died shortly afterward, and I'd heard that the old restaurant on Fifty-Sixth Street, with its coral-colored banquettes and its carefully arranged jars of fresh roses on every table, had recently closed its doors for good.

My father and I flipped through the menus before our waiter arrived and talked about the affairs of the day. We talked about how we were able to chart our passage through the city by the various doomed luncheonettes and diners we'd frequented over the years. We talked about how Neil's was the latest, and possibly the last, in a succession of favorite Platt family restaurants, and about our favorite dishes, stretching back over the years to the dumpling houses of Hong Kong and Taiwan, to the Sick Duck in Beijing, to the pan roast at the Oyster Bar when his father was alive, and to the jellied clams on the bountiful antipasti cart at Giovanni's, rolled up and down between the tables by the waiters before the pasta course arrived. We talked about the magical power of a favorite family restaurant, which, like a neighborhood church or a familiar, well-tended garden, provides a brief, cocooned illusion of comfort and dependability in a changeable, often uncomfortable world. We talked about how my brothers and I piled into the worn and familiar leather booths at Neil's after our mother's funeral, still dressed in our rumpled dark suits, to dine on club sandwiches and comforting platters of patty melts, stacked with thatches of steak fries.

We talked for a time about the usual things as the timeless

room, with its old collection of pies on the counter and faded photos of sitcom stars on the walls, began to fill up with other regulars coming in for their lunch. We talked about the weather, and my doctors' appointments, and the End of Days weariness I'd been feeling on the job. When the waiter came around, my father ordered his usual BLT, and I ordered my BLT too, and the waiter brought the old ambassador a large squeeze bottle of mayonnaise to go with his sandwich, like they always do. "Bring my son the restaurant critic a salad with his BLT," said my father, as he handed his menu to our waiter with a merry smile. "He tells me he's about to embark on another one of his crazy diets."

LATER THAT WEEK, AFTER DILIGENTLY FASTING FOR HOURS AND possibly days, the way portly people do when they set sail filled with optimism and purpose on a new diet, I find myself standing in the bright afternoon sunshine not far from another legendary diner in the city, Joe Junior Restaurant, on the corner of Sixteenth Street and Third Avenue. The other Joe Jr.'s near our apartment, where I used to take my daughters for breakfast when they were younger, has been gone for years now, replaced by a more current, fashionable version of itself: a Brazilian-themed coffee shop where a new generation of headphone-wearing regulars crowd the uncomfortable wood chairs, peering silently into their laptops, sipping fair trade coffee from biodegradable paper cups. This surviving Gramercy area Joe's had once been owned, according to legend, by the same people who owned our long-vanished local Joe Jr.'s, and it was still famous among its devotees, some of whom were well-known chefs around the city, for the quality of its cheeseburger and for the omelets, which are rounded and creamy smooth and served with crunchy-topped hash browns and glasses of fresh-squeezed orange juice.

I slip into one of the seats at the counter as the regulars drift in and out, and watch the timeless ballet of the line cooks as they break eggs over the griddle and flip the shells into the garbage can behind their backs. I'd written a story about the death of big-city diners not long before and how this short-order ballet was slowly disappearing from the scene. I'd described how one of the grill men, whose name was Marcos, from Puebla in southern Mexico, sat down next to me at the counter to eat a salad during his lunch break.

"It doesn't matter what you order here, everything is good," he'd said to me with a weary smile, as I flipped through the menu; and he'd sounded the way Louie the waiter used to sound back in the day at the West Village Joe Jr.'s when that little establishment had been the unofficial dining club of my slowly vanishing neighborhood. Marcos is behind the grill today, as it happens, flipping perfect omelets and firing up the famous house burger, like he's been doing every working day since he started at Joe's over a quarter of a century ago in 1992. I order a glass of the fresh orange juice, and then, because it tastes so good and so fresh, I order another one. I order a Greek salad, and because I've been virtuously sticking to my diet, and because I'm in a delirious, semistarved state, a small bowl of steak fries. The fries are gone within seconds. I read a secondhand copy of the morning paper for a while, listening to the seductive sizzling sounds rising from the grill; and it's not long before I hear myself say with a little bit of the old André Duffy flourish in my voice, "Gentlemen, why don't you give your friend here a little taste of that blessed cheeseburger."